# Eloquence in Public Speaking

## HOW TO SET YOUR WORDS ON FIRE

**KENNETH McFARLAND**

Englewood Cliffs, N. J.
PRENTICE-HALL, INC.

*TO MY FAMILY:*

Often alone while the author was getting the speaking experience that made this book possible.

PRINTED IN THE UNITED STATES OF AMERICA

27476—MO

# Preface

A corny joke in my high school annual of 1924 has a teacher asking a student to define a vacuum. The youth responds by saying, "Well, I've got it in my head but I can't tell it." In the confusion of our modern world one thing is becoming increasingly clear—you may as well have a vacuum in your head if you can't *tell* what you do have in there. *If you can't tell it, you can't sell it.*

Almost all the positions and distinctions that are desirable in life seem to hinge more and more upon the individual's ability to successfully persuade others. In an age of bigness and mass living, halting conversation with one person at a time is too slow. Only those will be recognized who can stand up and speak out. The modern generation is becoming increasingly intolerant of leaders who cannot literally point the way.

This book is designed to help any person who earnestly wishes to speak more effectively. It is not a text book. It is much more than the traditional "speech book." It proceeds on the principle that one cannot speak with sincerity and conviction unless he is a sincere person who lives by his convictions. It declares you cannot separate the speaker from his speech, that it is folly to expect things to come out of a person that are not in him.

In this volume you will find all the techniques and devices you need for constructing and delivering a speech, but it frankly tells you these are not enough. As important as these things are, they are still the scaffolding. In these pages you will perceive that the author is deeply concerned with helping you kindle that inward spark that sets fire to your words and burns them into the memory of your hearers. The book seeks to help you develop your own dynamic philosophy of living that is so essential to continued success in speaking.

A little dictionary in my pocket defines "eloquent" with one word—"forcible." I believe an eloquent spokesMAN is an eloquent MAN who has *learned* to tell others effectively about the things that make *eloquent lives*. This book will achieve its purpose if it helps you increase your *capacity* to live eloquently, and increases your ability to eloquently tell others how to do it.

# Table of Contents

IV. PREACH WHAT YOU PRACTICE (*Continued*)

experience, knowledge, faith. Hearers must recognize speaker as genuine person. Persuasive speech must be from heart to heart as well as mind to mind. Platform no place for phoney. Still no substitute for knowing. Cannot separate what you say from what you are. The Fifty-Rose Man. Things you can do.

Why do you lack confidence? Wholesome fear helpful. Confidence defined. You are greatest authority on yourself; stand on your own experience. Illustrations. You should have as much confidence as those who invited you to speak. Experiences of "little people" important. Those who "could do it better" are *not* doing it. Illustrations. Confidence comes with knowing you know. Don't apologize to audience because you are you. You are deliveryman with important message. Over-emphasis necessary to push ideas across footlights. Speaking in official capacity adds confidence. Suggestions on appropriate dress for speakers. Be confident but not over-confident. Be confident you can improve.

Most important things named with little words. Simplicity gets to the points. Big ideas in homely words. Grass roots people. "Let down your buckets where you are." Powerful simplicity illustrated.

Speeches classified as to purpose—to inform; to motivate action; to entertain. Speeches judged in terms of their objectives. No standard pattern for straight entertainment type. Examples. Action and Informative speeches fall in standard three-part pattern: Introduction, Body, Conclusion. Responding to Introductions. "Softening-up" exercises. Illustrations. The fast start. When to state objective. How to state. Illustrations. Identify with audience interest. How to build Body of speech. Topical outline plan recommended. Reasons. Conclusion should nail down and clinch objective. Types of Conclusions illustrated.

An all-important device. Skillful speaker rests audience between flights of oratory. Technique described and illustrated.

## XIII. USING HUMOR (*Continued*)

and sincerity. Test yourself before telling stories. Humor not essential. Let humor come in if it wants to; do not drag it in. Humor must harmonize with both material and audience. Should always be kindly. Caution on jokes dealing with religion and race. Dialect stories risky. Don't fly off the nest if you lay an egg. Humor, like balance of speech, should be *yours*. Genius of story telling. When is story "proper"? You need be neither "low brow" nor "blue nose." Tests for appropriateness. Humor in selling. Summary of Points to Ponder.

Vitality is quality most desired in speech. More than enthusiasm. Speech titles should reflect vitality. Examples. Deal with things that make a difference. Devitalized "Speech for All Occasions." Examples of modern speaking and writing with vitality: Charles H. Brower, Adlai Stevenson, Bryson Reinhardt, H. G. Wells, Don Herold, Charles T. Lipscomb. Examples of making points with punch. Conclusion.

# Unprecedented Opportunities Demand a New Approach

*Never have so many understood so
little about so much.*

Sir Harry Lauder used to say the ability to hold an audience must be a gift, or else no Scotsman would possess it.

A prominent public relations man, whose work requires him to be on the receiving end of innumerable speeches, declares that if the ability to speak is a gift, then "someone must have shot Santa Claus."

We shall soon have 200 million people in the United States. The educational level of the general population is being constantly pushed upward. Virtually all of our people speak English. Yet the percentage who can speak well enough to command an enthusiastic following is infinitesimal. Experienced program chairmen, whose organizations can attract the best of the nation's speaking talent, lament that there are scarcely two dozen people in all the land who are "sure fire" speakers—after dinner, before dinner, during dinner, or any other time.

This criticism is not offered as a blanket indictment of the current and traditional avenues of speech instruction. There is, and there will always be, a vital place for regular speech courses, debating and declaiming, presiding and toastmastering. However, it is becoming increasingly obvious that our traditional instructional techniques need to be supplemented.

What accounts for our dearth of effective speakers? Is it because there is no longer a need for such ability?

There are many chronic cracks about public speaking. One of the most threadbare of these is, "If all the public speakers in America were laid end to end—both they and the audiences would be more comfortable." Still, virtually every serious student of the modern scene concurs that there has never before been such a crying need for leaders who have ideas, and who can effectively express those ideas. The reasons for this obvious truth are rather easy to discern.

### The Country Is Wired for Sound But the Sounds Are Not Improving

Our modern society has enormously increased the *facilities* for dispensing facts, information, and propaganda. The average citizen is bombarded with information on an ever-increasing scale. Newspapers, television, radio, books, and other media are shoveling out facts and data in a volume that defies comprehension, and the future promises an acceleration of this trend. The average citizen is literally drowning in a sea of information. This, coupled with the fact that the educational attainments of the people are being steadily increased, means the average citizen now possesses more *facts* than ever before. But, oddly enough, this same average citizen is currently more *confused* than ever. He frequently finds himself with complete sets of facts that completely contradict one another. The possession of more and more information alone has not given our people better judgment, more peace of mind, better balanced personalities, or firmer convictions as to the course of action they should pursue.

It can almost be demonstrated that the better informed a person is the more likely he is to be confused. I know a man who drives a delivery truck. He has been making the same rounds for a decade. He reads no newspapers nor periodicals. He avoids all newscasts and "educational" programs. He has reduced life to its simplest terms and has almost no problems that he recognizes. Of course, he is a "simple" person.

Of those people who do have "informed" opinions on current problems, I find the ones are most secure who have but one source of information. They never clutter up their minds with the rest of the evidence. They are often wrong but never uncertain. The people who really need help these days are the sincere citizens who earnestly seek the facts from all the sources available to them.

Some observers declare that much of our modern day hysteria is the result of people being constantly loaded up with information which they are not prepared to process and handle. One frustrated soul recently wrote his radio station an urgent plea to quit broadcasting tornado alerts. His letter said in part,

> We don't have any more tornadoes than we used to have, but now we hear about them all the time. My grandpappy never worried about a tornado until he saw it coming over the hill toward his house. He only saw two in 86 years and they both missed him.
>
> I have decided I would rather take a chance on being in a tornado once in a while than to worry about them all the time. Besides my house sets on a solid concrete slab, and there is no place for me to get anyhow. I reckon if a tornado hits us dead center, I'll just end up on another slab. In the meantime, I say nuts to the whole business —let's all relax!

While the above viewpoint may not be worthy of emulation, it does illustrate something of the frustration that may result when one constantly swallows more information than his system can digest. The need is for short cuts, for summarization processes, for pointing out what the facts *mean* in *terms of intelligent action* that the individual can successfully pursue.

The big need in our time is *perspective*. In the crush of modern living the average citizen may be likened unto an infantryman in the midst of a great battle. He is right in the thick of it, yet he cannot see its broad outlines, nor how it is shaping up generally. He has a lot of first-hand information yet he often cannot even determine whether he is winning or losing. He must have someone who can get up above the din of the battle to *tell* him how the day is going.

Walter Lippmann said in an interview that Churchill and De Gaulle are the greatest leaders of this century because of their ability to "goalize" the needs of their day and to lead people to the solution of problems.

A cartoon in *The New Yorker* depicts a housewife saying to her bellowing husband,

"Why can't you lead a life of quiet desperation, like everybody else?"

Another modern cartoon shows a store clerk explaining a weird "tinker toy" to a mother. "This toy," the clerk explains, "prepares the child for modern living—no matter how you put it together it won't work."

The current scene is literally crying out for more media that help people develop a workable *philosophy of living*. We need more media for *transposing facts into a philosophy*. We need improved methods of *translating information into understanding*. Many of the nation's fine editorial pages make a great contribution in that direction, but unfortunately they are not widely enough read to meet the problem on anything like an adequate scale. Books and periodicals will always serve splendidly in their historic role of formulating sensible wholes out of a maze of data. Certain public interest features on television and radio are wonderful for cutting through mountains of minutia and emerging with clearly stated problems, or solidly supported conclusions. Still, perhaps the greatest of all media for transposing facts into a living philosophy is the medium of the public speech. Indeed, much of the radio and television contributions to current problems are made by simply multiplying the number who may hear a speech. Again, the news columns can do their best job of shaping public opinion on current issues by reporting the words of those who have thought those problems through, and have subsequently delivered public utterances concerning them. Indeed the reporting of a speech is one of the few ways of getting an opinion-shaping "editorial" on the front page. Thus, we have vastly improved the *facilities* for getting the thoughts of speakers to the multitudes and have placed their potential capabilities almost beyond limit. But, strangely, we are making no corresponding progress in improving the quality of the speech arts themselves.

Here we have one of the mysteries of modern times. The *need* for effective public speaking is the most intense of all time, and it is a need that is destined to sharply increase as our society becomes more complex. The media for reaching larger and larger numbers of people is keeping pace with the increase in the need. We find ourselves in the strange situation of having a good market, a growing demand, and a fine distribution system—but no corresponding increase in the *quality of the product*.

Following the Democratic National Convention of 1960, Columnist George Sokolsky wrote:

> "One thing about the Democratic Convention: oratory seems to be dead. Not one orator appeared on the rostrum. Not one speaker showered the spectators with wit, humor, pathos, flights of language, or flights of thought. There was no William Jennings Bryan; there was no Bourke Cockran. The silver tongues had become base metal. . . .
>
> If the conventions are going to permit television to expose them, they will have to adopt new devices. Oratory is a glorious art. It is designed to make words act psychologically as music. The true orator must have language, voice, and gesture—a combination that eats into the mind and soul of the listener.
>
> . . . the prompter machine . . . is a device of the devil . . . Did Demosthenes require a prompter machine to tell him what to do? Or did Cicero? What weaklings machines have made us. We shall not only lose our legs, we shall have voices like chickadees." [1]

Most observers agreed the 1960 Republican Convention orators were more talented than their Democratic counterparts, but Sokolsky's appraisal reflects another facet of the existing shortage of speaking talent.

It has been said that "nature abhors a vacuum." If there is a demand for a product or service, there will not long be a shortage. New operators come onto the scene, competition is created, and unnatural shortages soon disappear. In fact, this is a basic tenant of our free enterprise system. But in the case of the demand for more and better public speakers nature's law seems to have been set aside. There *is* a vacuum and it is *not* being filled.

## Never Before Were So Many Interested in Speech

The current dearth of effective speakers, then, has not been occasioned through lack of need for such service. Could the answer be found by concluding that there is simply not sufficient

[1] *The Topeka State Journal*, Topeka, Kansas, July 19, 1960.

interest among capable people who could supply the need? Here again, the trend is overwhelmingly in the opposite direction. There have never before been so many intelligent and able people who were so deeply desirous of increasing their effectiveness in the speech arts. The gamut ranges all the way from dreamers and theorists to the most practical minded politicians and hard headed leaders in business and industry. Every man with something to "sell" his fellow men—whether it be an idea, a service, or a product—is intensely interested in telling his story better.

Let us note one bit of evidence in support of the above contention. The enrollees in the Dale Carnegie course now number some 100,000 and the future promises steady growth. This writer has on several occasions addressed national conventions of the Dale Carnegie Alumni Association. From all over the nation came the faithful, paying their own expenses, and often using their vacation time to make the pilgrimage. Any outside observer could not fail to be impressed with the intelligence of the group and the great power of their motivation. That motivation is an honest and abiding desire to improve their proficiency in the speech arts. Similar interest is being shown in other organizations designed to teach these things by correspondence, or in person.

Are these people just simple souls who are floundering in a sea of misconceptions as to the importance of speech in our modern world? Not on your life! Over two thousand American industries have cooperated with the Dale Carnegie organization alone in an endeavor to improve the speaking effectiveness of their executives and prospective executives. These industrial concerns include such names as Coca Cola and General Motors. And who will say such training does not fill a need? Few of the 100,-000 now enrolled are there because of outside pressure. The pressure comes from *within* these individuals. It is the pressure of a burning desire these people have to improve themselves by improving their proficiency in a field which they know is tremendously important.

### The "Revolt of the Inarticulate"

For a variety of reasons "men of affairs" are becoming intensely interested in effective public speaking. Some of these reasons are as elemental as the law of self-preservation. One of America's leading industrialists had this to say in a private conversation,

"I attended a national convention of educators at Atlantic City and heard a speech delivered by one of our prominent labor leaders. I was both envious and alarmed at how effectively he told his story. The spokesmen for management who appeared on the same program were pitiful by comparison. I have rarely ever seen labor represented in an important program by an individual who could not tell his story well. We are going to have to develop the same skills in management *or there isn't going to be any management.*"

Another champion of the American free enterprise system remarked to the author that he had never seen the British Labor Party represented on an American platform by a poor speaker. This man had the humiliating experience of following such a Laborite speaker on the platform of an American university. In relating his experience later the industrialist said,

"It burned me up! That left-winger won the battle for his side with a bean shooter, and I had an arsenal full of atomic weapons on my side—but I didn't know how to *fire* them!

"I came home and went to work on this speaking business. I'll never again go to a meeting and read a paper prepared for me by the public relations department. From here on in, I am going to stand up on my hind legs, look 'em in the eye, and *tell* 'em!"

*The Wall Street Journal*[2] reports a rapidly expanding new business of ghost writing speeches for business executives, with one public relations man stating that he receives $1000 for each such speech he prepares. *Newsweek*[3] made a round-up of the growing number of corporations that are not only training their own executives to speak better, but are also retraining professional speakers to put their story over to the public.

### Interest in Speech Comes from Both the Top and the Bottom of the Ladder

In every segment of our modern life more and more leaders are becoming acutely aware that the causes they hold dear cannot survive unless they develop people who can stand up on their hind

[2] *Wall Street Journal*, January 4, 1960.
[3] *Newsweek*, November 23, 1959.

legs, "look 'em in the eye, and tell 'em." From the 4-H Clubs,
through the university graduate schools, and out through the
uttermost segments of the social order there is a new appreciation
of the importance of effective communication. Constantly greater
grows the demand for the individual who can truly excel in effective speech. Such skilfully conducted organizations as the American Institute of Banking are placing increasing emphasis upon
speech training as they prepare the future executives of their businesses. Still the vacuum between supply and demand persists.

Another strange thing about the present situation is the keen
appreciation of good speaking ability that exists among those who
have managed to succeed without it. One rarely ever hears the
significance of effective speech discounted by successful people
who do not possess it. This fact seems to reverse an almost universal human tendency for the individual to minimize the importance of attributes which he does not himself possess. It is a
notable exception to Shakespeare's statement, "We rarely like the
virtues we have not." In a midwestern city a university professor
annually conducts a speech course for top executives. Every student in these classes is an individual who nearly any observer
would agree has "arrived." Yet each week for three months these
men devote one of their valuable evenings to the all-important
business of better speech—and rarely does one miss a class. They
come to the sessions with their homework well prepared, and
they are eager to get on with the learning. Some of them are
equipping themselves to become full-time "missionaries" for private enterprise when their retirement releases them from the
burdens of routine administration. Others are equipping themselves to be "top top-executives," and still others are there because
they have "just got to have more tools for getting through to the
employees, the customers, and the public."

A well-known and eminently successful construction contractor
on the West Coast is gradually turning over his managerial responsibilities to his capable son. While this man has never even
made an attempt at public speaking himself, he does not plan to
release full responsibilities to his son until the younger man has
become adept at expressing himself in meetings. This successful
and respected industrial leader states his view this way,

"I made it to the top despite the fact that I was virtually tongue-tied. But this is a new day. My son could not get to the top with the same handicap. In fact, I don't think he could even stay at the top if I started him there. I believe the time has come when a man has either got to speak up, or move over."

Another top executive enrolled in a short course in management at a state university. When asked what he considered his most acute shortage, he promptly answered, "Speech." Then he added,

"Give me everything you can in public speaking, and let me leave here set up to continue the study on my own. I've got a belly full of being outpointed in company meetings by people who don't know as much as I do, but who can tell it better."

Another enrollee in a special speech course for top executives said,

"I'm here because of a speech I heard. The speaker said, 'There is always room at the top because so many people up there go to sleep and fall off.' He called this process 'rusting on your laurels.' There were 1800 men in the audience and I was twenty rows back, but he hit me right between the eyes. I made up my mind then and there that I am not going to be the stumble bum of our outfit."

Yes, there seem to be two sources of motivation behind the current drive for more proficient speech—it comes from those who *can* speak and from those who *can't*. But a single fact stands out in bold relief—the present dearth of top-flight public speakers *has not been occasioned by any lack of interest on the part of the people.*

*Leaders Who Once* Talked *to a Few Must Now*
Speak *to Many*

Down through the ages nations have kept their social, economic, and religious life intact by the leaders of each generation teaching the succeeding one in the most direct manner possible— that is simply *telling* the new generation through day-to-day association. A great deal of our troubles in America in the past three decades comes in the fact that this system has broken down. The leaders who should be *telling* the story to the new generation *are no longer in daily and direct touch with the people.*

In industry, for example, there was a time when the "boss" was the foreman, the plant manager, the president of the company, the chairman of the board, and all the stockholders. He owned the place and he ran it personally. He had five or ten employees. He knew their first names, their wives' first names, and their kids' first names. This meant "top management" was right next to the man on the line. They all rubbed shoulders every day. The employee got the economic facts of life "straight from the horse's mouth." He learned that the key word in the American system is *opportunity*. Through his daily association with the "boss" he found out how people succeeded under the system—they *earned* progress through *individual proficiency*. When "top management" was teaching these things daily and directly we were getting along a whole lot better than we are now.

Today top management is no longer standing next to the man on the line. Instead of five or ten employees, the plant may now house five or ten thousand. Top management is far removed from the daily life of the worker. The top executives are just as fine fellows as they ever were—*but the man on the line does not know it like he once did*. He *can't* know it. He simply does not know the "big boss" and has no opportunity to observe his personal qualities. But far more damaging is the fact that the "big boss" is no longer telling his story directly. Furthermore, *the big boss, who could talk very well to five or ten, usually does not possess the technique for addressing five or ten thousand*. He is now issuing directives and bulletins, and writing an occasional article for the official company publication. He is holding meetings of his assistants and discussing "personnel" problems. The man on the line whom the boss (or maybe the boss's predecessor) called "John," is now a unit of "personnel." And the big boss sits in his office wondering why John and all his buddies "don't understand the American system like they used to." He wonders why they are looking to sources outside the company to provide their leadership and solve their problems for them.

*New Kind of "Company Man" With New Opportunities*

There is one tremendously significant and hopeful fact in our modern business and industrial picture in so far as "personnel problems" are concerned. A new kind of management has come into the picture. In between top management and the man on the line has come the new group we call *middle management*. *This means there is still a "company man" standing next to the man on the line.* The salvation of the American industrial picture now lies in the hands of *middle management*. We must teach this group to *speak up* for the American system of competitive enterprise. This group must develop more able *spokesmen* who will champion the fundamental principles that made America great. Present day top management could do no finer or more effective thing than to increase the speech proficiency of middle management. Top management must equip and inspire the middle management group to become both teachers and missionaries. When properly told, the story of what free enterprise and the other institutions of freedom have done for the average man and his family will inspire a cigar store Indian. When ably and dramatically compared with this, the stories of Communism, socialism, paternalism, "security" and government handouts fall flat. But the poorer story is too often told by the skilled spokesman, while the true story is either related by a dub, or not told at all.

American leadership in all phases of our society has made the ghastly mistake of thinking our people somehow inherit a knowledge of our system in their bloodstreams. There is no such easy way to transmit great basic principles from one generation to the next. The truth is *not* self-evident. Good work does *not* speak for itself. *People must speak for it*—ably, constantly, and effectively. Most industrial and business leaders realize this principle in selling their products, but too often they do not recognize that it applies the same way in selling *ideas*. Yes, the greatest opportunity of all time now lies at the feet of the eloquent spokesman.

One major industrial executive has faced the opportunity offered in public speaking and caught fire with it. In addition to putting full time at his office every day, he fills speaking engagements on an average of three evenings a week. In fact, he begins some of his addresses by saying,

"I am a pillar of brass by day and a cloud of gas by night."

This leader reports that his speaking experience has honed his thinking until he is solving his own problems with greater sharpness than ever before. He has discovered that in order to explain things to other people he needs to increase his own understanding of them. He says,

"I would be selfish indeed if I do not hope that my speaking activity is helping other people solve their problems, because there is no doubt it is helping me come up with better answers in our own business."

### *"American System" Has Returned Home But Is Unrecognized*

We are currently witnessing a strange phenomenon in the United States. The American system of free enterprise is again working as it was originally designed, but it has not been functioning that way for so long that the majority of the citizens do not recognize it when they see it. The customer is again "calling the shot."

Back in the great depression of the 1930's the system was not working, the people were not working, and little of anything was functioning as designed. The customer could have been king in the Thirties if there had been any customers. But as one writer put it, "things got so bad that even the people who didn't intend to pay, quit buying."

Then came the Forties and the whole situation was completely reversed. Everything worked. Everybody who wanted a job was working. In most lines of endeavor this situation prevailed all through the Forties and through the first half of the Fifties. We had great prosperity in that fifteen years but one of the basic elements of free enterprise was missing—the customer still was not king. It was a seller's market all the way.

Now we have the customer back in the saddle for the first time in over 30 years. A research department was recently charged with the task of determining what percentage of all the people now working in America came into their first work experience since 1929—or since the "American system" was fully operative before. The figure that came out was 69.6%. Of course, this percentage grows larger with each passing year as older workers retire and younger ones replace them. Two out of every three Americans currently earning money in all the professions, vocations, careers, businesses, and jobs, are *now* for the first time in their earning lives seeing our American economic system work as it was designed! And we wonder why more of them do not understand it. We wonder why so many seem willing to trade it off for a mess of pottage—false security, foreign ideologies and Utopian promises.

The fact is we are faced with a teaching job of such proportions as to defy the imagination. It reminds us that nothing is ever finished—it is all yet to be done, or to be done over. As someone has well said, "Leadership is not a destination—it is a journey." With so terribly much that needs to be taught, why should any speaker be at loss for a subject?

## *Americans Are Organized to Speak and Organized to Listen*

The American people are frequently declared to be the "meetingest" people on the face of the earth. Someone said if you let three Americans get together they will form an organization and elect one as president, one as vice-president, and the other one as secretary. These things have usually been said in jestful criticism. But the time has come to look upon all these myriads of organizations as the magnificent assets which they can be. We must start at bedrock. Everything must be taught or retaught, and the leadership of every segment of the society must be responsible for *teaching its own.* We not only need, but we must have, organized groups of a continuing nature that represent the leadership of all kinds of endeavor. If they will but respond to the wonderful opportunity for service now offered them, our civic clubs, trade associations, women's organizations, Chambers of Commerce, professional associations, farm groups, fraternal societies, and religious groups can achieve a greatness that in most cases could not possibly have been originally visualized—even by their own founders.

For example, let us take the civic club. For this illustration we can use Rotary. This currently great international organization was originally founded to increase the business and professional contacts of its members. But a membership classification system was developed that is truly genius. As it has evolved through the years, the Rotary classification system is designed to bring into the club's membership the top people from a wide variety of endeavors, which, taken together, represent an almost complete cross-section of a community's business and professional life. The local Rotary Club does not ordinarily sponsor specific projects, but endeavors to "tone up" its members through weekly meetings which effectively expose them to vital problems along with suitable solutions. The theory of the organization is that the Rotary members will return to their particular brackets in the community's life and exercise more effective leadership therein. This organization alone is now represented across the nation in "every Middlesex, village and farm." And it has become "international" to such an extent that it now operates in more countries than are enrolled in the United Nations. What a perfectly magnificent forum for disseminating information, inspiration, and understanding through the medium of effective speech!

What can be said of Rotary can be said of hundreds of other groups. Each of them has a thousand avenues through which basic truth and motivating inspiration can be delivered to its membership. Yet it is frequently declared that the heyday of such organizations has passed! If this be true, then it is because we are missing one of the most tremendous opportunities of all time. Each of these groups should be a great *forum*—where the truth rings out and echoes down the corridors of the community, and enters every door until it finally reaches the minds and hearts of all who are represented in that group, both directly and indirectly. The time has come when "service" clubs must really *serve*. But such forums can be effective only as those who participate in them are effective. The current great opportunity of our many organizations in America therefore becomes tied inextricably with the need for improving the speech effectiveness of their membership, and of all those who address the membership.

## The Idea Builder Must Keep
## Pace with the Engineers

A recent speaker [4] revealed that in the next four decades we are faced with the most gigantic building project of all time—we

---

[4] Dr. George Cline Smith, Vice-President and Economist of F. W. Dodge Corporation, in speech for New York Society of Security Analysts, July 1, 1959. Reported by the *Denver Post* of same date.

must build a second America. The data presented by this speaker indicates that our present population will double in the next forty years, and by the year 2000 it will stand at approximately 340,-000,000. If our economy is to expand sufficiently to meet this growth, it means we must build as many buildings and facilities in the next forty years *as we possess now*. This means literally that we must build another America in the lifetime of one forty-year mortgage. Our chances are excellent for having the 64,000,-000 new housing units ready that we shall need by the year 2000. We shall in all probability build the streets and sewers to go with them, as well as the necessary fire stations and public buildings. But are we prepared to equip the *occupants* of all these structures with certain built-in *truths* and principles which must be possessed by at least a simple majority of them if our great heritage of freedom is to be passed on? Edwin Markham [5] said it well:

> We are all blind until we see
>     That in the human plan
> Nothing is worth the making, if
>     It does not make the man.
> Why build these cities glorious
>     If man unbuilded goes?
> In vain we build the world, unless
>     The builder also grows.

To meet this gigantic task we shall need to do the greatest teaching job in history. And the most effective method of teaching is the same now as it was in the days of Socrates and of Jesus. It is "nature's method." It is *speech*. Great teachers often wrote, but the greatest teachers did not write very much, and the Greatest Teacher did not write at all—except a few words in the sand. Yet He *spoke* more effectively than anyone else ever has, and His Sermon on the Mount is the all-time masterpiece of speech construction.

If the Sermon on the Mount were to be delivered today, virtually all the people in the world could hear it simultaneously.

---

[5] Braude, *Speaker's Encyclopedia of Stories, Quotations, and Anecdotes* (Englewood Cliffs, N. J.: Prentice-Hall, 1958), p. 285.

But our marvelously improved mechanical facilities are not used often enough to carry the words of great teachers. More often they scatter over the earth the words of the dictators and demagogues who can command such facilities.

Almost half of all the people in the world cannot read nor write—some 700 million of them. But they can all *hear*. To counteract the voice of each dictator we must lift a "thousand little voices of freedom." Current studies are being made to determine what is termed the "aura of influence" of an individual. Already the early results reveal something of the ultimate significance of these studies. In an investigation made in one small community the least influential individual observed was found to be influencing 160 different people in the course of a year. Think, then, of the tremendous possibilities that may be achieved by people who are skilled in using nature's method of teaching, and who are also equipped with all our modern facilities and know-how!

### *New Opportunities Require a New Philosophy*

In this chapter it has been demonstrated that the need for effective speakers now and in the future is so terribly urgent as to be literally a matter of life and death. The great truths which we "hold to be self-evident" are not really self-evident at all. They must be *taught* and *explained* if they are to survive. This opening chapter has shown that on the one hand there is a great need for more effective speech, and on the other hand there is a sincere and increasing desire among the people to supply that need. Yet between the two factors there remains an unnatural vacuum. It becomes obvious that we need a *new approach* to this vital problem. In the pages that follow it will be contended that a new *philosophy* of speech is needed, and a sincere effort will be made to set forth the main features of that philosophy, as well as the best techniques for its implementation.

# 2

# Thought on Fire

William Jennings Bryan defined eloquence as "The speech of *one who knows what he is talking about* and *means what he says—it is thought on fire."*

At another time Bryan said eloquence results when a speaker is "tremendously enthused about worthwhile things concerning which he is thoroughly informed."

It is most significant that in neither his definition nor his descriptive statement did Bryan say anything at all about the *mechanics* of speech. He did not say what percentage of the discourse should be devoted to the introduction, how much to the main presentation, and how much for the conclusion. He did not state how the speaker should stand, how far apart his feet should be, nor when he should gesture. There was no mention of how one forms those pear shape tones with the voice.

We come now to one of the basic premises upon which this book is based. It is developed on the conviction that *effective speech is a medium of service to one's fellow men.* The eloquent speaker is a person of profound *convictions* who sincerely *feels* he can help his fellow men by conveying those convictions in such an effective manner as to inspire others to adopt them, and to mold their lives and actions in the light of those beliefs. He must be a person with an important story to tell. Possessing this truth has helped the speaker in his own life, and he has an *obligation* to get the story out to others.

The traditional method of speaking is to learn the mechanics of

17

speech and then look about for a suitable subject. This treatise contends that there are great and burning subjects on every hand that are literally crying out to be heard. When a speaker is filled with such information he will be highly motivated to find the most effective means of transmitting it to his hearers. He then develops the mechanics of speech that are most *natural* and suitable to *him* in expediting the telling of *his* story in the way best suited to *his* *total personality*.

*Don't Wait Until the "Spirit Moves You"—*
*Move Yourself*

I want to interject right here that the writer never belonged to the "naturalist" school of public speaking. The art of public speaking must be carefully *studied* and deliberately *mastered*. The major part of this book is devoted to the construction and the delivery of the speech. When you have read those chapters you will realize that effective speaking involves much more than "just doing what comes naturally." You cannot succeed at it as quickly as the fat girl won the shimmy contest. Her formula was "just move quick, and stop quick, and let nature take its course."

It was in Red Rock, Mississippi, that a colored minister invoked divine aid in his preaching in the following prayer:

> "O Lawd, give Thy servant
> This mornin' de eyes of de eagle and de
> Wisdom of de owl; connect his soul with
> De gospel telephine in de central skies;
> Luminate his brow with de Sun of
> Heaben; pizen his mind with love for
> The people; turpentine his imagination;
> Grease his lips with 'possum oil;
> Loosen his tongue with de sledge
> Hammer of Thy power; 'lectrify his
> Brain with de lightnin' of de word; put
> 'Petual motion on his ahms; fill him
> Plum full of the dynamite of Thy
> Glory; 'noint him all over with de
> Kerosene oil of Thy salvation
> And sot him on the fire.
>
> Amen!"

It is extremely important that we understand *there is no set pattern of eloquence.* There can be almost as many styles of good speech as there are good speakers. The important thing is to be literally *filled* with a message that you *know is terribly important.* In your sincere desire to make your message serve other people you will be constantly motivated to find the clearest and most effective way of telling your story. The almost inevitable result of such a combination of factors is that you will become eloquent. And what is more important, it will be *your own brand* of eloquence.

## The "Slow of Tongue" May Become Eloquent

The record is filled with illustrations of people who became effective speakers when a great *need* arose. Moses is a dramatic example. This man was a sheep herder. One could scarcely imagine an occupation that would offer any less opportunity for public speaking. Then one day as he tended his sheep at the "backside of the desert," God spoke to him from a burning bush, and told him he was to go to Egypt and free the children of Israel from their bondage.

The reaction of Moses to this statement was as natural as it was human. In effect he said,

"Who, *me?*"

Then he said something else that was perfectly natural. He offered an excuse that millions are still using every day for not speaking up and dispatching their citizenship obligations. Moses said,

"I am not eloquent . . . I am slow of speech, and of a slow tongue."

And God replied,

"Who hath made man's mouth? . . . Have not I, the Lord? Now therefore go . . . and I will be with thy mouth, and *teach thee what thou shalt say.*"

God told Moses he could take his brother Aaron with him because he "can speak well," and God added,

"And thou shalt speak unto him, and put words in his mouth: and I will be with thy mouth, and with his mouth, and *will teach you what ye shall do.*"

Moses told Aaron what had happened. God had addressed him from a flaming bush, yet after the flame had ceased to burn the bush was intact. It had neither been destroyed nor damaged by the fire. God had transformed Moses's staff into a serpent, and before his eyes had changed it back into a staff again. He had caused Moses to be afflicted with leprosy and then healed him instantly and miraculously. Then God had commanded him— Moses, the sheep herder—to go into Egypt and free the people of Israel from Pharaoh's bondage. And Aaron was to go with him.

It is most significant for the purpose of this discourse that Aaron apparently *believed* all of this fantastic report which Moses gave him. There is nothing in the record that says he doubted its truth and its validity. This means Moses must have done a mighty effective job of *telling the story*. It was quite a selling job for a man who was "slow of tongue."

Moses then went to see Jethro, his father-in-law, and told him that he and Aaron could not herd the sheep any more. They had been commissioned by the Almighty to go down into Egypt and serve their people. Here again it should be noted that Jethro *believed* him. There is no record that Jethro said,

"Dig these crazy mixed-up kids!—Now you get back out there into the desert with those sheep!"

On the contrary Jethro blessed him and said,

"Moses, go in peace."

The point here is abundantly clear. When God gave Moses a *job* to do, a *story* to tell, a *message* to deliver, and a *service* to render—*these things made Moses eloquent. And these factors will make anyone eloquent!*

*Little People with Homely Experiences May*
*Develop Great Power*

Some years ago it was the author's privilege to address the annual convention of the Minnesota State Junior Chamber of Commerce. A feature of the program that evening was the winner of the state oratorical contest, who was to present the winning speech. This proved to be a remarkable event.

The winner was a girl from New Zealand who had come to

Minnesota to live with a farm family and attend high school. Her name was Kathy. Her speech was a magnificent example of the platform power that can come from a sincere desire to make one's experiences and convictions contribute to the lives of others.

Kathy related that when she was a little girl, living in New Zealand, she used to be impressed with the cowboys who rode by her home on their horses. There was a *"look"* in their faces. She never understood it exactly, but it was always there. When she reached San Francisco, on her way to Minnesota, she got her first view of a big city. There under the neon lights she saw the people's faces—and in them was that "look"—that same *something* she had always noted in the cowboys back home.

Kathy reached Minnesota and sat down for the first meal with the wonderful farm family with whom she was to live while she attended high school. There, as the family sat around the table with bowed heads, the father returned thanks. Out of the corner of her eye Kathy stole a glance at the faces of the family—and there it was again! In the family's faces was that same *something*. Kathy decided "it was *freedom*—that's what it was!"

When the time came for the oratorical contest Kathy made up her mind to enter. She decided she would talk about what it was she had seen in the people's faces—in New Zealand, San Francisco, and Minnesota. But she could not make a whole speech out of this one observation. She had to decide *what freedom is*. And she came up with a remarkable definition. Kathy said, "Freedom is the right all people have *to be as happy as they can*."

The people in the audience that evening had heard the classic definitions of freedom from Aristotle down through Thomas Jefferson, Woodrow Wilson, and down to now. But this definition was *Kathy's*. She had *lived* it. She had figured out what that *something* was and she put it into her own words. She felt deeply about the subject, and she felt compelled to get up and tell people about it. She talked with her teacher and found out how to smooth up her technique. She got instruction to correct her deficiencies *at the time she felt the need for such help*. Here we have all the elements for a good speech. Kathy could not fail to win with a hand like that—and she did win.

## Franklin D. Roosevelt

Now let us take a quick overview of one more extremely successful speaker—Franklin Delano Roosevelt. This speaker was most fortunate that his first campaign for national office followed the advent of the radio as a common means of communication. (Most competent observers agree William Jennings Bryan could have been elected President had the nation been wired for sound in his day.) Indeed the radio was the key to Roosevelt's phenomenal success with the public throughout his unprecedentedly long occupancy of the White House. The radio fitted his need perfectly because Roosevelt's greatest asset as a speaker was his voice. It was a voice that came into millions of homes in "fireside chats" and on many other occasions, and somehow made millions of people feel the man himself was in the room—talking to each of them personally. With some 80% of the nation's newspapers politically opposed to him, Roosevelt used his voice to talk directly to the people and a resounding majority of them believed him. It is not the purpose of this brief description to discuss whether the doctrines that voice promulgated were economically or politically sound. We are examining Roosevelt only in his capacity as a speaker.

When Franklin Roosevelt stood to address a public meeting it was necessary for him to constantly support himself with one hand. Thus he had but one hand free with which to turn pages and gesture. He was also completely restricted as to physical movement. To offset these handicaps he developed remarkably expressive facial movements, and "gestured" with a flip of his head, or a tilt of the chin.

Roosevelt studied his delivery technique with great care. He is reported to have remarked to Orson Wells, "You know, Orson, you and I are the two best actors in America." [1] John Gunther reports that after Roosevelt saw himself in a newsreel once he grinned and said, "That was the Garbo in me." [2] These admis-

[1] Ernest Brandenburg and Waldo W. Braden in Hochmuth, *History and Criticism of the American Public Address* (New York: Longmans Green and Company), Vol. III, p. 516, 1955.

[2] John Gunther, *Roosevelt in Retrospect* (New York: Harper and Brothers, 1950).

sions of acting were fuel for the flames of his critics who were already convinced he was insincere. But even such a bitter critic as John F. Flynn conceded that "Roosevelt possessed a golden voice and a seductive and challenging radio technique." [3]

One of President Roosevelt's most disarming devices was to align himself with the listener. He would preface a statement with such remarks as "You and I know . . ." Very often the listener would then accept what he would have otherwise held in abeyance, or rejected. Subconsciously he was thinking that if he did not know this "fact" before, then he *should* have—because the President *assumed* that he did—and had obviously *expected* him to know it. As a speaker, Roosevelt said "We" instead of "I." Or, "This we must do for *our* children." While he never attempted to disguise his Groton-Harvard accent, he nevertheless developed a technique and terminology that were downright "folksy" in their over-all tone.

*Good Speakers Vary Widely But Have
One Thing in Common*

The brief sketches of the four speakers we have set forth here should be sufficient to show that there is no fixed mold into which one must fit in order to be a "good" speaker. All of these were good speakers and yet their techniques and general approaches bear almost no resemblance to one another. It is therefore obvious that *you do not need to ape someone else in order to be a superior speaker.* This fact becomes more pronounced as one continues to add names of prominent speakers and study their identifying characteristics. But there is one common denominator —all of them used speech *as a medium of accomplishment.* Moody was saving people's souls. Rogers was saving people's sanity. Washington was the "humble representative" of his race who directed every speech toward the same general goals. Roosevelt knew a man cannot be a successful statesman unless he is a successful politician, so he used speech to explain procedures and enlist support.

In each of the four cases examined, the speaker used speech as a *vehicle* to deliver what he believed was a *service.* In each

[3] Flynn, *The Roosevelt Myth* (New York: Devin-Adair Company, 1956).

case the speaker was convinced there was a vastly important *job to be done and that he was the man to do it*. Certainly it must now be obvious that this kind of speaking is a far call from the simple, mechanical approach of studying the devices of public speaking, and then looking about for a subject that we can pour into the fixed forms we have learned to build.

One will not run far afoul of a desirable course if he will follow Booker T. Washington's simple rule of speaking only when he has something to say. A freshman member of the House of Commons once asked the great Disraeli if the old members were wondering why the new member did not speak in the House. "Young man," said Disraeli, "it is better to have them wondering why you do not speak, than wondering why you do."

By ignoring Disraeli's advice the young speaker could have become as involved as in the classic example of another Member of Parliament who was haranguing his colleagues with a dry-as-dust discourse. At the end of the first hour he paused and took a sip of water. Then again facing the House he said,

"I pause to ask myself a question."

A member on the back bench cried out,

"And it's a damned dull answer you'll get!"

## The Wrong Kind of Practice Doesn't Make Perfect

There is a common belief that we learn by doing—that practice makes perfect. If you want to be a speaker, then you should prepare by the simple and direct expedient of making speeches. Unfortunately, to follow this policy without embodying any of the philosophy set forth in this chapter will not bring the desired results. There is no use practicing your mistakes.

The writer knows two men who entered politics at the same time to run for the office of mayor. Both were without experience in public speaking. Both started the campaign with virtually no oratorical skill. The campaign was an almost ideal arena for "learning by doing." The schedule frequently called for a half-dozen speeches in a day. One of the candidates warmed to the challenge. He was not only elected but he went into office with the confidence of a proficient speaker. The other candidate was ignominiously defeated at the close of a pathetic campaign. He apparently learned nothing after the first day. On election day his platform technique was as awkward and ineffective as it had been in the beginning. Furthermore, his voice was worn out and unpleasant. What accounts for the difference?

Granting that there was a difference in the native ability of the two candidates, the major part of the difference in their campaign results can still be accounted for in one fundamental fact. The first man sincerely believed that he and his fellow citizens were getting a "lousy deal" at the city hall. He had tried to correct the problems by making speeches *to* the mayor. He finally decided he would run for mayor himself and make his speeches to the voters. He was thoroughly fortified with facts and completely sincere in his motives.

As he progressed through the campaign he picked up additional points that were troubling the voters, along with "live" illustrations to go with those points. In this manner he not only kept his material fresh, but he constantly increased his power. He got so much information in his arsenal that he became confident and adept at conducting question-and-answer periods following his speeches. He repeatedly said in closing his campaign speeches,

"Friends, if you will make me your mayor, I will use the power of that office to deliver to you these things that are rightfully yours. But, if you elect my opponent, then I will still be grateful for the opportunity this campaign has given me to say a lot of things that desperately needed to be said."

The second, and unsuccessful, candidate in the above illustration ran for office because he had the *time* to "serve the people"— he was temporarily out of employment anyway. He really had no platform. The big "issue" was to get the incumbent out and himself in. He prepared one speech according to the best "form," and harped on that one string throughout the campaign. After a few days of campaigning he was as bored with the speech as were his listeners. Soon he could not even fake any enthusiasm for his points. He never really learned anything after the first day. At the close of the campaign this candidate claimed he had had "sixty straight days of speaking experience." Actually he had just one day of experience—sixty times.

*Your Opportunities to Serve Will Increase*
*in Proportion to Your Capacity*

It is hoped that we have now established that the eminently successful speaker uses speech as a *vehicle* to deliver something to his hearers that will be a *service to them*. Does this mean one cannot become a good speaker unless his vehicle is filled with such weighty loads as those operated by the great divine, the world-renowned statesman, the university president, or the eminent industrialist? Indeed not.

When Will Rogers was talking informally with his audiences at the Ziegfeld Follies, he could not possibly foresee what a great figure he was to become through his daily column, his speeches, his radio appearances, and his movies. He was merely delivering something that was useful to the people who *were in front of him then and there*. He sincerely felt people needed to be lifted out of their daily ruts, to look at themselves with humor and perspective—and he believed he could render that service to the people who came to the Follies. As he enlarged his *capacity* to serve, his *opportunities* for service increased. This is the usual experience of the sincerely motivated person. If you have a sincere desire to serve in the field of religion, you do not have to start out as a Billy Graham, but you can teach that class of young adults in your Sunday School. If that class grows, it means you are growing. Presently you will not only be serving more people every Sunday in the class, but you will find additional opportunities for larger sounding boards outside the class.

You do not have to diagnose the weaknesses of the United Nations to have a topic worthy of development before your local civic club. Perhaps some of the club members desperately need to develop special interests, or hobbies, to give them a change of pace, and preserve their balance under the pressure of their responsibilities. You may give them a fascinatingly interesting discourse upon something about which you are thoroughly familiar and tremendously enthused. It may be gardening, or boating, or books, or music. And when you share your enthusiasms you are saying to tired souls, "Go thou and do likewise." And some of them will go—and they will rise up and call you blessed because you helped them. As you help the smaller numbers in the smaller things you are increasing your own ability to help larger numbers in larger ways, and eventually the "multitudes will hearken unto your voice."

## A Good Speech Is Genuine Service

A well-prepared and well-delivered speech is a service because of the following factors:

1. It saves the time of the hearers. The grain has been separated from the chaff before they were invited to the meeting. When you save time you save life, because, as Franklin said, time is the stuff that life is made of. In the rush of modern living people are grateful to those who save their time by showing them short-cuts for acquiring valuable information.

2. As has been previously pointed out, a good speech does the job of *transposing* information into understanding. A properly prepared presentation sends the hearers forth with measuring sticks for meeting their problems. They go away better organized as *individuals* and more capable of determining what things are really important.

3. Frequently a well-prepared address will not only state problems and suggest solutions, but it will also *inspire action*. "When Cicero spoke the people said, 'How well Cicero speaks!' But when Demosthenes spoke, the people said, 'Let us march against Carthage!' "

4. Finally, the effective speech very often conveys vital information and inspiration to people who simply never would get it in any other way. There are many people who will never grasp certain facts unless some able individual stands up, looks them in the eye, and *tells* them. Maybe we are becoming a nation of "intellectual sloths," as one columnist recently declared. If so, we had better increase our facilities for meeting this fact, as well as stepping up efforts to reverse the trend.

## Proficiency in Speech Is Not Achieved Without Sacrifice

To serve others through the medium of public speech is not an easy undertaking. It requires careful preparation, real "deep sea" thinking, and an unbelievable amount of effort in a variety of ways. When it is done on an ascending scale it often means one works all day, travels half the night (or all of it), and works the next day along side the people who slept the night before. It is an activity that requires an incredible number of evenings that could be otherwise devoted to recreation, relaxation, and rest. It is the kind of work one never "finishes." When carried on rather extensively, speaking activities constitute something of a perpetual three-ring circus—one must think simultaneously in terms of what he has done, what he is doing, and what he is scheduled to do in the future. It requires a constant shifting of one's mental gears.

Gene Flack, a veteran sales speaker, occasionally used a gag in his opening remarks that demonstrated how confused a speaker can get. When he was introduced to a group such as the National Manufacturers Association, or a Chamber of Commerce, he would rise, take some notes from his pocket, and say,

"Mr. Chairman, head table guests, and fellow members of the A. F. of L.—C. I. O." He would then hastily return the notes to his pocket and say, "Pardon me, ladies and gentlemen, that is my speech for *tomorrow* night." The device was always good for a laugh.

One who loves his routine and 40-hour weeks should stay strictly away from the speaking field. It is a situation that recalls the story of the man who told Jesus he wanted to be a Disciple, but he did not want to leave home. Jesus could not use this man. When one accepts the philosophy that speech is a *service* he must accept the things that go along with that concept—hard work, irregular hours, a thousand inconveniences, and often a frustrated feeling that he could have done better, or he could have done more. But there are also heart-warming rewards.

### The 1960 Presidential Campaign Brought New Significance to Speaking

The 1960 presidential campaign brought a new and unprecedented importance to public speaking. The day after the election, Robert Kennedy, who served as campaign manager for his brother, said,

"Without the television debates Jack would not have had a chance."

The above fact may revolutionize the campaigning of the future. Perhaps no man will ever again be elected President of the United States who cannot effectively address fifty to one hundred million people at one time.

The 1960 campaign also brought forth a new device for disrupting a speaker. It is called the "silent heckler." This type of heckler says nothing but merely stands in front of the speaker with a placard that boldly displays a slogan or statement designed to let the speaker know the heckler opposes him. For example, each time Richard Nixon drove home a point with one New York crowd a large sign was held up in front of his face which read, "Please Say Something." Both candidates had to adjust themselves to such unnerving tactics as they made their unheard-of number of personal appearances.

Dr. Edward Rosenow, formerly with the Mayo Clinic in Rochester, Minnesota, told of the experience that caused him to become associated with the field of medicine. When he was a small boy living in Minnesota, his brother became acutely ill. The family sweated it out until the doctor arrived. As the physician examined his sick brother, Edward Rosenow kept his eyes riveted on the anxious and anguished faces of his parents. Finally, the doctor turned to the parents with a smile and said,

"You can relax, folks, your boy is going to be all right."

Young Edward Rosenow was profoundly impressed with the change that announcement brought over his parents. In relating the incident in later years he said,

"I resolved then and there that I was going to be a doctor—*so I could put light in people's faces.*"

In all the world there are few experiences more rewarding than putting light in people's faces. It is a reward that comes often to the speaker who becomes thoroughly imbued with the concept of speech as a service—whose thoughts catch fire and become a torch to light the way for others.

# 3

# Speaker Must Be *Informed*

*"A feller can't no more explain what he don't know than he can come back from where he ain't been."*—Mountain Philosopher

It will be remembered that a basic provision in William Jennings Bryan's definition of eloquence is that the speaker *"knows what he is talking about"*—that he must be *"thoroughly informed."* It has been made clear in the opening chapters of this book that the good speaker can be developed only after two basic conditions have been met: First, he must possess information that can render a valuable service to others. Secondly, he must himself be fired with the enthusiasm that comes with the realization that he has an obligation to literally *deliver* that service.

The effective speaker must possess a great deal more information about his subject than he uses at any one time. It is only in this manner that he can speak with complete *understanding* upon the points that he does use. His presentation should be only the refined product of much research, experience, and thought. He should reserve the skim milk for those who wish to remain intellectually and spiritually thin, but he should deliver only the cream to those whom he wants to build up rapidly.

An intelligent audience will invariably sense when a speaker is "scraping the bottom of the barrel" to develop his presentation. The difference between depth and shallowness is too obvious to avoid detection for very long. The speaker who has unlimited resources upon which to draw will muster confidence as he develops his topic, and that confidence will in turn relax his audience into a mood of acceptance. When the hearers are convinced "the guy knows his stuff" they settle into a "listening mood" that adds still further to the speaker's effectiveness. Conversely, uneasiness and doubt grow in an audience if the people sense that the speaker is "pushing the foot feed clear to the floor" with every statement, and that he has nothing left for the hill. They have a vague feeling that he cannot stay in business very long because he has all his merchandise in the show window. He is trying to sell them a bushel of apples by putting all the big ones on top. The very fact that he thought he could get away with a shallow presentation is not very complimentary to his hearers. The result is an increasing skepticism that makes the speaker's problems mount as he attempts to sell his ideas. To sum it up one way, there is nothing more pathetic than an empty speaker addressing a full house.

Braude [1] tells of a farmer who attended a church convention and listened to the speeches on how to get people to attend church. When it was his turn to speak the farmer said,

"I have never heard a single address at a farmer's convention on how to get cattle to come to the feed rack. We spend our time discussing the best kinds of feeds."

It seems customary of late for television entertainers to quote their "grandpappies." Perhaps it will be in order at this point to quote my Scotch grandmother who said,

"When there's feed in the trough, the sheep will come ta it."

### *"The Main Ingredient of Ignorance Is the Desire to Prove It"*

If the speaker is not fully informed and thoroughly prepared, he should not accept the invitation to speak. He should *never* accept the invitation and then begin his remarks by announcing that he is not ready. If he has "nothing to say," he should not let anyone induce him to say it. Few experiences are more exasperating than to have a speaker announce in his opening remarks that

[1] Braude, *Encyclopedia of Stories, Quotations, and Anecdotes* (Englewood Cliffs, N. J.: Prentice-Hall, Inc.), 1955.

he is unprepared and then take a half-hour of some important people's valuable time to prove the truth of his first statement. His hearers will accept his statement on its face value if he will just omit the proof, and he will have preserved their good will for that day when he comes back into the arena fully armed and ready.

Without any prior notice whatever, an experienced speaker was called upon by an inexperienced chairman. Not only did the chairman's introduction come like a bolt from the blue, but he even announced the subject he wanted the speaker to "briefly develop."

The speaker was in a state of temporary shock, but he was a veteran. He smilingly acknowledged the introduction and told the audience how flattered he was that the chairman apparently thought him capable of handling so difficult a subject with no advance notice. He then told the classic story of the farmer who was whipping a team of mules up a muddy hill road in a frantic effort to get a load of potatoes to the top. Unbeknown to the farmer, while he was flaying the mules, the end gate of the wagon came open and all of the potatoes rolled out. Even then the wagon bogged down and came to a stop. The team could not budge it. It was at this point that the farmer looked around and discovered the wagon was empty. He summed up his situation neatly by saying,

"Stuck, by Gad, and nuthin' to unload!"

After relating this incident the speaker smilingly said,

"Let's face it, folks. This is exactly my situation right now."

And he sat back down, with the good will of everyone in the room.

*No One Has Ever Found a Satisfactory Substitute for Brains—Nor for* Preparation

Many of the people who seek to become speakers these days are products of the schools as they were operated under the extreme Progressive educationists. This school of educational philosophy de-emphasized the acquiring of facts and substituted the developing of good attitudes and "balanced personalities." America was rudely blasted out of its complacency by the firing of the first Sputnik, but the influence of the Progressives lives on. It is evident in speeches where the "word count" is high and the "idea count" is low. Too many speakers are trying to substitute "personality" for information. The same tendency is true in the fields of sales, business, education, and elsewhere.

Many speakers turn out to be mediocre for the same reason that limits achievement in countless other endeavors, and that is just plain laziness. They like the spotlight but they do not like the hard work that makes one look good under the spotlight. It has been well said that artistry consists of making the difficult look easy. This necessarily implies *mastery* in whatever field one may want to be an artist, and mastery comes only with work. There can seldom be any deviation from the formula that spectacular achievement must be preceded by unspectacular preparation.

## Make Sure the "Something New" You Are Using Is Not "Old Stuff" to Your Hearers

There is also danger that the fledgling speaker will "discover" a gem that is so hackneyed as to incite open revolt if he uses it again. For example, when a speaker recently started to quoting "The Bridge Builder" an audible groan escaped from his audience. The people had been across that bridge so many times through the years that they simply could not face the boredom of crossing again—"in the twilight dim," or at any other time. A similar reaction took place with another audience when a speaker launched into "Somebody said it couldn't be done . . ." The crowd couldn't believe the poor old poem could be done *again*—but here the man was doing it!

A classic cartoon depicts an audience attending a recital by a baritone. The facial expressions of the audience reveal that they have "had it." The soloist has just announced another number when a frustrated little man in the balcony stands and cries out in anguish,

"No, Sir! My God, Sir! *Not* the Road to Mandalay!"

The speaker should remember that the same mental rebellion is likely to occur among his listeners as he recites such bromides as,

When the One Great Scorer comes to write
      against your name—
He writes not whether you won or lost,
But how you played the game!

Actually, if you are using this kind of material in your speeches, you should be grateful for the above truism—because *you've* lost! It may be true, as the poem indicates, that the Great Scorer won't hold it against you—but your audience will!

When your speech preparation brings you across something "new," be sure it is not just new to *you*. One recalls the classic story of an Englishman, Robert, and a Frenchman, Pierre, who worked side by side in a New York factory. They were old buddies. Each morning they met on the same street corner so they could walk together for the last three blocks to the factory. After work each evening they went to a neighborhood bar and drank wine together before parting company for the night.

One morning when Robert arrived at the corner, where Pierre was waiting as usual, their routine was rudely changed. Without a word of warning Pierre flattened Robert with a fist to the jaw. With his jaw and his feelings both badly hurt, Robert struggled to his feet and asked in shocked surprise why Pierre had done such a thing.

Pierre said, "Because you British burned our Joan of Arc at the stake!"

"Why," said Robert, "that happened over 500 years ago."

"That may be," said Pierre, "but I just heard about it last night!"

The speaker must make sure before he breaks out with a newly discovered "gem" that it isn't something very old that he has just heard. While anything in this bracket is hard for an audience to swallow, the speaker can never be forgiven who tells an old, beaten-up joke as something that just happened to him as he "was coming to the meeting." Nothing is more certain to horrify an audience than to have a speaker relate some classic illustration or story as a true, personal experience.

### *One Misstatement of Fact Can Discredit the Rest of a Good Speech*

One rule of public speaking is a rule of good reporting—get the *facts*. As Oliver Wendell Holmes said, "No generalization is worth a damn—including this one."

In preparing his materials a speaker will be motivated to make sure of his facts if he will but remember that someone in his audience will probably be well-versed on most of the factual points he will present. Perhaps one of the listeners will be thoroughly familiar with one point, while another hearer is well-informed on another phase of the speech. Taken all together, the speaker should proceed on the basis that no factual point will be presented that is not known by someone in his audience. The larger and more heterogeneous the group, and the larger the geographical area represented, the more likely is this general thesis to be true. It is a rather sad commentary, but true, that some people like nothing better than to catch a speaker in error on a point, even if it is a comparatively insignificant one. There is a type of personality that will gladly wait around for half an hour after a lecture just for the privilege of pointing out an error to the speaker personally. Such a person can usually be recognized by his approach to the speaker. "I enjoyed your speech very much, *but* you said Hillsdale is 17 miles from Pottsburg, and it is only 15½. I was born at Pottsburg and have gone over that road to Hillsdale a thousand times."

It is not the trivial errors a speaker makes, or allegedly makes, that pose the serious threat. There is a real danger in a straight-out error of fact, or a deliberate omission in the facts used to support a conclusion. In the courtroom a lawyer dearly loves to damage his opponent's case by doing what is called "discrediting a witness." If the attorney can demonstrate to a jury that *one* part of a witness's testimony is incorrect, then he has cast doubt over *all* of the witness's testimony. The same thing applies to the speaker. If certain people in the audience know the speaker is incorrect about a point with which they are thoroughly familiar, then they naturally become suspicious of the validity of the balance of the speaker's discourse, even though they have no specific grounds for such doubt.

## A Speaker Should Constantly Increase His Sources of Supply

How does one acquire the information, spirit, poise, and judgment to consistently produce speaking viewpoints that render real service and consequently command respect? W. G. Hoffman gives us some of the answer:

One should be abreast of the thought of his day. He should know what people are thinking in politics, business, education, science, and art. He should be familiar with right- and left-wing thought. He shouldn't be a contemptuous radical nor a pious conservative. He should read the newspapers but realize it isn't the business of the newspapers to go deeply into the meaning of things they report. There are books and magazines that can do that better, but they should not be read without a certain amount of challenge and suspended judgment. Opinions should not be formed by one book. Intellectuals, as well as others, go haywire.[2]

In addition to the above helpful suggestions the successful speaker must *live on many levels*. He must be at home in a variety of groups and his interests must be both varied and sincere. As Emerson said, "Speak with the vulgar and think with the wise." One of the greatest speakers of all time, Daniel Webster, gave us a golden key to the door we are now trying to unlock when he said,

"Converse, *converse*, CONVERSE, with living men, face to face, mind to mind—that is one of the best sources of knowledge."

The successful speaker must learn to be a part of life and yet apart from it. He must flow right through life, touching it on all sides, and yet keep his own personality and his own identity intact. It is not a job for either the recluse nor the playboy. It takes quite a tall individual to keep his head in the clouds and his feet on the ground, but that is something of what is demanded. One of the best things about such a challenge is that most anyone who strives to meet it is bound to grow taller in the trying.

[2] William G. Hoffman, *The Speaker's Notebook* (New York: Whittlesey House, 1943).

*How the More Youthful May Impress the More Mature*

Reflection upon the proper preparation for a successful speaker seems to always place the advantage with the person who has a lot of experience under his belt. Such a person can have something more than knowledge—he can have wisdom. He has judgment that is based on knowledge and general maturity. He is better qualified to talk about the general business of living because he has personally experienced more of it.

How, then, can the younger speaker overcome the handicaps of immaturity and inexperience? To overcome a lack of mature understanding based upon broad backgrounds of living, the younger, or less experienced speaker may safely rely upon two techniques. First, he can in the beginning limit his discourses to subjects where his comparative youth is not a handicap. He should avoid subjects that require him to come forth with preachments to people that are older than he. He should stick to subjects where he can rely more on undeniable facts, and deal less frequently in fields that call for broad-gauge conclusions.

This does not mean the less experienced speaker need limit his remarks to statistics or other types of cold facts. His speeches need not be devoid of any of the elements that give meaning an on-goingness to an address. But he should usually develop presentations where he lets the audience conclude from the facts he presents, rather than simply asking them to accept certain conclusions out of respect for his own authority.

There is a second and better method whereby the younger, or less experienced speaker can meet a more mature audience on equal terms. That is for the speaker to draw both his data and major conclusions from sources which the audience will readily concede are superior to its own. The author well remembers a striking example of how this technique was used with great success in an extremely difficult situation.

On a Friday noon in September a beautiful little girl in the writer's hometown went home for lunch from a third grade room at school. Someone at the home said,

"Honey, will you go over to the neighborhood grocery and get a loaf of bread?"

The little girl started to the store. She stepped into the street from between two parked cars, was struck by a delivery truck, and killed instantly. To make matters worse, she was an only child. And to make the situation about as bad as it could get, her mother had been killed in a car wreck just the preceding June.

I attended that little girl's funeral the following Sunday afternoon. The situation I found would have been a challenge to anyone, no matter how vast his experience. A large crowd of friends and relatives had assembled. One could sense they were completely demoralized. The people were so shocked, grieved, frustrated, and confused that they were literally falling apart. Toward the front sat the young bereaved father. It had been only a matter of weeks before that he had possessed a wonderful family. Now, here he was—horribly alone.

The writer could not help but feel great sympathy for the minister who was to conduct that service. He was obviously on a terrible spot. What *would* he say to the young father? What *could* he say that would do any good at all? What would he say to all the others assembled? They had come there desperately wanting something. How could it be given them?

When the minister came forth to take charge of the service, the prospects looked more hopeless than ever. He was very young. He seemed frightfully immature. In fact, he did not look equal to any part of what the occasion demanded. But this appraisal proved entirely unfounded.

The young minister looked over the crowded room and in an even voice he said,

"Friends, I am not going to begin this service this afternoon by telling you that the thing that has brought us together is God's will. The God I worship doesn't kill little girls. He doesn't kill their mothers, either. This is just stark tragedy. I would not for a moment try to make anything more than that out of it. And I certainly would not for a moment pretend that I understand why things like this have to happen. I am as confused and hurt this afternoon as any of you could possibly be.

"If we were depending upon my resources to meet the needs of this hour, we would be in a bad way. I have not lived very long. I have not lived very broadly, either. I have never lost a member of my own family. I am not prepared to speak to you from personal experience with grief. Nor can I speak with the general wisdom of maturity.

"But, thank God, *we are not depending upon my resources.* Thank God, that I, who know so little, *can* bring you the words of Him *who knows all.* I can bring you the words of Him who did lose His only Son. I can bring you the words of the Son, too, who was himself a 'Man of sorrow and acquainted with grief.'

"Let us begin this service with a prayer. Something of a two-edged prayer. First, a prayer of *gratitude*—that this magnificent help exists for us when we need it so desperately. Secondly, a prayer of *guidance,* as to how we can best take advantage of this help."

As the young minister prayed that afternoon one could literally *feel* strength come into the situation. I thought to myself, "The young man's prayer must be going *straight up to the throne of God.*" I remembered that God was pleased with Solomon, not because he asked for wisdom, but the *reason* for which he asked it—to better *serve* his people. That was exactly what this young minister was doing!

When the opening prayer was completed, the youthful minister read powerful portions of Scripture that sustain and strengthen us in times of trial. He summarized and commented upon the Scripture reading, briefly and effectively. There was a closing prayer. And that was it. The service was over. But the situation had changed completely. The people were still grief stricken, of course, but they were not demoralized any more. The transformation that had taken place in the young bereaved father was almost miraculous. When the service ended he walked out on his own power, with his head high, and his eyes dry!

As I left there that afternoon I found myself uttering my own little prayer, which went something like this,

"Dear God, You were not afraid to give your own Son terrifying responsibilities because He was young. Thank You for trusting another young man to help us today."

## How This Technique May Be Used by Young Salesmen

It should be remembered that comparative youth, or inexperience, does not prevent one from meeting authority with *better* authority from outside himself. This fact can be of great help to the beginning salesman. No fledgling salesman should make the mistake of sitting down across the desk from some heavy executive and telling him,

"Now, Mr. Smith, here is what *I* think you need . . ."

In all probability Mr. Smith will not be listening. He will probably be thinking how he was running that business "before this nincompoop was born." How did he ever get along without knowing what this young squirt thought he should do?

Suppose, on the other hand, the young salesman starts out with this approach,

"Mr. Smith, our *company* has been in business seventy-five years. We have grown bigger and stronger throughout that time for the same reason your own good company has grown. We have made it our business to *serve* people. Today I am just a little piece of our company sitting in your office, but I am officially authorized to serve you with every bit of the resources and know-how that our whole organization has accumulated in three-quarters of a century. That is the only justification I have for taking your valuable time, and I sincerely believe you are going to feel that the news I bring from my company is *good* news."

In this approach the younger man nullifies the advantage the older man originally held in the matter of experience, success, and maturity. The young man took himself out of the picture as a personality. He became his company's official representative, and he then *represented seventy-five years of successful experience and service*. He is not there to tell the older man what he thinks, nor what the older man should think. He simply stands ready and able to help. The field is now clear for doing business.

One new sales representative made a smash hit with his company's top accounts in his territory by using this simple approach with the executives upon whom he was calling for the first time,

"Mr. Williams, the Morgan Company is still your old friend, just as it has been through all these years. But the firm got a new *delivery wagon* for this territory—and I am it. They told me to deliver more service to you than you ever got from anybody before and that is just what I am going to do!"

Dr. G. Herbert True developed a device which effectively overcame his comparative youth as a speaker. Preliminary to meeting a speaking engagement for a company or organization he sometimes makes a survey of problems pertaining specifically to the group he is to address. His speech then takes the nature of a *reporting* job. This plan has an advantage in that it is obvious the speaker did not create the facts and problems which he discusses. On the contrary, the audience must more often take the responsibility for the problems, and the speaker is in the favorable position of being there to help find solutions. In using this technique the speaker can further increase his objectivity by also making recommendations based upon the results of other studies and surveys.

### Extemporaneous and Impromptu Speaking Does Not Eliminate the Necessity for Preparation

In any discussion of the information and preparation of a speaker the question invariably arises: What about the art of extemporaneous speaking? It is a common mistake to confuse *extemporaneous* speaking with *impromptu* speaking. While these words are frequently used as synonyms, they do not mean the same thing in speech. In the extemporaneous speech the speaker has planned the *ideas* he wishes to present but has not reduced them to an exact wording he will use when he speaks. He may say the same things in different ways and in different terminology, but the speech itself is organized in advance.

The term "impromptu" usually indicates the speaker makes the speech without advance warning. This type of speech is given in response to a sudden call or unanticipated opportunity.

It may seem paradoxical but it is true that both the extemporaneous and the impromptu speech may be carefully planned in advance, and even rehearsed. In fact, if they are good speeches of their type, they, in all probability were carefully prepared. In a later chapter it will be recommended that the "extemporaneous" speaker should work from a carefully prepared outline and rehearse his remarks until he is saying the same things "in about the same way." This plan avoids the defects of both the memorized speech and the unrehearsed one. Similarly, the good impromptu speech is one that is carefully thought out. Most of it may have been rehearsed and delivered on one or more

previous occasions. It is impromptu only in the sense that it is
called forth without much advanced notice for the *particular
occasion*.

There is nothing in the art of extemporaneous and impromptu
speaking that does violence to the basic tenets of this book. The
best speeches of these "informal" types are so thoroughly prepared that they *appear* "extemporaneous." Any speaker, experienced or inexperienced, who goes to meetings without preparation and depends upon the "spirit to move him," is doomed to
failure. He may find the "Lord was with him" for one occasion,
but the next time the Lord will be busy helping somebody else
and he falls flat on his face.

The writer once heard an "impromptu" speech which impressed him tremendously. At the close of the speech he rushed
over to a newspaper reporter who was present and said, "I hope
your notes are sufficient to give this speech good coverage."

The reporter said, "You can read it word for word in the
morning paper. It was all set up in type before the chairman
ever 'surprised' the speaker by calling on him for a 'few words.' "

Mark Twain said it took him about three weeks "to prepare a
good impromptu speech."

Extemporaneous speeches can be built in advance somewhat
like prefabricated houses, and then merely *assembled* on the
sites. Of course, the speaker needs a little more latitude than an
architect would permit on a house. The speaker gets everything
ready before he goes to the site. After he arrives he must consider what his neighbors, the other speakers, have already built.
Then he decides in the light of the total situation how many of
his rooms to assemble. He may use all of the ones he had ready
or he may eliminate some. He may even add a few new features
on the spur of the moment. But he has the main structure in
mind before he goes to the meeting place, and he makes sure
that the completed job contains all the essentials, and possesses
good balance.

Secondly, it can be pointed out that good extemporaneous and
impromptu speakers are usually loaded with certain key thoughts
and core materials that can be easily adapted to most any situation. For example, there are certain points that are sure to

interest specified types of audiences at a given time. Citizenship themes apply with more or less equal force to all groups. Regardless of how widely divergent may be the ways in which people make their living, they have a common denominator in general citizenship themes. They all love their families and they want conditions of peace and prosperity in which to raise them. Community problems may be generally assumed to be of interest to most all the people who live in the community. Most people have an interest in spiritual values, and can also strike a common chord in many things of a cultural and ethical nature. Again, certain timely facts and observations on sales, finance, labor, management, advertising, and industrial matters can be quickly tailored to reach a wide variety of groups that all fall in the general bracket of "business." These techniques are among the things that account for the successful "extemporaneous" speaker.

### *It Is Necessary to Think Before Speaking, But You Must Also Think* While *Speaking*

None of this should be construed to mean there is no premium for the art of *"thinking* on your feet." The individual who does not improve his ability along that line will not be on his feet often before public meetings. The extemporaneous speaker, like all speakers, will find plently of need to think—even when he is loaded with worthwhile materials. Thinking is so terribly important in the art of speaking that one should do as much of it as possible in *advance.* Then the thinking he does while on his feet can be the "frosting on the cake." It can mark the difference between "boring 'em and flooring 'em."

H. Roe Bartle, of Kansas City, Missouri, a widely-known speaker, has recounted an experience that emphasizes the importance of "thinking on your feet." When Bartle was a struggling young lawyer in Tennessee, a woman came down out of the hills and engaged him to sue the railroad. Bartle was mighty anxious to sue somebody, and he eagerly entered into his preparation of the case. Some days later his client, the hill woman, came to his office to inform him that she wanted another lawyer. When Bartle registered surprise, she explained she was not firing him—she wanted two lawyers. Realizing that this meant splitting his fee, Bartle explained that he felt he had the case well in hand and he did not feel he needed any help. But the hill woman persisted. She said, "I found out the railroad company has got two lawyers. I figure it this way: While one of their lawyers is up there talkin', the other one is goin' to be settin' there *thinkin'*. But when you're up there talkin', they ain't goin' to be *nobody* thinkin'!"

Surely this is the key to many lost causes! Somebody up there talkin', but nobody thinkin'.

There will always be a premium for fast thinking at the time the action is taking place. As the Scotsman said, in telling his friend of his car accident,

"We would have collected no insurance a'tall if I had not had the presence of mind to kick my wife in the face just as our car was turnin' over."

As a young speaker, Dale Carnegie [3] had already learned to think on his feet. He was doing an illustrated lecture on the Far East. He had never visited the area and gave his speech from memory. One night a slide was flashed on the screen, but Dale could not think of the words to go with it. Without a hitch he said, "Ah! Here is another beautiful picture of the East. Let us enjoy it in silence."

In the art of effective speaking there can never be any substitute for reservoirs of information, for reserve power, and for defense in *depth*.

When Daniel Webster was in the midst of the monumental debate with Senator Hayne on the nature of the Union, he found himself with little time to prepare. Hayne's attack was so devastating that it had to be answered when the U. S. Senate convened the next day. The paramount question in the minds of the harried union forces was whether Webster could be ready. With so short notice, how could anyone make an immediate counter attack that would be strong enough to carry the field? Yet Webster met the challenge with power to spare. In his "Reply to Hayne" Webster reached one of the all-time highs in the history of oratory. A jubilant Senate colleague expressed

[3] Maxwell Droke, *Encyclopedia of Creative Thought* (New York: Maxwell Droke Publishing Company, 1941).

the wonderment of many when he said, "How did you prepare such a masterpiece *overnight*?"

Webster answered, "I didn't. I have been preparing that speech for *thirty years*."

Webster merely *assembled* the speech overnight, but he had inexhaustible sources from which to draw. He brought into play all the logic of a brilliant mind that had been made razor sharp in the practice of law, in political campaigns, and in legislative halls. His subject was the meaning of the U. S. Constitution—a document he had virtually memorized when he was a small boy and had carried it with him, printed on a silk handkerchief. And his motivation was to *save the United States,* which he loved with a passion that could not be excelled—and none could express it more eloquently than he. Add to these attributes the advantage of a completely overpowering platform personality and you can begin to assess what Daniel Webster brought with him to the Senate floor that day. Indeed, he did not get ready overnight!

There is a legend that President Lincoln dashed off the immortal Gettysburg Address while enroute to the dedicatory exercises for the famous cemetery. As a school boy wrote in his essay, "Lincoln wrote the Gettysburg Address while riding to Gettysburg on an envelope." Yet when we cut through the mountains of myth that surround this monumental event the facts emerge in quite a different light. Lincoln was accompanied to Gettysburg by Mayor James B. Frey, who said later the President did no writing on the trip.

Lincoln's Gettysburg Address was delivered November 19. It is significant that when he spoke informally to a crowd on the White House lawn the preceding July 4, he said,[4]

"How long ago is it? Eighty-odd years since, on the Fourth of July, for the first time in the history of the world, a nation . . . declared, as a self-evident truth, that 'all nations are created equal.' "

It can be noted in the above that more than four months before the Gettysburg address Lincoln was getting close to the classic,

[4] Earl W. Wiley, in Brigance, *History and Criticism of American Public Address* (New York: McGraw-Hill, 1943), Vol. II, p. 870.

"Four score and seven years ago . . ." Careful study of the facts causes Wiley [5] to conclude:

"Revision and yet more revision characterized Lincoln's composition method. The few score words he spoke at Gettysburg were months in the making. In a sense, the composing of that address had no beginning that we can identify, for the concepts that stimulated those words had long been in Lincoln's heart. The process of recasting tended to purge his style of its impromptu crudities and embellish it with the craftsmanship of vivid extemporaneous expression. This is an important consideration refuting the all-too-popular fallacy heard that the Gettysburg Address was the off-hand utterance of a man inspired."

This gets us back to one of our basic contentions—that no one can for long separate what he *says* from what he *is*. It is from this springboard that we can plunge into the next chapter.

[5] Earl W. Wiley, in Brigance, *History and Criticism of American Public Address* (New York: McGraw-Hill, 1943), Vol. II, p. 871.

**4**

# Preach What You Practice

*"What is in the well of your heart will show up
in the bucket of your speech."*

One claim this book may have to being different from
most volumes on the general subject of public speaking comes in
the fact that it does not plunge immediately into the specific techniques of speech. However, the reader who is impatient to get on
with the specifics may readily do so by simply turning to the
proper chapters. Meanwhile, it seems sound to continue developing this treatise on the foundational fact that the right kind of
thoughts cannot consistently come out of the wrong kind of people. You cannot separate the speaker from the speech.

This chapter does not purport to tell you what to say nor how
to say it. But it will help you build the platform of sound understanding upon which most every successful speaker must stand.

If you aspire to improve your effectiveness as a speaker, ask
yourself these questions:

1. Am I the kind of an *individual* whose opinions are respected?
What can I do to increase such respect?

2. Do I possess a basic philosophy of living that keeps me on
a steady course, or am I an opportunist who plays it by ear from
day to day?

3. How can I develop a philosophy that is so sound that it will
not only keep me moving in the right general directions, but will
permit me to take others along with me?

4. Do I really understand the *chief* causes of success and failure,

or am I merely mouthing a series of unrelated formulas that seem appropriate for the moment?

5. Am I expecting my speeches to pour out things that are not inside of me?

6. What are the simple virtues that give a personality *staying power*?

This chapter should help clarify your thinking on the above questions, and perhaps fill in some of the gaps in what you can firmly believe. It should also cause you to fortify your living philosophy with additional data and illustrations of your own, which you can in turn use to help others.

A basic premise of this book is that effective speech must be an out-pouring of one's own convictions, ideals, experience, knowledge, and faith. The speakers platform is no place for a phoney. Shoddiness shows up quickly under a spotlight. When you stand up to admonish others, you can never completely avoid the effect of saying, "If you do as I say, you will be like I am." If your hearers do not want to be like you are, then you have sharply reduced the effectiveness of your preachment.

Nothing in the above should be interpreted to mean that speeches should be made only by the lily white Adonis with a halo around the outside of his head, and an I.Q. of 175 on the inside. It is not necessary that your hearers should envy your appearance, your voice, your position, your success, your wife, or your bank account. Maybe they can out-score you on every one of these points and a lot more. But it is essential that your hearers should say to themselves, "Here is a *genuine person*. I can *believe in him* as an *individual,* and *therefore* I can *believe what he says*."

In December, 1959, President Eisenhower made his historic tour of eleven nations in nineteen days. Between nine and ten million people saw him personally. After the President had returned an editorial writer in my hometown had this to say,[1]

With a customary inclination to put everything away in pigeonholes, some critics, not at all unfriendly to President Eisenhower, already are calling the message of his 24,000-mile Friendship tour the "Eisenhower Doctrine."

[1] *Topeka State Journal,* December 22, 1959.

This has too dry and stale a sound for the vital, friendly, warm-hearted, almost person-to-person appeal of Eisenhower's extraordinary meetings with the masses of Asia and the Near East. As television cameras caught them, the faces of Asiatics along the way were lighted with mixtures of feelings—bonhommie, curiosity, fellow feeling, hope, trust. It is as if they were saying to this man, especially when his arm shot up in greeting or his face broke out in a grin—

"I think if I could talk to you, you would understand me and believe me; I like your looks; your smile isn't put-on; you're not kidding me or teasing me or mocking me; I know; you're not a phoney like so many of them; you're a real person."

People are all alike under the skin; all of us have the same starvation for affection and understanding, for sincerity and truth, for believable words and believable people.

It cannot be over-emphasized that nothing, absolutely nothing, can take the place of sincerity in a speaker. As Bryan said, "Persuasive speech must be from heart to heart, as well as from mind to mind."

A national organization of industrialists employed an ordained minister as a full-time speaker to tell the story of free enterprise to various groups across the country. This writer heard the speaker at an annual Chamber of Commerce Meeting. The speaker started out with a series of stories that were definitely "off color." He followed each of these stories by remarking, "Oh, I forgot I am a preacher." Then he would add, "Well, I am on leave-of-absence," or, "I am taking a vacation." His opening stories were greeted with a small amount of laughter, but the speech was doomed. What the man had done was to take a vacation from *personal integrity*. He was marked as a phoney. His hearers were not stupid. They could easily deduct this way:

"If this guy did not believe what he himself preached from the pulpit, why should we believe him *now*?"

Compare the above illustration, if you will, with that of another minister appearing on a program of a non-religious nature. Some years ago it was my privilege to address a breakfast meeting of the Los Angeles Sales Executives Club. It was one of those sessions where the group has breakfast and then sits around the table for an all-morning session with several speakers. Appearing ahead of me was a Los Angeles minister, Dr. James William

Fifield, Jr. After responding to his introducer with a few pleas-
antries that were in excellent taste, Dr. Fifield said,

"I am a minister of the Gospel. I am sure your committee knew
this when I was invited to speak here. I am also sure your committee knew I would never haul down my true colors and run up
a false flag for the privilege of speaking *anywhere*. So, I shall
speak to you this morning as a minister. Does this mean I cannot
bring you a message that is appropriate to a sales group? Not at
all. I want to tell you this morning about the Greatest Salesman
that ever trod the earth, and I want to show you that His selling
methods are more effective now than ever before."

The response to Dr. Fifield's speech was tremendous. When
the meeting was over no one was still asking the question that
some had raised in the beginning. "Why did they get a preacher
to speak to salesmen?" Dr. Fifield had demonstrated that the
word *man* means the same thing whether you add it on to make
sales*man* or clergy*man*.

After the writer had addressed a company-wide sales meeting
for a nationally known concern the surprised general sales manager made this statement:

"Your clean stories went over better than my dirty ones, and I
thought I *knew* my gang!"

*People who aspire toward proficiency in speech are asking for
positions on the faculty in the school of life, and they must be sure
they are fully qualified to "speak with authority."* They must not
only *know* something for this job, but they must *be* something as
well.

### Speakers Must Help Dispel the "Darkness of Mass Living"

Dwight Moody used to say, "Character is what a man has in
the dark." At a Tennessee bankers convention the writer shared
the platform with Dr. Ralph Sockman, and heard him deliver a
great address in which he expanded upon Moody's theme. Dr.
Sockman declared, "The darkness of our time is in *mass living*."

Dr. Sockman grew up in a small Ohio community. Most everyone in town knew most everyone else. As he puts it, "I knew
that if I got into any devilment everyone would know it, so I

didn't get into much." Dr. Sockman has now been living in New York for more than forty years. Throughout most of that time he has not only been prominent locally, but he has also been prominent nationally. He has been on television regularly and appeared personally before thousands. Yet, in his Tennessee speech Dr. Sockman said, "I can still walk the streets of New York for half a day at a time and never meet a single person who recognizes me."

Our rapidly growing and rapidly shifting population in America, our fast transportation, and our great concentration in urban centers are among the factors that make it easy for people to try to be several kinds of personalities all at once. Increasing numbers of relatively strong characters seem to be breaking down in the darkness of mass living. People are desperately in need of *anchors,* and such anchors can frequently be supplied through the medium of speech.

No amount of "human" qualities can be substituted for the point established in the previous chapter that the speaker must be informed. But facts and skills cannot be substituted for character either. Success comes to those who have a sufficient amount of knowledge and skill on the one hand, and the proper *human* qualities on the other. When you *know* something you have a glove on one hand, and when you *are* something you have a glove on the other. Public speaking is a two-fisted business. If you want to win, you had better go in the ring with gloves on *both* hands.

### Do Some Speakers Successfully Separate What They Say From What They Are?

It may easily be argued that in the field of speech a man *can* successfully build a wall between what he *says* and what he *is*. For example, it has been pointed out that such evil men as Hitler and Mussolini were most effective speakers. Yet they scarcely represent the type of character that we would want to emulate personally. Upon closer examination, such illustrations do not negate the premise of this chapter, as they may first appear to do. These men observed part of the rule we have advocated in that they used speech as a *vehicle*. They made it serve a purpose, and as previously pointed out in another connection, they *commanded* enormous *facilities* for the spreading of their words. But how did these speakers *finish the race*? What is their standing today? Do their utterances have an honored place in history?

The writer was in a motion picture theater in Heidelburg when an old newsreel was flashed on the screen. It was Adolph Hitler addressing a throng at the Sports Platz. The great mass of humanity shown in front of the dictator was apparently enthralled. But the crowd in the theater fifteen years later *laughed*. At first the laughter was rather subdued and nervous, but as the dictator continued his harangue the laughter grew louder and unrestrained. The fake prophet has no honor left—in his own country, or anywhere else.

### The Fifty-Rose Man

Some years ago the writer addressed a meeting in Portland, Indiana. Some 500 people of Jay County had gathered to honor one of their own, a physician who had served them faithfully out of the same office for half a century. He was Dr. E. C. Garber of Dunkirk, Indiana.

Dr. Garber was an intern in a Dayton hospital when Orville and Wilbur Wright were operating a bicycle shop in that city. He took up practice at Dunkirk, and served the people of Jay County all the rest of his life. He delivered more than 2500 babies in that county. Scores of "Doctor Garber's babies" were present when he was honored at Portland that evening.

Dr. Garber was brought forward, and in a simple ceremony he was given a bouquet of fifty beautiful roses—one for each year that he had served his people. The writer was so inspired by the occasion that he radically changed the speech he had planned to give, and regrouped its basic thoughts under the title of "The Fifty-Rose Man." I believe the Almighty wanted to join the rest of Dr. Garber's admirers in doing the old physician honor that night, and I believe He used me as His instrument. I have always felt good about that speech. I have addressed many meetings that would easily "out rank" the one at Portland. They were many times larger, national or international in scope, and the settings were far more sumptuous. But I have rarely assisted with a meeting that gave me more lasting satisfaction.

Here is the answer to those who ask, "What of the Hitlers and the Mussolinis?" Our goal should be citizenship of the fifty-rose variety. The scheduled playing time for the game of life is three-score and ten, and to win all the way requires *staying power*. What kind of citizenship will your speeches reflect? The flash-in-the-pan or the fifty-rose man?

It is important to realize that we do not all have to be Bryans, Ingersolls, or Websters. Each person can develop the *talent he has*. A little man talking to a 220-pounder said, "If I was as big as you are, I'd be the heavyweight champion of the world."

The big man said, "What's keepin' ya from bein' the lightweight champ?"

It is easily possible that a reader of this book may say it is "too idealistic." That it leans too much toward the spiritual side for its evidence and its illustrations. For the sake of the record let it be said that the writer is no theologian. He has no license to preach. But it is inevitable that the writer or speaker who sincerely seeks to serve his fellow men by telling them the truth, will find himself looking more and more often to the Source of Truth. The writer is very much a "practical man." He has always had to be a "doer." He likes to think of himself as just as much of a he-man as the next fellow. This does not mean he cannot be an idealist too. In public speaking it is always well to remember that the most *practical thing in the world is an ideal in action*.

One summer Sunday evening my family and I were driving down a country road in Tennessee. We stopped near the open windows of a little country church where the congregation was standing to sing the hymn that would conclude the evening's services. No one had a book, but they all seemed to know the words. Two lines I shall never forget were these:

> Many things about tomorrow
> I do not understand,
> But I know Who molds tomorrow and I know Who
> holds my hand.

Are you seeking assurance in this age of uncertainty? Do you have something better than this? If not, I can commend it to you until you can find something better.

### Things You Can Do

Clean house *personally*. Get the dirt out from under the rug of your own life. Then you can speak with *conviction*. Then you can say, "This I believe with all my heart." In this way you develop the indispensable quality of *sincerity*.

Test what you believe in individual conversations. Talking and explaining will sharpen your own thinking. Fill in your low spots as they are revealed by such examinations. When you can state your viewpoints interestingly and effectively to one person, or several persons, you are becoming prepared to tell them to an audience.

Examine ideas that move you. Learn to state them in ways that move other people. Presently you perceive that life revolves around a few big ideas: the dignity of the individual; that success comes only through service; that knowledge is indispensible and that character delivers it to the right places; that basic morality is the "right answer"; and that one must continuously restore himself by drinking from the Source of Truth.

Grasp the fact that in our modern day the "old-fashioned virtues" are actually vocational, professional, and business *necessities*. Learn to hammer these facts objectively—in ways that are not "preaching."

Tie in with enduring things. Avoid being typed as a flash-in-the-pan and build to become a fifty-rose man.

# 5

# Confidence in Public Speaking

*Thank God, a man can grow!*
  *He is not bound*
*With earthward gaze to creep along the ground;*
  *Tho' his beginnings be put poor and low*
*Thank God, a man can grow!*
                —Florence Earl Coates [1]

*Do you lack speaking confidence*
  *Because others can do it better?*
  *Because your life is uneventful?*
  *Because you just can't bring yourself to try?*
  *Because you keep thinking—"Who wants to hear me?"*
*If so, this chapter will help you.*

I t is not necessary to banish fear in order to gain confidence. A wholesome fear of failure is one of the best guarantees of success. In *Moby Dick* we find Captain Ahab declaring, "I will have no man on may boat who does not fear a whale." Seasoned and successful actors begin to worry when they no longer have "butterflies" in their stomachs prior to a performance. It is like the kangaroo who told the psychiatrist, "Doctor, I'm worried because I don't feel jumpy any more."

Virtually all studies pertaining to the subject seem to agree that

[1] Margery Gordon, Anthology, *Verse of Our Day* (New York: Appleton-Century-Crofts), 1923.

confidence is not only a basic ingredient in successful public speaking, but it is also a key component in success generally. It is, therefore, appropriate that the treatment given this element should be rather broad in scope.

In tracing the derivation of the word "confidence," we find it originally meant to *"believe with."* Or, as we say these days, to "get with." What is it we are supposed to get with? This is not good sentence construction but it is a highly significant question. The late Robert E. Lee Hill, well-known Missouri speaker, used to say, "Your sentence construction ought to be the proudest thing that you are of."

If you wish to achieve confidence in the field of speech, you must first *get with yourself*. It should be obvious that no matter how far you go you must start *where you are now*. This may first seem discouraging, but actually it is a most fortunate fact. *You are the world's greatest authority on yourself*. The one subject upon which no man can even pretend to rival you is *yourself*. Thus, you can start with the confidence that comes with being an unquestioned authority.

The next step is to draw upon yourself for certain fundamental convictions that have come out of your own life and your own experience. These can be simple basic truths which have been shared by most of your hearers in their lives. In this way you have established a common bond with your audience early in your presentation. That common bond causes the audience to "accept" you. The listeners will begin to relax. They know what you are saying is the truth, because they, too, have experienced it. Once they have decided you are "sound," then *they have confidence in you,* which will in turn give you increased confidence in your ability to handle the situation.

## Take Off from the Launching Pad of Your Own Experience

It is not necessary that your life be filled with earth-shaking experiences in order for you to draw from your own reservoirs for your foundational materials. It is usually better to use a simple, powerful illustration that is yours than to give a second-hand version of some more dramatic incident. After all, the most convincing witness is always the one who can say, "I was there." Similarly, the speaker has infinitely more power when he says, "I know this thing is true because I have *lived* it." And from his own simple principles and convictions, the speaker can branch into the issues he wishes to discuss. By the time he gets to the points he wants to "sell" he will have the double-barrelled advantage of more confidence in himself and more from his audience.

For an example of launching a speech from one's own experiences let us look at the "kick-off" of one of the writer's addresses that was entitled "Thinkin' Tall." The original examples in this book are not offered as models of speech perfection. They are presented merely as original examples of the point under discussion, and because the author knows they "worked."

Folks sometimes ask me where I went to school. They think I will tell them about Stanford University or Columbia University. But I usually say, "I went to school to Miss Georgia Brown at Caney, Kansas."

I was blessed with a number of great teachers along the way, but none had such influence with me as this simple Kansas woman, born in Montgomery Country, Kansas, the same as I was. She taught us arithmetic and reading, and she made us learn them. But she *inspired* us. She made us look beyond the narrow confines of our little town and up toward the stars. She said in later years she had never judged a student by the address on his enrollment card. She used to say to me, "Kenneth, you're growing tall, but are you *thinking* tall?" As I think back over the wonderful things she did for me I realize that her genius was in her boundless faith in the fundamental goodness of the human race.

Miss Brown used to say, "Kenneth, do you know there is a ladder that goes right up through the roof of this school house? And you can climb up on it just as high as you want to go. But the base of the ladder is in the school. This is where you get on it. This school is your passport to anywhere you want to go. Don't ever look at the school as something you like to get out of—get down on your knees every night in this world, boy, and thank God you have this school to get in *to*!"

One can see how easily a major address can take off from the above spring board. The *present* need is for "Thinkin' Tall." It means getting up above the scramble and viewing our problems with perspective. From that vantage point we move easily into a discussion of current matters—local, national, or international.

Perhaps a second original speech illustration will suffice to serve the technique of building confidence by beginning on the rock base where you are standing and proceeding from there. The following paragraph occurred near the opening of an address made for a national convention of Parents and Teachers Association:

My wife and I are trying to do what a lot of you folks are attempting, and that is to raise some kids. It happens that neither my wife, nor I, spent our own childhood years dancing around a bowl of cherries. I could have been born with a silver spoon in my mouth— my mouth was big enough—but there was no spoon. In fact, if it were raining soup, I would be there with a fork. So at our house we have been working pretty hard at the same job a lot of you have taken on —trying to make sure the kids have things a little better.

But lately we have begun to wonder about some things. We find our friends are also worried about these same things, and I'll let you in on it, too. Here's the question:

Have we become so engrossed in giving our children all the advantages we did *not* have, that we are failing to give them some of the advantages we *did* have?

From the above launching pad the speaker can fire as many rockets as his materials, time, and the other speech factors may determine. It is simply a matter of determining what *are* the advantages we had that our children do not have. These are the points we are trying to reach. They constitute the real purpose of the speech. Among the points that can be developed are these:

1. Closer home ties. Fewer outside intrusions on family life.
2. The doing of "chores." They not only taught children responsibility, but the children could see plainly they were *needed*.
3. Family worship.
4. Parental authority. Parents confidently filled the roles of husband and wife, father and mother. They were not neurotic from trying to be "playmates" for one another and the children.

Nothing in this chapter so far is intended as an exclusive method. To be sure there are other ways of moving confidently into a speech without drawing solely from your own experiences. However, it should be remembered that the recommendation was that one draw from his own experience and *convictions*. Naturally one's beliefs and convictions are derived from many sources, direct and indirect, personal and vicarious. Indeed, there are some writers who contend the first-person approach should be shunned in speaking as well as writing. It will be noted the author of this book makes no attempt to be "consistent" by referring to himself as "the writer," or by simply saying "I." As in speaking, we are trying to get a story told, and we are doing it in the simplest and most direct way possible.

It should be remembered that people speak because they were *invited* to speak. If you are the person so invited, it means that someone in authority wanted to hear what you had to say. Then why should you be coy in saying it? To say, "The present speaker feels . . ." is a milk-water approach that can do nothing but weaken the discourse. Do you suppose school children would be memorizing his speech if Patrick Henry had said, "Your speaker knows not what course others may take but as for him, give him liberty or give him death"?

Again, the approach will depend largely upon the nature of the speech. A discourse that is highly scientific in nature will be entirely objective. The more detached is the speaker, the more objective is the report. However, such presentations are usually read—to insure accuracy, to provide the necessary detailed data, and to provide a complete manuscript for the record. This same holds true of certain legal treatises. Because of these limitations, "papers" are not considered here as falling under the regular rules of speech. Furthermore, it does not require nearly so much confidence to read a paper as to make a straight-out speech.

Let us consider an example of how a speech may confidently begin with the speaker and his audience standing on common ground, without that common ground being part of the speaker's personal experience. The technique here is to begin with an interesting observation that is not generally realized, and yet can be quickly supported. In an address before the United States Chamber of Commerce in Washington, D. C. the writer said,

There is a popular fallacy that communism is the natural result of low living standards. That it is invariably spawned in poverty. We should face up to the fact that communism does not *naturally* spawn anywhere. It is something that is deliberately *brought* in by people. Witness how quickly prosperous Czechoslovakia fell under the communist yoke, while poverty stricken Finland went to war against enormous odds to stay free of communist domination. Taken as a nation, Turkey is frightfully poor, yet it is a tower of strength against the communists.

There has been poverty in the world since the beginning of time, but communism in the world is a phenomenon of our life time. The government of every enlightened nation should use its intelligence and resources to eradicate the cruelties that poverty inflicts upon people. But, at the same time, governments must realize that *the spread of communism is stopped by militant governmental policies against it.* This is the difference between Czechoslovakia and Finland. Czechoslovakia, after being betrayed at Munich and weakened by the Nazi yoke, let communism come in and take over. Finland met it at the border with bayonets.

## The Ideas and Experiences of "Little People" Can Be Important and Interesting

Every so often someone raises the question, "Why should 'little people' be interested in speech?" One man said to the writer, "I haven't been anywhere much and I haven't seen anything much. Why would anyone want to hear me?"

Lincoln had not been "anywhere much" when he tied into Senator Douglas in the great debates. Lew Wallace had never been outside North America when he wrote *Ben Hur,* but his settings are as accurate as if he had personally visited every scene mentioned in his book. Some of the greatest speeches, greatest writings, and greatest works of art were created by people who "hadn't seen anything much." But they got information through the sources that were available to them, and they had sincere *convictions* about the importance of some things they knew.

Charles Reade says, "Not a day passes over the earth but men and women of no note do great deeds, speak great words, and suffer noble sorrows. Of these obscure heroes, philosophers, and martyrs the greater part will never be known till that hour when many that were great shall be small, and the small great."

It was a wise person who said,

"Speak up for those who cannot speak for themselves—even God may be listening."

One of the best ways for "little people" to gain confidence is to realize how important little people are.

*Do Not Hesitate to Speak Because "Someone Else
Could Do It Better." You Do It—and Get Better*

One's confidence in his potentialities as a speaker will be increased if he will but realize that he is *needed*. Of all the worn out reasons why people do not strive for proficiency in speech, none is used more frequently than, "There are so many others who can do it better." If this same measuring stick were applied to everything, then no one would have the heart to enter *any* new field. The hesitant and reluctant speech maker's confidence would be restored on this score if we could somehow write these words in blazing letters across the sky: *"Maybe others can do better, but they are not doing it!"* As pointed out in the opening pages of this book, the job is simply not being done.

The writer once poured his heart into an address, and poured out his heart delivering it. It was a speech declaring that the greatest danger to our democratic institutions does not come from the enemies of freedom—from communists, demagogues, outlaws, and hoodlums. The people in whom freedom should live in mortal fear are the *good people* who "believe" in all the right things—*and never do anything about them*. They affiliate with the right groups. They subscribe to the right causes, and they are generally considered "right" people,—but they stand mute when the day comes to stand up and testify. Do you remember the great lesson of G. A. D'Auria's novel, *High Noon*? The good people of the town left the marshall to stand alone in defense of law and order. The marshall desperately needed help. He did not ask for volunteers from only the sharp shooters—from the ones who "could do it so much better." He would have been grateful to any man willing to pull the trigger for what he believed. And any such man could have nobly served. But the marshall was left to go it alone.

A defeated candidate who had sincerely tried to serve his community said after the election, "I had the solid support of all those good people who didn't go to the polls."

A man once asked Evangelist Billy Sunday, "What must I do to go to Hell?"

Billy Sunday said, *"Nothing."*

"Why," said the inquirer, "Shouldn't I fight the church?"

"No," said Sunday, "just don't attend church. Just don't believe in it. Just don't do anything."

"Wouldn't it speed me on my way to Hell," persisted the man, "if I actively opposed all the good people and all the good things?"

"Don't work at it so hard," said Sunday. "Relax. Just *don't help* with the good causes. Just don't do *anything,* and you will get where you want to go all right."

Someone well said that public opinion is no force when it is expressed only in private. Amien put it this way: "Truth may not only be violated by falsehood; it may be equally outraged by silence."

Many people earnestly desire to influence their fellow citizens by becoming speakers, but they are afraid their first efforts may be awkward and beneath their dignity. E. J. Karnes answered these people when he said, "There is nothing so dignified as a corpse all laid out for burial, and there is nothing so awkward as a growing child who is just starting to go places."

Modesty can easily reach a point where it ceases to be a virtue. During a political campaign, Sir Winston Churchill said of his opponent, Clement Atlee, "Clem is a modest little man who has a great deal to be modest about."

Remember, the man who is too big to learn is as big as he will ever be.

### Confidence Comes With Knowing You Know

Since confidence means to "believe with," or to "get with," the second suggestion in the broad outline of this chapter is that to achieve confidence in speech we should get with our materials. The necessity for thorough preparation was the theme of Chapter 3. It is not necessary to reiterate points previously covered in order to link up careful preparation with confidence. In sales work we urge people to acquire confidence by being so completely versed on their product and service that they can never be crossed up in an interview, no matter what turn the discussion may take. No amount of versatility or personality can substitute for this.

To "get with" your material in a way that will bring confidence in presenting it, you must both *know* it and *believe* in it.

The materials can come from sources as wide as the universe, but the speaker is most effective who can transpose them into life needs. Here again he can be safe and secure if he has made the experiences a part of his life, and speaks with the resulting conviction.

In a series of sales meetings in Florida, the writer shared the platform with Rick Rickenbrode. Rick is one of those sales speakers who picks up steam as he progresses. His success with sales groups comes from playing to his strong suit, and that is his own unquestioned success in the sales field. Rick started out with nothing, and at the age of 39 he retired on an income in excess of $35,000 annually. Every foot of this long climb uphill was made under his own power and in the field of sales. Rick could spend the balance of his days by the swimming pool at his Florida home. But he is rendering another service to selling by *telling* the other folks how he did it.

Many speakers might go before a sales group and say, "If you will do as I advocate, I am sure you will succeed in this business." But Rick Rickenbrode, and some other people in his same general experience bracket, can say, "I *know* it can be done because I *did it*. Neither the Lord nor my parents endowed me with a thing you guys don't have. Now here is the way it's done . . ."

A man with this sort of hand can become thoroughly confident in speaking, especially if he makes most of his speeches in the general field where he succeeded. His own record of accomplishment automatically answers the hearer who says his stuff won't work. My father used to tell of the old man who waved a red lantern and stopped a night express train. The conductor and engineer rushed down the track to where the old gentleman stood and asked, "What's the matter? Is the bridge out?"

The old man said, "No. Everything's all right. I just want to mail a letter."

The conductor shouted, "What! What are you saying! Don't you know you can't stop an express train to mail a letter!"

The old gent said, "By Gad, I *did!*"

There are no more convincing arguments than facts accomplished. When the writer addressed a meeting of the New York Insurance Agents Association in Town Hall, he heard a speech by a star insurance salesman from New Jersey. The man had been a school teacher who married somewhat later in life than the average. This made him especially grateful when he and his wife were blessed with the birth of a son. When the little boy grew old enough to talk, he and his daddy would go through something of a ritual each morning as the teacher left for school. The lad would kiss his dad and say, "Good bye, and come back."

One morning on the way to his school the teacher said to himself, "Someday I might not come back. *Then, what would happen to my boy?*"

That question was the launching platform from which he soared into orbit in the insurance business. He wanted to make sure his family would be taken care of *regardless*. And if insurance was the answer for *his* family, why wouldn't it be needed just as much by *all* families. His story was just as logical and just as powerful as that. Thousands of people had been selling insurance for many, many years. But in came a *new* man with *his own experience,* and another success story was written. When this man told his story to the New York audience he did it in the same, straightforward manner that he had told it to hundreds of individuals. It was sure-fire. He couldn't miss. As T. W. Higginson said, "Originality is simply a pair of fresh eyes."

*Do Not Wait Until You Are Ready. Accept the Invitation and* Get Ready

If you are reading this book, you must be interested in speech. If you are an experienced speaker, it is hoped you may find something in these pages that will reinforce you in certain basic convictions. If you have little, or no, speaking experience, then you may have great need for developing confidence. No doubt you have already thought of speech topics which you feel are vitally important, or highly interesting, or truly entertaining. You have found in talking with individuals, or in some groups, that others share your appraisal of these topics. Then think how you would tell your story if you were doing it for fifty or a hundred, or several hundred. Then *accept the first invitation* you get to make your speech. Do not hesitate. Just say, "Yes, I shall be pleased to do my best for your group. Thank you for asking me."

Under no circumstances should you say, "Oh, my! I never *did* make a speech. I'll probably hook one toe on the other heel and fall off the platform. This should be the speech to end all speeches!"

Just accept the invitation before you think of all the reasons why you shouldn't. And then do not let yourself nor anyone else talk you out of it. It is much easier to accept an invitation for an engagement that is some weeks or months away. Smart program chairmen know this, and plan their programs well ahead. If the date is too close, the inexperienced speaker panics and the experienced one is "too busy." Acceptances for distant dates are easier to get.

If I were illustrating this point in a speech, I would probably relate the story of the minister who asked the little boy if he wanted to go to Heaven, and the kid said, "No."

The minister was somewhat astonished and said, "You don't want to go to Hell, do you?"

The lad said, "Oh, no, I don't want to go there, either."

"Now, look," said the preacher. "When you have grown old and feeble, and you come to die, you *will* want to go to Heaven, won't you?"

The boy said, "Oh, yes, sure! You see, Parson, I thought you was gittin' up a load to go *now*."

## Learn to Pitch One Inning, Then a Game, Then the Series

A safe general rule for developing confidence in public speaking is to begin with the smaller topics and smaller groups and develop to the larger ones. Whether this rule should be followed in a given instance depends upon the speaker and the audience. A beginning speaker may be a person of small affairs and limited experience, or he may be a man with a tremendous amount of experience and success. In either case it is best not to try too big an effort for the first time. Place sharp limitations on your initial efforts, whether you are discussing tropical fish or guided missiles. Select two or three clear-cut points upon which you really know your stuff, of which you are confident, and that will be of interest to the group you are to address. Pitch those balls over the plate

and quit while you are ahead. You will find you have strength-
ened your arm for the next game. You can go the full nine
innings later.

Do not be afraid to progress from smaller to the larger crowds.
Once you get going you will find 500 are usually easier to address
than 50. The point is to *start somewhere* and *keep going*.

From your personal conversations you have learned that certain key ideas and stories from your stockroom of experiences
"catch on" with people. A danger with beginning speakers is
that they forget such items when they are invited to make a speech,
and attempt to do something more profound.

### Do Not "Beg the Indulgence" of Your Audience

Beginning speakers should never apologize to their audiences
for their lack of experience. It should not be mentioned at all.
Get your audience's collective mind off *you*, as soon as you can,
and over to what you are *saying*. In that respect, the more you
can detach your personality from your discourse, the more confidence you will have. Furthermore, to apologize to your audience for your inexperience, lack of preparation, or incompetence
is an indictment of the persons who invited you. That is scarcely
a proper way to treat your hosts who had confidence in you, and
had a right to expect you would publicly vindicate their judgment.

Occasionally an "apology" can be indirectly made by a novice
speaker if he uses it in a humorous form. One of the best beginnings I ever heard from a fledgling speaker was made at a city
Rotary meeting. He said,

"It must seem strange for you to hear me introduced as the speaker
of the day. You all know I have always been too timid to lead the
group in silent prayer. Compared to me, Silent Yokum of the
comedy strip is a blabbermouth. I have been a member of various
organizations for forty years and have never had the courage to even
second a motion. I come by this shyness naturally. If my father
hadn't been so bashful, I would be four years older. I've decided
that since I can never found an organization, I may as well con-
found one. I accepted the committee's invitation for today because
I have something which my years of listening to speakers has convinced me is rather rare—I think I have something to say. (Laughter
and applause.)

"They say you should have your speech well in mind before you start. This one is on my heart. It has been on my heart a long time. If it doesn't come up as easily as it should, please understand it is because it is deeply rooted."

This approach relaxed and disarmed the crowd. It got the hearers out of the mood where they had been sitting with folded arms and figuratively saying to the speaker, "Entertain us, if you can." The audience gave no further thought as to whether the speaker would make it, as an individual. The hearers were now anxious to hear what it was this long silent member considered important enough to discuss with them.

From there on the above speaker made a walloping presentation for a new Y.M.C.A. building in his city. It was a 20-minute endeavor in which he deliberately aimed every word as though he were firing bullets from a gun. It was the first of many speeches he made on the subject and a new Y.M.C.A. building now stands in his city as an everlasting monument to his courage.

## *Think of Yourself as a Deliveryman With an Important Message to Get Through*

The illustration of the Y.M.C.A. champion leads us naturally into the third thing we must "get with" in order to develop confidence in speaking, and that is to get with our cause, our convictions, our purpose. Shyness and fear can be surmounted by the speaker who believes so much in the efficacy of what he is saying that it has "just got to come out." That trait undoubtedly accounts for much of Abraham Lincoln's genius as a speaker. Observers frequently remarked that he invariably "started slow." At that stage the crowd was aware of his awkward appearance and his lack of a pleasing voice. But as Lincoln warmed to his topic "his face would light up and he became a different man." From then on he poured out his heart to his listeners and they forgot everything else as they took his words to their hearts.

Dr. Frank C. Laubach,[2] who is listed as an international authority on literacy, addressed a conference on that subject at Baylor University. His address was remarkable for the ring of

[2] Dr. Frank C. Laubach, "Each One Teach One," *Vital Speeches*, Vol. XXV, No. 19 (July 15, 1959), p. 587.

conviction that it carried. It was truly a call to action. He obviously believed with all his soul that the basic factor underlying the world's troubles are the ills that stem from illiteracy. Near the end of his speech he said:

> But, friends, time is running out. As I stand here before you, I'm trembling, because I know that history is swiftly rushing toward Niagara . . .
>
> We could have the whole world as our friends easily if my country would be completely, totally Christian enough to reach and take it; for it waits to be taken. This is the reason why our meeting is not just a nice Christian thing we're doing—it is a part . . . of the Army of Compassion under the banner of Christ that is going out to save the world.
>
> . . . Tell everybody about it! Try to get a company of a hundred organized in the Army of Compassion, in your own church and your own school or club. Then this can be one of the most important meetings ever held in Texas, because of what will happen afterward.

Dr. Laubach's cause is a world-wide literacy campaign called "Each One Teach One." But he teaches thousands—and does it with absolute confidence that comes with profound belief in a cause.

### Don't "Water Down" Your Convictions. It Requires Over-emphasis to Push Facts Across Footlights

Believing in a cause, or the basic principles and truths which you espouse, inevitably gives you a confidence that reflects in your speech. The great, moving speakers have spoken with resolute assurance that comes to one who feels from the "bottom of his shoes to the top of his head" that he possesses the truth.

It is significant that the immortal utterances of history have invariably been *confidently* spoken. They are consistently devoid of qualifying phrases.

What do you think would have been the results in history if Churchill had said something like this:

"Now I may be wrong about this, but it would be my suggestion that we fight them on the beaches. I also feel we should engage them on the landing grounds, and in the fields and streets, if necessary. There is a possibility we may fight them even in the hills. Some of you may not agree with me, but if I have my way, we shall never surrender!"

A milquetoast preacher became disgusted with his congregation and decided to "lay it on the line" for the members. But when he faced them he weakened and his watered-down remarks went this way:

"Some of you—now understand, I don't mean *all* of you—but some of you are not supporting the church as you should. Perhaps I shouldn't say this, but I have become more or less disgusted. I hope you won't feel these words are unbecoming of your pastor, but unless some of you change your ways you are likely to end up in Hell, or at least, you are, to a certain extent, headed in that general direction."

Perhaps the minister could have taken a lesson from the two brothers who operated a clothing store. They had one account that was long overdue and decided to write the man concerned a "straightforward" letter. It was decided one brother would draw up the letter, but both of them would read and discuss it before it was mailed. They agreed they did not want to do anything "rash." When the one had written the letter, the other read it over carefully and said,

"I believe that reflects our thoughts very well. Yes, I believe it is all right. There are a couple of little mistakes you should correct before mailing it. You spelled 'lousy' with a 'z' and you have just one 'k' in 'skunk.' "

The more one studies the subject, the more one is impressed that the speeches which endure are positive in tone. The speaker was confident because he had *confidence in what he was saying*.

### Speaking in Your "Official Capacity" Is an Easy Aid to Confidence

It is well to remember that speakers are frequently invited to speak in their official capacities. A particular audience wants to hear a particular person at a specified time because he can speak as the mayor, the boss, or an official representative. In such cases the speaker can gain confidence by the realization that *no one else will do.* Maybe others could speak more eloquently, but the hearers want to get the word straight from headquarters—"from the horse's mouth."

A. H. "Red" Motley, President of Parade Publications and popular speaker, relates an instance which well illustrates the above point. He was a passenger on a non-stop flight from New York to Miami. The plane was droning along in dense fog. Red and the other passengers kept looking nervously out the window although they could not see as far as the wing tips. Presently a confident voice came over the loud speaker:

"Good afternoon, ladies and gentlemen! This is your captain speaking. We are now over Wilmington, North Carolina, and flying at 11,000 feet. We shall be in Miami on schedule at 2:55. The sun is shining in Miami and the temperature is 82 degrees."

In relating this incident to an audience, Mr. Motley said,

"After that announcement the other passengers and myself were completely relaxed. I looked out the window and I still couldn't see the wing tip. But we all felt fine. *We had heard from headquarters.* The man who was running things knew right where we were, where we were going, when we would get there, and exactly what the conditions would be upon our arrival."

In contrast with Motley's account is the story of the airliner that was rolling and lurching in a violent storm. The passengers sat silently and glumly with seat belts fastened. Suddenly the door to the cockpit opened and the captain emerged wearing a parachute, and announced to the passengers,

"Everyone keep calm. I am going for help!"

General managers, business leaders, public officials, and others in key positions who dread speaking assignments should gain much confidence in the tremendous advantage they have in being the official voice of headquarters. If you are an individual with such an opportunity, then take advantage of it—literally, rise to the occasion. Regardless of whether you are the "head man," remember whenever you are invited to speak that *you* are the one the people *wanted* to hear. They did not ask that you be a Demosthenes. They only asked that you come down and tell them what *you* think. And you are the only person in the world that can do that job *officially.*

*Dress Appropriately for the Occasion and Then Forget
How You Look*

The manner in which a speaker is dressed can be an important factor in his confidence, or lack of it. He should not be overly dressed, but he should be well groomed and appropriately attired for the occasion. The quality of his clothes should compare well with the best dressed of his hearers. In this manner the speaker will not be conscious of any deficiency in regard to his raiment. He should *know* he is well dressed, and then forget it, as he concentrates upon delivering his speech.

Occasionally we hear of speakers who take a devil-may-care attitude in regard to their appearance. Others think it proves they are "fire eaters" if they peel off their coats and jerk off their neckties as they warm to their subjects. The writer has never subscribed to this school of thought. Speakers who can't make an address while fully clothed should join a nudist colony. The general principle involved here is that radical deviations from the accepted pattern tend to be distractions from the speech itself. Of course, sometimes a speech is so bad that any distracting deviation is merciful. However, the speaker's manner of dress and all other considerations should be aimed toward the goal of giving the speech itself a clear field in which to develop.

For most speaking occasions, both day and evening, men should best wear suits of varying shades of gray, blue, "oxford" and black. Black shoes are highly preferable to any other color. This fact somewhat determines the categories of clothing shades that may be worn. Speakers making day-time appearances for meetings held in resort settings can appropriately conform to the dress tempo of the meeting. However, in such cases the speaker's attire should tend toward the more conservative part of the crowd. The speaker who appeared on the platform in Bermuda shorts for a summer insurance convention over-estimated the sophistication of his crowd, even though everyone was attired in sports wear. Too many of his listeners concentrated less on the speaker's knowledge and know-how, and more on his knobby knees.

Maxwell Droke tells of a speaker who accepted an invitation to address a nudist colony. Believing that "when in Rome he should do as the Romans do," he came in the back stage door and divested himself of his clothing. When he was introduced he stepped out on the platform only to find—that out of respect for him—his audience was fully clothed.

A speaker's carelessness in dress or manner can easily be interpreted as a discourtesy to his audience. I once contracted a nationally famous columnist and commentator to do a lecture on a series for which I was chairman. When the columnist arrived in the city, he was wearing a red shirt, yellow tie, brown suit, and tan shoes. He needed both a shave and a hair cut. When he appeared before the audience that evening he was still wearing his red shirt, yellow tie, brown suit, and tan shoes. His need for a barber was more obvious than it had been earlier in the day. His whole bearing was characterized by what one member of the audience later described as a "nuts-to-you attitude." He would have gone over great guns with an audience in Greenwich Village, or the left bank of the Seine, but he was speaking in the relatively conservative Midwest. He had some excellent materials to present and made a penetrating analysis of some highly significant situations on the then current scene. But his discourse suffered a serious discount with his audience who felt he had not shown it sufficient respect.

Even Lincoln did not continue to depend upon oratorical skill to overcome handicaps of dress. When he returned to Illinois from his trip east, where he had made the Cooper Union speech, he confided to a close associate that his clothes had made him ill at ease before his eastern audience. He purchased an entirely new outlay of clothes before his next engagement.

Whether a speaker dresses formally is largely determined, of course, by the occasion and what others are wearing. If it is a dinner jacket affair throughout, there is no problem. The same applies when the head table or platform guests are all in formal dress. The speaker merely conforms. A problem arises when some of the head table guests are dressed formally and others are not. In such instances, one can usually be safe in going along with the chairman's wishes and example. A few professional speakers feel it compliments an audience for the speaker to dress formally for all evening meetings regardless. As a matter of practical policy, the speaker doing a "solo" in dinner clothes would probably be more appropriate for the Federated Women's Club than for a mixed audience representing a normal cross-section of the community. Also, local customs and traditions are factors. Formal clothes are worn more often in Boston than in Butte.

This discussion has dealt with the matter of correct dress as though all speakers were male. Of course, the writer makes no such assumption. In briefly discussing how speakers should dress he is merely following a practice which he recommends for speakers, and that is to stick fairly close to that part of the subject that one understands. Furthermore, men usually need more council in such matters, as women are normally more sensitive to the problems of dress. The general rule for women speakers is to present the "tailored look" rather than the "frilly" impression.

An energetic civic club leader was elected district governor of his club's international organization. During his term of office his own home community celebrated a centennial year and many of the men grew beards for the occasion. Among those who went "behind the bush" was the District Governor. It enhanced his popularity in his hometown and with his home club, but it completely killed the official visits he made to other clubs in the district.

## The Speaker Should Not Give the Impression of Over-confidence

It is important to point out that there is a great difference between confidence and cockiness. An audience dislikes both the blowhard and the intellectual bully. Never throw your mental weight around. Remember a speech is not a good speech unless it is good for the particular audience to which it is addressed.

The writer sat in an audience where the speaker's problem was not one of lacking confidence, but one of over-bearing over-confidence. He was the hero of every illustration he used. He would follow some point by saying there are three ways of doing this, and he would enumerate them. Or he would rapidly enumerate "the five ways" of doing something. That invariably meant *his* five ways, and there were no others worth considering. To top off his egotistical exhibition he referred constantly to his book. One readily deducted from his tone and frequent references that his book was the Alpha and Omega of all essential knowledge. Anything worthwhile that was not covered in his lecture could be found in his book. He constantly looked at his audience with the disdain of one who reluctantly continued to cast his pearls.

When the speaker finally concluded, after announcing for the seventh time that his book was on sale in the lobby, a friend seated near me said, "I nominate him for President of the 5-H Club."

I said, "Do you mean 4-H?"

He said, "No. I mean 5-H—Hell, How He Hates Himself!"

Droke [3] contends one should be glad if he is concerned about his ability to deliver, because the "real simon-pure bore is the individual who never has the slightest doubt of his ability to entertain, uplift, and instruct the multitudes." On the other hand, William Jennings Bryan always said a big head is still preferable to a pin head. He contended a big head can be reduced in size, but a pin head is hopeless.

Confidence is a key ingredient in business, in the "success personality," and in public speaking. It is something the speaker can learn to acquire and to impart to his audience.

### *You Cannot Always Be Confident of Success But You Can Be Confident That You Will Improve*

The acquiring of confidence is a process which is often spoken of as *gaining* confidence. There is more opportunity for making gains in the distant runs than in the dashes. Confidence is gained over the longer course. One must stay in the race and keep driving. Accept that first speaking invitation and keep on accepting them. Make each speech a little better because of the experience gained in the last one. Build *in* your strengths by building *out* your weaknesses. Learn to know your materials so well that you can concentrate on your delivery.

The hero in a popular novel of a few years ago came out of the swamps to run for governor. He started out as the laughing stock of the campaign but he grew stronger and more confident

---

[3] Maxwell Droke, *Encyclopedia of Creative Thought,* Maxwell Droke, Publisher, New York, 1941, p. 721.

as the campaign progressed. In the final days of the campaign he was closing the gap fast, but there was not enough time. He lost the nomination. When the election returns were in, a crowd gathered to cheer the winning candidate. While the nominee was making his victory speech, the loser stood out in the fringe of the crowd. Turning to one of his campaign cronies, the losing candidate said, "I found out something in this race, Johnny. I found out how to *win*."

If you have read the novel, you know he did win the next time, and founded a political dynasty.

Robert Mohler used to illustrate confidence with the story of two scientists who were on a field trip in the mountains when they discovered a baby eagle in a nest on a craig below them. They very much wanted the eaglet. They tied a strong rope to a heavy wicker basket that was large enough to hold a mountain lad who was serving as their guide. The plan was to lower the boy in the basket to the nest, have him put the eaglet in with them, and hoist the boy and the bird back up. But the boy steadfastly refused to go. Even when the scientist offered him a week's pay for the one day, he declined. Finally, the scientist in despair said, "Do *you* have any suggestions as to how we can get this bird?"

The mountain lad said, "Shure. I'll go down there for nothin' if you'll get my Dad to hold the rope."

That is confidence. It is to "believe with." It is faith in people and in things because we know them to be true. When a person possesses truth and a burning desire to put it into *service*, he will become confident, and he will gain the confidence of others.

# 6

# Simplicity Is Power

*"The greatest truths are simplest, and so are
the greatest men."*

A fundamental principle in public speaking lies in the
fact that the real power is in simplicity. We can clinch this fact
at once by noting the things that mean the most to us, in both this
world and the next, have all been named with little words—life,
love, wife, home, food, heart, hope, health, death, God.

Note how short are "immortal words":

"Four score and seven years ago . . ."

"The Lord is my Shepherd, I shall not want . . ."

"To be, or not to be: that is the question."

"Greater love hath no man than this, that a man lay down his
life for his friends . . ."

"The only thing we have to fear is fear itself."

"I have nothing to offer but blood, toil, tears, and sweat."

"Intellectuals" sometimes love to toy with fine shades of meaning in words. They revel in "eight-cyclinder" words, letting them
loll on their tongues like old wine. It is well to develop a vocabulary that will let one express exactly the shade of meaning he
desires. This kind of exercise not only sharpens one's word
power, but it is a great aid to clear thinking. It is only by this
process that we can tell ourselves exactly what we mean. Then
after we have done that, we should transpose the thoughts into the
best possible words for the audience we are to address. There is no
use for a person to carefully weigh in his own mind which of two

words more nearly expresses his meaning, if the audience he is to address does not understand either one. Remember, a speech is not a good speech unless it is good for the audience for which it is given.

In analyzing the sermons of Dwight L. Moody, Huber [1] discovered that approximately 79% of the words he used were of one syllable, 16% were two syllables, and 4% were three syllables. No doubt this contributed to the fact that the "common people heard him gladly."

Moody's background was that of a salesman rather than an "intellectual." Still, intellectuals can achieve the common touch and they are invariably better for it. Speakers of scholarly backgrounds sometimes surprise general public meetings by their down-to-earth presentations. The hearers later express surprise that they "understood every word." Whether the listeners realize it or not, such statements are tributes to the speaker's scholarship. He understood his scholarly subject so well that he could make it plain to those with less equipment for comprehending it.

*Seek to Reduce Both the Size and*
*Number of Words Needed to Clearly Express*
*Your Ideas*

Theodore Parker was the minister at Horace Mann's church. It was he who said the scholar should "think with the sage and saint, but talk with common men."

Occasionally the audience for which a speech is intended is not the one in front of the speaker. Perhaps the immediate audience is a sounding board and the more important one is listening on radio or television, or will read the speech in the morning papers. In such cases the terminology of the speech can be geared to the bigger audience, even though it may be at some points slightly out of touch with the immediate hearers. However, this technique is never recommended for novice speakers, and should be rarely used by any speaker. A safe general rule is this: After you have clearly expressed your thoughts,

[1] Robert B. Huber, *History and Criticism of American Public Address,* ed. Marie Kathryn Hochmuth (New York: Longmans' Green & Company, 1955), Vol. III, p. 240.

then seek to *reduce* both the size and the number of words necessary to faithfully tell your story. It was Emerson who said, "An orator or author is never successful until he has learned to make his words smaller than his ideas."

In an excellent little book entitled *Power in Preaching,*[2] W. E. Sangster devotes one chapter to a plea to "Make it Plain." In listing the common errors of style he states that the style is sometimes "grossly flatulent." Perhaps the preachers would understand what that error is, but most of the parishioners wouldn't. The question is: did the writer "make it plain" when he said, "Don't be flatulent"? The speaker must always think in the terms of the listener. Do you recall the account of the man who requested his wife not to cuss in public. He depersonalized his criticism by saying, "It's not that *I* give a damn, but it sounds like hell to other people."

It is said the rule in preparing government directives is: never use a hundred words if a thousand will do. Stangster demonstrates this with the delightful story of the plumber who wrote a government bureau in Washington that he had discovered clogged drains could be cleared by using hydrochloric acid. The bureau wrote back, "The efficacy of hydrochloric acid is indisputable, but the corrosive residue is incompatible with metallic permanence."

The plumber wrote the bureau members another letter to express his satisfaction that they concurred with his findings, and he received this in return,

"We cannot assume responsibility for the production of toxic and noxious residue with the use of hydrochloric acid."

The plumber wrote again to tell how pleased he was that his discovery was apparently a useful one. The bureau's third letter to the plumber was evidently written by a new employee who was not yet schooled in governmental procedures, and consequently came straight to the point. He said, "Don't use hydrochloric acid. It eats hell out of the pipes."

2 W. E. Sangster, *Power in Preaching* (New York and Nashville: Abingdon Press, 1958), pp. 64–65.

### The Prayer Perfect

Many thousands of Americans have enjoyed Moss Hart's and George S. Kaufman's delightful play, *You Can't Take It With You*. And who could ever forget the simple and powerful way in which old Grandpa Vanderhoff returned thanks before meals. As the eccentric but lovable family sat around the table with bowed heads, Grandpa would stand informally at one end of the table. Looking up he would say,

"Well, Lord, we are all here. We're just agettin' along fine, and we're sure much obliged. Amen."

When this prayer is analyzed, it becomes almost the prayer perfect. It says everything. First—and it *is* first—Grandpa said, *"We are all here."* That is the big thing! No fact transcends that one. The members of the family had all been spared to sit down together. There was no empty chair to make their plenty less. Secondly, he said, "We're just agettin' along fine." That actually covers *everything else*. But Grandpa was not through. He had a *purpose* in his prayer. Since they were all there and getting along fine, he did not feel it was necessary to *ask* for anything more. But he did want to express gratitude for what they already had. So he said, "We're sure *much obliged*."

### Youthful Audiences and Adult Audiences Both Like Speeches That "Get to the Point"

One year when I was a superintendent of schools, we had an undefeated football team, and as the season progressed, we started getting a lot of static from some of our jealous competitors. Incidentally, I have never known a losing team to be investigated. The situation got so bad that our football team and student body began fighting back through the newspaper columns and other means at their disposal. Finally, we called a special assembly to talk about the situation. I recently ran across the notes from which I spoke that day, and I found I had said this:

There are two kinds of administrative problems that go along with athletic teams. You have one kind of problem when you are winning, and another kind when you are losing. You have very real problems either way. Now, personally, I prefer the problems that go along with success. The kind of problems we have right now are the kind I would *choose*. If I had my "druthers," I would "druther" have this kind.

When you are successful, your enemies howl to high heaven. You must expect that. But let me caution you not to expect too much enthusiasm from your friends, either. Do not become embittered about human nature if your friends don't get out the brass band to celebrate your successes in life. Remember this: your friends usually like to see you do well—but not *too well*. Our team is undefeated and unscored on. That's *too* well for a lot of folks to swallow. So some people are saying some nasty things about us. And some of our friends, who should be standing up for us, are not doing it. Now one of the "problems of success" is: what should we do about it? To answer that question is the purpose of our meeting.

May I suggest first to you squad members, and to the whole student body, that you put these critics down as people who sincerely *appreciate your superiority*. Let's give them credit for that. A person just *can't* be jealous of another whom he knows is not doing as well as he is. You can't do that if you try.

So first you give your critics credit for recognizing your superiority. Next you mark the whole thing off your list and forget it. If you start throwing back their mud balls, you won't be superior any more. Booker T. Washington said one time, "One man can't hold another one down in the ditch without staying there with him."

This was a simple story told in simple language. But the results of the meeting were good. These things, and other things said by other speakers, were understood by the teen-age audience. It is interesting that such simple language works just as well with adults in the rough, tough competition of business. I was in Miami for a meeting of the Eastern Airlines management. Ahead of me on the program was "Mr. Eastern Airlines" himself, Captain Eddie Rickenbacker. One of the items on the agenda was how to ward off some brick bats that were at that time being heaved at Eastern by a competing airline. Captain Rickenbacker's discussion was so down-to-earth that he could have made it at the school assembly. He said:

As I review my active life, I realize I have never been kicked in the seat of the pants by a man who was in front of me. The only way we can get our pants kicked from the front is to turn around and fight the guys who are behind us.

Do you remember the mother who asked her kid why he had kicked his little brother in the stomach? The kid said, "I didn't know he was

going to turn around." Now you and I should let these folks behind us
keep on kicking us where they are kicking us *now*. We can take it
*there*. Each kick just boosts us farther down the road on which we are
already ahead—and in the direction we want to go.

## Big Ideas in Homely Words

The art of simply illustrating a powerful idea is pointed up in
the old story concerning William F. Wrigley, the chewing gum
magnate. He was riding in the club car of the famous old Broad-
way Express when one of his assistants opened the *Saturday
Evening Post* to a two-color, two-page spread on Wrigley's chewing gum. The assistant figured out how many packages of gum
Wrigley had to sell to pay for that one ad, and the total was
astounding. Showing these figures to the "boss," the assistant
asked:

"Why do you keep on making such enormous outlays for
telling people about Wrigley's chewing gum? You've got everybody chewing gum now. Things are going along fine. Why
don't we ease up on this effort?"

Wrigley said, "How fast is the train going, boys?"

One of the men answered, "Seventy miles an hour."

Wrigley said, "It's sure going along fine, isn't it? *Why don't
they take the engine off?*"

Wrigley could not have said more in a sixty minute sermon of
six-syllable words.

There is never a time to take the engine off. The basic facts
of our business, social, cultural, and spiritual life must be told
over and over and over again.

Here is a simple confession of faith that I have made many
times in public speeches. Nearly all the meetings in which I have
made this statement have been layman groups—businessmen,
industrialists, professional people, civic groups, and broad cross-
section audiences. Our mail has included hundreds of letters
attesting to its power, and I believe its impact has been occasioned
by the fact that it is a timeless truth stated in homely language.
Here it is:

"I believe there was a wonderful Man who lived a wonderful
life; He died, and now He lives again. And I believe that *because*

He did it, *I* can do it—*you* can do it—*and anyone can do it*. That's the way I believe it, and I am not going to let anybody mess that up with so much theology that I can't understand it any more."

The simple life saving facts must be hammered incessantly in solid words that sell.

In working with sales people we constantly implore them to tell the story simply in terms of service. To illustrate this need one might take the story of the elderly lady who went into a hardware store and inquired about a heating stove. The clerk was hep on heaters. He had mastered the manual. He fired forth the facts on how the stove was insulated, how many BTU's it could develop, and all the other data that would have interested an engineer. At the close of the formal presentation he asked, "Now, do you have any questions?"

His gentle customer pulled her shawl closer around her shoulders and said, "Will it keep an old lady warm?"

The following illustration is taken from a speech the writer heard made before a civic club during Brotherhood Week. Notice how it goes straight to the point, and also conditions the audience for the ramifications that were to follow:

My home life would be much more serene if my four-year-old son didn't ask so many penetrating questions. The other day he said,
"Daddy, what are *people?*"
Now, gentlemen, if you like questions—*there* is a humdinger!
I said, "Well, your mother and I are people. Mr. and Mrs. Roberts next door are people. All the folks we know are people."
Then came the shocker. My son said, "What about the ones we *don't know?*"
If that kid of mine had not floored me with that question, I would not be attempting this speech. I now begin to see the meaning of Brotherhood Week. We all need a dedicated occasion when we can stand up in public and answer the question for the kids and the adults alike.
"*Yes*, they are *all* people—*even the ones we don't know.*"

Let us use an extract from another speech to note how simply and powerfully a speaker gets to a point that grips both the intellect and the emotions. It was important to reach both the mind and the heart in this speech because it was an appeal to raise funds for a boys' home. As in the case of the Brotherhood speaker, this appeal was made by a layman who understood the power of simplicity:

Last week I called at the home of Mr. and Mrs. Charles Burns on Ridgewood Avenue to discuss our fund raising campaign for the new Boys' Home. As we sat in their pleasant living room I said, "Did you know your neighbors, Mr. and Mrs. Elliott, are giving $5000 to the new home in honor of their son who was killed in Korea?"

Mrs. Burns turned to her husband and said, "Charley, let's give $5000 in honor of our son."

"Why, Honey," Mr. Burns said, "our son was not killed in Korea."

With grateful tears in her eyes Mrs. Burns said, "Let's give our $5000 because he wasn't killed."

## Grass Roots Truths Can Be Told Best By Grass Roots People

We must use the speech arts to continuously preach that the enduring things of life are the simple things—homely things we take for granted until they are suddenly and forever lost. This is why the speaking must not be limited to the few who live glamorously, or dangerously, or conspicuously. The powerful stories of life come from the grass roots where the *real living* is done, and those stories can best be told by people who *know* them.

Ernestine Schumann-Heink, the great contralto, covered the world in her tours. For fifty years she was the toast of princes and paupers alike. Near the end of her long and brilliant career a reporter said to her, "Madame Schumann-Heink, you have personally known the great throughout the world. Whom do you say is the greatest living person?"

Madame Schumann-Heink said, "I would have no idea who is the world's greatest person, but I am sure it must be someone we never heard of."

Do you know some of these great people who have never been heard of? Have there been some of them in your life? Is one of them living in your block now? These people *can* be heard of —their stories can be heard by the people who are *listening to you make a speech.*

The writer was in a newspaper office when a reporter dialed a local mortuary and asked, "Did anyone *important* die today?"

Was there any *unimportant* heart that stopped beating today! If that event was noted by Him who marks the sparrow's fall, who are we to sit in judgment as to who is important?

The father of the Chinese Renaissance, Hu Shih, says in his book *Living Philosophies*:

As I reviewed the life of my dead mother, whose activities had never gone beyond the trivial details of the home but whose influence could be clearly seen on the faces of those men and women who came to mourn her death, and as I recalled the personal influence of my father on her whole life and its lasting effect on myself, I came to the conviction that everything is immortal. Everything that we are, everything that we do, everything that we say is immortal in the sense that it has an effect somewhere in the world, and that effect in turn will have its results somewhere else, and the thing goes on in infinite time and space. A man is what he thinks and everyone who has influenced him—from Socrates, Plato, and Confucius, down to his parish preacher and his nursery governess—lives in him.

In the drugstore in the block where my offices are located, a scene took place that is repeated countless times every day throughout our land. A dreamy-eyed teen-age girl shuffled up to the newsstand, purchased a copy of *True Romances,* and headed home with it. The child did not know she could have looked across the breakfast table that morning at her mom and dad, and probably could have seen more true romance than she would find in a carload of such magazines. Webster says "true" means "real," "genuine," "right," "firm and steady," "faithful," "not false," and "loyal." Do these words describe the kind of "romance" that makes the headlines these days? Romance that is really true is rarely news. If youths are going to know about it, they will need to be *told*. Because of its unsensational nature it is extremely difficult to find the story in print. This does not mean it cannot be presented in ways that are interesting, and even fascinating. Here is a magnificent opportunity for the modern public speaker.

*Important Things That Can't Be Read Must Be Said*

In one of his brilliant lectures, Channing Pollock told of meeting an old friend, John, on the street one morning. (How could a story start more unglamorously than this?) John was going to work at the same place he had been going every morning for forty years. That particular morning he was wearing what he always wore—a shiny, old blue serge suit. As Channing Pollock said, "You know how blue serge *can* shine, and *where* it can shine."

Channing said to his friend, "John, I am glad to see you. I've been wanting to tell you a couple of things. The first one is this: you have done a job. You never made a good salary in your whole life. Yet you have raised a fine family; you bought a house and paid for it; you got the kids through college. Now your son is doing well in medicine, your daughter is happily married, and you have those lovely grandchildren. Any way you look at it, boy, *you've done a job*.

"Now that is the first thing I wanted to tell you. The other is this: You have taken care of everyone in the picture with the exception of yourself. John, there is no use of you and I kidding ourselves. We've got a lot of miles on our speedometers. We couldn't have many years left. I am going to treat myself a little better from here on in, and I want you to tell me that you will take better care of John."

John said, "Channing, it's nice of you to think about me, and I want you to know I appreciate it. You are my friend, and I can be frank with you. I am carrying a lot of insurance now. I should have started my program back there when I was a young man and the premiums were small. It isn't that I didn't know it. It's just that I couldn't do it then. I didn't have the money, that's all. I had the house to pay for. We got in the depression and my income went down; the kids got older and it took more money for them every year. So I have had to start my main insurance program late and the premiums are awfully high. Channing, I don't mind telling you that it's got me strapped. But I know you will understand this—*I've just got to make sure that Martha will be provided for when I'm gone*."

Channing Pollock said, "As John turned to go on down the street to work, a stray sunbeam fell across his shoulder, and I didn't see shiny serge any more. I saw *shining armor!* I saw John as a knight with his lady's colors worn across his coat of mail. Sir Lancelot went out and fought forty minutes for the lady he loved, but John went out and fought for *forty years!"*

### *In Your Search For Speech Materials—*
### *"Let Down Your Buckets Where You Are"*

Where will true romance be found? With the stars of movies and television who *play* at love in front of the cameras and change wives with the weather? *True* means *enduring.* There is romance in holding steady—steady like the tick of a clock in a thunderstorm. This is the kind of romance we all have around us every day—but the story *is not being told.* Develop discourses that help others to *see* what they are looking at, and you will become a great public speaker. I like to say to college audiences, and younger folks everywhere,

"The world won't pay you every Saturday night for the biggest job you have to do—and that is to *be a man.* But that is where the only true pay-off is to be found. It not only pays off all the way, but it is the only kind of a record to stand on at the finish. When Sir Walter Scott lay on his death bed, he spoke his last words to his old friend, John Lockhart. Scott said, "Be a good man, Locky. Nothing else will give you any comfort when you come to lie here."

### *In Reading Kit Carson I Overlooked Aunt Sarah*

When I was sixteen years old, I went from my home in Southeast Kansas to a family reunion at Fort Collins, Colorado. My great grandmother was there from Portland, Oregon. We all called her "Aunt Sarah." The train trip to Colorado was most uncomfortable. It was August and there was no air conditioning. Western Kansas and Eastern Colorado were having a "dry spell." I tried to get my mind off my discomfort by reading a novel about Kit Carson, which a fellow passenger permitted me to borrow.

When the family reunion got under way at Fort Collins, I was relating the hardships I had endured coming out on the train. When I finished, Aunt Sarah looked at me and said,

"Young man, when I was your age, I *walked* from Ottumwa, Iowa, to the Pacific Ocean. Most of the wagons in our wagon train had four horses. We had two. There was no money for more horses, so our family had to make a choice. We could either ride, and leave our precious family heirlooms and household things behind, or we could take these beloved things with us—and walk. We knew we would need everything when we got there and that we could not buy replacements. So, you see, there wasn't even a choice, really.

"My father never snapped the lines on our team the whole trip. He walked beside the horses all the way, and I walked beside him."

I said, "Didn't you ride *sometimes*?"

She said, "Maybe a total of twenty miles out of the 2000. Dad explained it to us. He said, 'When we get there and get our fruit farm going, we can get more horses, and everyone can ride. But the first job is to get there, and we must do that with what we've got now.' Of course, that was just plain sense, that's all. We understood how it was. And we *walked* to our new home in the West."

After hearing that story, I forgot about the romance of Kit Carson. I spent hours enraptured by that wonderful woman whose name was in the newspaper just one time in eighty years. That was when she died. But her influence lives on in me and in countless others. And now the readers of this book know her magnificent story. As Hu Shih said, "A man is what he thinks and everyone who has influenced him . . . *lives in him*."

*Simple and Forceful Illustrations Can*
*Be Taken from Anything You See,*
*Hear, Read, or Experience*

To be sure, one is not limited to his own personal experiences in order to come simply, directly, and forcibly to his points. For example, in the paragraph that follows note how quickly the stage is set for a speech that "views with alarm":

In 1912, the finest and safest vessel that has ever been built, the unsinkable *Titanic,* struck an iceberg and sank with pretty nearly everybody on board. "The staggering fact," an editorial commented, "is not that the ship went down, but that she went down after fifteen hours of radio warnings, her engines at full speed, her band playing, her passengers dancing, and, apparently nobody caring a damn that there was ice ahead." And that is the staggering fact about contemporary America—warnings everywhere, engines at full speed, bands playing, passengers dancing, and nobody caring a damn.

It is in the closing of a speech that we frequently need the greatest power. The result will most often be achieved by a statement or illustration that is powerful in its simplicity. The writer developed an address built on the theme that under the free enterprise system there is only one basic reason why some people and some firms succeed, while others fail: The successful ones *serve* more. In closing that speech an illustration was used that features two monuments in Washington, D. C.

I was born in the little town of Caney, Kansas, on the Oklahoma line. Seventeen miles east of Caney is Coffeyville, an industrial town. There is a trade school there that is named for me. I am very proud of that. It is good to have a building named *for* you instead of *after* you. It is difficult for people to understand these days that I could have been born in Caney and lived there thirteen years before I ever saw Coffeyville, seventeen miles away. But that is true.

When I was seventeen years old, I went to Washington, D. C. to a high school editor's conference. In those days the school did not "send" students on such trips. They "honored" you with the appointment, gave you a hearty cheer in the school assembly, and you were on your own. I saved my money for nearly a year in preparation for that trip, and paid all my own expenses. I was so homesick while I was gone that part of the time I was physically ill, but I was thrilled, too.

When I got to Washington, I found they had a guided bus tour of the city. I hesitated a long time before deciding to take it. The tickets cost seventy-five cents each and I didn't have anything in my budget for "miscellaneous." I finally decided to cut out three meals at twenty-five cents each, and I took the trip.

Our bus stopped in front of a great, tall mounment and the guide said:

"Folks, you are now looking at the highest monument ever built to the memory of a man. That monument is 555 feet high. We built it

here to the memory of the richest man in the colonies. You can go
see his home right down here in Virignia. He had more money, more
land, and more of everything than any of the other colonists had. But
when the great fight for independence came, he put everything he had
down on the altar of freedom, and he had more to risk than anyone
else. But he didn't stop there. He gave the whole movement his personal leadership, knowing full well the penalty for being an unsuccessful rebel against the king. It wasn't because he was rich that his life
is thus commemorated. It was because he *served more* and *served
better* than anyone else that we have built to him here the *highest*
monument ever built to the memory of a man."

A little while later on our tour we stopped in front of a beautiful
white monument with a spacious reflecting pool in front of it. The
guide again took over and explained:

"Folks, this is the *widest* monument ever constructed to commemo-
rate a life. This one we built to the memory of a poor man. He was
born in a log cabin in Kentucky. As far as we know, the cabin didn't
even have a south side in it at the time he was born. He moved out
to Indiana and on out to Illinois. He came down here to the capital
city just when the great battle for the Union was to be fought. Before
that was all over he had given everything he had for his fellow men—
including his life. But this monument is not here because the man gave
his life for his country. Many men have done that. Nor is it here because he was poor. It was because he *served more,* and *served better*
than anyone else, we built to him the widest monument ever constructed to the memory of a man."

In recent years I sometimes fly into Washington several times a
week. I know many of the airline captains, and I will ask the captain
of a Washington, D. C. flight how he is coming into the National Airport. After all these years, I still like to sit on the side of the plane
where I can see *both* of the monuments at once—the *highest* one here,
and the *widest* one over there. A lot of water went under the bridge
between the time I first looked *up* at those monuments, and the time
that I now look *down* on them. In that intervening time it has been my
privilege to know and associate with some of the truly great people of
the world. And it is upon the basis of *their* experience, not mine, that
I can stand here today and say to you, with all my heart and soul I
believe that when the time comes to build the monument that will be
the highest *and* the widest—it will be built to keep green forever the
memory of some humble person—*who served more than all the rest!*

In the above example the words are simple and the point is
simple. Yet, after hearing this illustration in a speech, a congressman came to me with his eyes moist and said, "I have lived in

Washington thirty-two years and I never really saw the monuments before. Thank you for reminding me that they symbolize *service,* because *serving more* is the keystone of success in any free society."

In the greatest of all speeches, the Sermon on the Mount, the terminology is amazingly simple and direct. Some of our modern day "success" books and speakers are criticized for making things appear too simple. They are accused of over-stressing such things as correct attitudes, the establishing of worthy goals, and the practicing of old-fashioned industry. These critics say the doors to success cannot be opened that easily. Yet the greatest Success Speaker said,

"Ask, and it shall be given you; seek, and ye shall find; knock and it shall be opened unto you."

# 7

# How Speeches Are Designed

This chapter demonstrates that there are three kinds of speeches and each kind has three main parts. Any one of the three kinds can be a "good" speech if it has a worthy objective and achieves it.

This chapter illustrates how to get speeches launched, keep them on course, and bring them in for good landings.

The next chapter illustrates how to keep your audience in a "buying mood" with the vital *change of pace*.

Chapter 9 deals with the actual construction of a speech, and provides a working model that incorporates the principles outlined.

Thus, taken together, Chapters 7, 8, and 9 could be entitled *Building Your Speech*.

In preparing a speech the first consideration is the one that is basic throughout—the *objective*. Whether or not you "arrive" with your speech can be determined only in terms of where you were trying to go.

I recently assisted with a guidance clinic at one of our great state universities. Some of the professors complained that their seniors were actually well-prepared but could not "sell themselves" to prospective employers. I learned that no public speaking was required for graduation. When I visited the campus book store I found the entire "speech education" section consisted of two soft-back books of the most elementary level.

In contrast, my own undergraduate work was done in the

Kansas State Teachers College at Pittsburg, Kansas. That college had a requirement which I recommend for all colleges—no one could get a degree without successfully completing at least one three-hour course in speech.

The vigorous department of speech at Pittsburg was headed by Dr. John R. Pelsma. Over the years he had managed to inspire a wholesome fear in the hearts of those who approached his required course. Dr. Pelsma had little regard for the mentality of athletes as a group, and around the athletic department he was about as popular as a hernia at a weight lifters convention. But he was the author of a good textbook on speech and he was an effective teacher. As a student in his class I got along famously with Dr. Pelsma and emerged with something which I later had framed when I learned it was almost the only one of its kind—a grade of A-Plus for his entire course. While I was under the sledge hammer tactics of his instructional methods I never dreamed I was making such progress. Dr. Pelsma never pampered his students. I shall be eternally grateful for many things he taught me, but the chief of these was the importance of the *objective* in making a speech.

My first and most lasting lesson from Dr. Pelsma came when I submitted to him the outline of a speech I had prepared to fulfill an assignment. Putting the outline before him on his desk, I said, "Dr. Pelsma, will this do?"

He never even looked up as he barked, "Do *what?*"

When you are asking yourself the question—"Will this speech do?"—always remember Dr. Pelsma's response. This simple test will keep you at the heart of the matter and avoid fatal digressions.

## All Speeches Fall Into Three General Classifications

All speeches may be classified according to their objectives. In general terms they are: (1) speeches designed to *inform*, (2) speeches designed for *action*, and (3) speeches designed to *entertain*.

Under the first classification come all lecture type speeches as well as many others of an inspirational nature. The second classification, the action type, includes all sales speeches, most political speeches, all "drive" speeches, and others designed to result in specific action on the part of the hearers. The objective of the "entertaining" type is obvious but by no means always achieved. Too often the hearer feels like the man who went to the box office after hearing an address by a "humorist" and requested a refund of his amusement tax.

It should be understood the three general speech classifications indicated here are not mutually exclusive. For example, the informative and the action types of speech may well include some entertainment features. Again the information type speech may well inspire the hearer to be a better citizen or a finer person. In this sense it is an action speech, although the action is of the delayed type. The results are not obvious at a specified hour or date, since there can be no deadline when the action must take place. The informative and inspirational types of speech frequently result in action but their fuses are cut longer. Regardless of his subject, Cato ended every speech with "Carthage must be destroyed!" Thus, an inspirational speech may be an action speech, and the action may be either immediate or delayed. Even a sales speech may fail to get a customer's signature on the order blank *that day,* but it may have planted a seed that results in an order at a later date. How, then, is such an action speech to be judged? Lincoln's debates with Douglas did not achieve Lincoln's goal—a seat in the United States Senate. But the speeches set up Lincoln to be the Republican candidate for President.

*There Is No Standard Pattern for Speeches Whose Objective Is to Entertain*

The one classification of speeches that seems to stand alone is that of the "strictly entertainment" variety. Since there is no set pattern for this type of speech we shall not be too concerned here with how it should be specifically designed.

A popular humorous speaker of our time is Ed Harding, the Tarheel Humorist of Washington, North Carolina. Ed's formula for building a speech is remarkably simple. He tells a story a minute. If you want a thirty-minute luncheon speech, Ed tells thirty stories. If the request is for a forty-five minute dinner speech, Ed adds fifteen stories to one of his luncheon speeches. Ed frankly admits he has no "theme" and is "not trying to save any souls."

In building a purely entertainment type of speech of the Harding variety, one merely needs to hook the stories together with a running line of patter. The stories should follow one another in a sequence that appears rather "natural," or easy. One story should seem to actually "remind" the speaker of the next one. If one story goes flat, the rest are usually unimpaired.

To demonstrate this easy going method, let us use the last sentence of the preceding paragraph to "remind" us of a story. A circus train arrived in a southern city in the middle of the night and started unloading the animals and equipment. Everything must be moved to the show grounds by early morning in order to get set up for the matinee. The handlers got all the elephants off the train and lined them up in the usual fashion—trunk-to-tail. At the given signal each elephant hooked his trunk around the tail of the one ahead of him. The line then proceeded around the end of the circus train and had started across the railroad yards when a night express came barreling through, hit one of the elephants and killed him. The next day the railroad claim agent called on the circus manager and inquired, "What do we owe you?"

The circus manager said, "One hundred seventy-six thousand dollars."

The claim agent was horrified. He said, "A hundred seventy-six thousand dollars! Why, we only hit *one* elephant!"

"I know," said the circus manager, "but you pulled the rear ends out of eleven more!"

Upon such a simple "chain of circumstances" as the above, one can keep the pure entertainment type of speech going indefinitely.

Some humorists build a speech around a particular event, specific business, special occasion, or personal life experience. Witness Irvin Cobb's "Speaking of Operations," or the speech Will Rogers made to the corset manufacturers. A speech of this type requires more careful planning than the Ed Harding variety, but its blue prints are still quite different from addresses of the regular informative and action types. The writer once asked Will Rogers how he planned his speeches. Will answered, "I don't plan 'em. A fellar doesn't need a road map if he ain't goin' anywheres in particular."

Still, Will's speeches for special occasions showed considerable advance thought. He used his enormous experience and wonderful wit to ad lib as he proceeded, but in the background an outline was perceivable. The stuff was too good to just happen.

James Gheen, Tom Collins, and other humorous speakers do follow definite themes. For example, Jimmy Gheen can wind a whole series of stories around the theme of "What makes things funny?" Tom Collins can do the same thing with a discourse on why we *need* to laugh. Both of these speakers and others can build entertainment into analyzing things that all of us observe regularly but have not given much thought.

There is another type of humorous speaker, of whom Jeff Williams, of Oklahoma, might be taken as a notable example. Jeff's speeches carry definite messages yet they are heavily interspersed with humor. Much of Jeff's humor goes beyond illustrating specific points of his speech and the mere advancing of his theme. They are inserted for purposes of audience enjoyment only. Although well educated and a prominent member of the bar, he likes to use the device of putting important facts in homely language. For example, in one of his addresses Jeff was developing the point that every war starts with the attacking side better prepared, and those on the defending side will lose unless they can *learn under fire*. To illustrate this important concept Jeff said,

In the old days the folks on one side could build a wall around their town. When the enemy showed up, they could simply go inside the walls and shut the gate. But one day the enemy showed up with something new. They had a machine that would chuck big rocks over the wall. That was *bad*. All the guys inside could do was to hunker down and hold until they could fix them a rock-chuckin' machine.

Other speakers of the "pure entertainment" variety use methods exclusively their own. For example, Cecil Hunter, as "Stuttering Sam," starts out with a hoax and ends up doing imitations. There is much more about the use of humor in a special chapter devoted to that subject.

For the moment, let us insert a word of caution to the novice

speaker attempting a discourse where the sole objective is to entertain. Make your first attempts *short*. Try out your wings. Try
flying across Mud Creek before you attempt to span the ocean.
Even in your short discourse you should mark a few cracks as
"ballast" which can be quickly jettisoned if the speech is losing
altitude. For your closing, have a story that is a real walloper and
keep in mind how you can go *directly to it at any time*.

Remember, it isn't everyone who can stand up and make a
speech, but anyone can sit down. As Confucius say, "You don't
have to be a cabinet maker to put a bottom in a chair."

Program chairmen bless the speaker who can apply his terminal
facilities at any time. The problem is particularly acute in the
case of local dignitaries who feel they must "respond" to introductions at all public meetings. In a small mid-western city lives a
retired general whose rank cannot be easily ignored by the program committees. At all community gatherings he is invariably
called upon for a "few remarks," and responds by refighting
World War II. Finally, the committee planning the town's annual
Chamber of Commerce banquet appointed an unusually able
master of ceremonies and charged him "to get the general seated
within one minute after his introduction." The M. C. accepted the
responsibility amid grave doubts on the part of the committee
members.

On the evening of the banquet the general was introduced and
was just beginning to develop the Battle of the Bulge when the
toastmaster handed him a note. The general glanced at it, turned
away from the podium, thanked the chairman, and promptly sat
down. Following the meeting the grateful committee members
asked the M. C. how he got the general to terminate so suddenly.
The resourceful toastmaster said,

"I simply took a note from one of the general's favorite speech
themes—'Strategy in a Crisis'—and wrote him a note saying,
'General, your trousers are unzipped.' "

For the immediate discussion in this chapter, let us assume the
humorous discourse is in a class by itself, and proceed to the construction plans for the more standardized types. For this purpose
the informative and the action type speeches may be considered
as one.

Three Parts in the Standard
Pattern of Speech

## PART 1—*THE INTRODUCTION*

Some astute student of the speech arts has made the penetrating observation that a speech must have three parts: a beginning, an ending, and something in between. Textbook writers call these parts the Introduction, the Body of the Speech, and the Conclusion. Let us consider them in the order they occur in the speech.

There is no agreement among speakers and "authorities" concerning the *form* the introductory phase of a speech should take. There is wide divergence of opinion upon how the thing should be done, but there is complete agreement that it is extremely important that it be done *well*.

This writer believes the first thing the introductory part of the speech should do is to *get the speaker and the audience favorably acquainted*. This might be called the Preliminary part of the Introduction.

Before an audience is ready to plunge into the main Body of a speech the hearers like to "size up" the speaker. Maybe they know in advance they like him personally, or at least they are favorably inclined. Maybe most of them are already prejudiced against him, or the theme he is going to champion. Most often the audience will be open-minded, with little or no preconceived opinion either way. The crowd is usually willing to be "sold" if the speaker can deliver, but the people want to make up their minds about *him* before they start buying his wares. Thus, the first purpose of the introductory part of the speech is to *favorably condition the audience*. The writer has come to refer to this part of the speech as the "softening up exercises."

### *A Flattering Introduction Won't Hurt You*
### *If You Don't Inhale*

To become favorably acquainted with his audience the speaker must let the folks know right off that he does not think he is God Almighty, nor even one of the Major Prophets. An Irish hod carrier, named Hooley, decided to enter politics. He did very well indeed. From a ward worker he arose steadily, and finally was elected to the office of mayor. Now that he was mayor "of all the people" he decided he should be democratic and mingle with all groups among his constituents. On the Sunday following his election he paid a surprise visit to the Methodist Church. When he came home, he jubilantly told his wife, "Them Methodists are mighty respectful, I'll tell ya. When I walked into their church this morning they all stood and sang, 'Hooley, Hooley, Hooley— Lord, God Almighty.' "

It is especially important that the speaker make some deflationary remarks if the introduction of him has been too flowery, or excessive in its praise. The speaker can quickly stick a pin in this kind of a balloon, but he should do it in a way that will not embarrass his introducer. After all, the chariman was simply trying to do his job. Maybe he did not believe the "blurb sheet" either.

After an introduction that contains a lengthy enumeration of his various titles and accomplishments, the writer has found it advantageous to respond in this manner.

"Thank you, Chairman Charley. That was a *good* introduction. However, you did forget to mention that I am a Notary Public."

There is something so utterly modest about the title of Notary Public that the crowd gets a good laugh and immediately relaxes. The natural psychological reaction to such a response is,

"This guy is all right. He doesn't think he is the oracle from which all important truth must flow."

Dr. Andrew Holt, President of the University of Tennessee, uses a most successful response of another type. He will say, "I was really *impressed* with that introduction. I believe you actually are fortunate to have me here."

Another disarming response can be made following an introduction which states a "survey" determined "our speaker this evening is the most popular . . ." or the "most in demand." The speaker can say,

"I can vouch for the validity of the survey that found me to be one of the country's (or community's) most sought-after speakers.

You see, I was the one who conducted the survey. After publishing the results I destroyed the data. But you can take our chairman's word for this, as you all know him to be an honorable man."

Sometimes an introduction is obviously too long. The chairman forgets his job and becomes the "first speaker." In such cases the audience wants the chairman deflated in a nice way. Such a device relieves the tension and makes everyone happy again. For example, after a very long introduction I have successfully used this story:

When I was a young school superintendent in Kansas, the great William Allen White was scheduled for an address in our town. I was given the honor of introducing him. I worked on my introduction for two weeks. When Mr. White came to town, I went down to his hotel to confer with him. He looked over all the introductory material I had prepared and said, "I'll tell you what. You just tell the folks I'm here, boy, and *I'll* make the speech."

A. H. "Red" Motley has a special device for responding to introductions when the program has been too long and the hour is late. He will look at his watch and say, "My schedule said I was to address this meeting on October 16. (Or whatever is the date of *that* day.) I believe if I hurry I can still make it."

Dr. Thomas H. Briggs was addressing a state teachers meeting. Following the long "preliminary program" the chairman made an endless list of anonuncements. "Mary Smith please meet Justamere Axelbender at the phone booth in the lobby at 10:00 P.M.," "Be sure to see the art exhibit sponsored by the Society of Unwed Fathers," etc., etc., etc. Finally, Dr. Briggs was introduced. He opened up by saying, "Just one more announcement."

The crowd almost groaned.

Briggs continued, "Immediately following my address delightful breakfasts will be served at all the leading hotels of the city."

A speaker who found himself introduced at 11:00 P.M. to address an annual Chamber of Commerce meeting started out this way:

"Your chairman explained to me why this is called the *annual* Chamber of Commerce meeting. He says it was set up to last 'damned near a year.' "

After receiving an exceedingly long introduction, a southern speaker arose, looked around over the audience, emitted a sigh, and said, "*Now,* are there any questions?"

The direct response to the introduction is merely one device, or step, in the "softening up" exercises. The speaker wants to establish with the audience what the French call *rapport*. A good story or two where the joke is *on the speaker* will find him moving in the desired direction. Witness Ed Harding's story of how his wife wore a hearing aid. As he watched her knitting peacefully in the living room of their home, Ed spoke up, "You know, I'm kinda proud of you."

His wife looked up and said, "Yes, and I'm gettin' tired of you, too!"

Again, the writer has successfully used the account of the mother who enthusiastically rushed to the platform following one of his addresses. She was holding a little boy by the hand. She exclaimed, "I'm just filled with your message! I declare, I'm just *filled* with it."

Beamingly I turned to the boy and asked, "Little man, how did *you* like the speech?"

He said, "I've got a belly full of it, too."

Other examples of introductory stories are included in the chapter on Humor.

Another device which may be successfully used is to tie your preliminary remarks into something that has preceded you on the program. For example, several favorable and specific references to the preceding program could be followed by this story:

"This has been such a splendid program. I hope I do not come along now and spoil it for everyone. Over in Scotland they were telling me of a funeral they had. Everything was going according to plan until suddenly one of the pallbearers fell into the grave and broke his leg. Incidentally, there is what I call an awkward situation. The next day the local newspaper undertook to report the funeral. The news story said,

" 'At Donald Graham's funeral yesterday Blacky MacGregor, one of the pallbearers, slipped into the open grave and fractured his limb. This unfortunate incident cast a gloom over the whole occasion.'

"Now, I don't want to play the Blacky MacGregor role on *this* program . . ."

After you have created a few laughs at your own expense, the audience will not mind your "having one on the house." An Indiana toastmaster presiding at an annual businessmen's banquet in Indianapolis said this,

"I always enjoy being with a group of prominent and successful businessmen . . . And I even enjoy spending an occasional evening with a group like this."

Sometimes a speaker can make a ten-strike by using something from the preceding program as a springboard from which he plunges directly into the main objective of his speech. A brilliant example of this was demonstrated by Congressman Adam Clayton Powell in a speech in Chicago in the Presidential campaign of 1956. Although a Democrat, Powell was opposing Stevenson and supporting Eisenhower. The huge crowd in Chicago was predominately colored. On the program preceding Powell's speech a colored chorus sang, "All God's Chillun Got Shoes."

When Powell was introduced he "brought the house down" by starting out this way:

"That singing did my heart good. It was wonderful to hear that choir sing 'Everybody talkin' about Heaven ain't goin' there.' Friends, I got *news* for you this evening! *Everybody talkin' about that White House ain't goin' there either!*"

The question is naturally asked, "How long should the preliminary part of the introduction be?" There can be no set answer to this one. It depends upon the nature of the occasion, the speech, and the audience. It will also be determined by the amount of time available. Naturally, one would not want to tell as many stories at the Old Ladies' Home as he would at the Junior Chamber of Commerce. Of course, there would be no place at all for them in such things as state messages and occasions where the key consideration is rigid dignity.

## Humor Is Not the Only Device for Warming Up An Audience

There are many devices in addition to humor for "getting with" your audience. One the most effective is the technique of finding

the common denominators. Early in the speech you can touch
on points, experiences, background, or beliefs that you share with
your hearers. A guest speaker for a Civic Club made an immediate hit with a western city by starting this way:

> When I got off the plane this morning I asked the cab driver to
> take me to 1212 Charleston Street. On the way in from the airport I
> told the driver I wanted to see the house at that address, since that
> is the one my grand daddy built for himself after he surveyed and
> laid out this town in 1872.

When Josh Lee was stumping Oklahoma in his first campaign
for the United States Senate he started every speech the same way:

> "I first saw Oklahoma from the back end of a covered wagon,
> and the team was headed west."

Oklahoma is a young state. Thousands of Lee's hearers had
first seen Oklahoma the same way, and most of the others had
heard their folks tell them about it. Josh was elected.

Humor combined with the common denominator is also effective. A former Kansan who had been away from the state for
many years was invited back to address a rally of Young Democrats. He was an immediate hit with this:

> I am not just glad to see so many of you here this evening—I am
> amazed. When I lived here many years ago there weren't this many
> Democrats in the whole state. In those days we Democrats were sort
> of like the coyotes—folks knew there were some around here some
> place, but they didn't *see* one very often.

The speaker should never over-stretch himself in an effort to
create common denominators where none exist. There is a classic
example of this mistake in the case of the politician who said to a
farm gathering:

> "I love you people because you are *my* people. I always say
> the Morgan County farmers are the salt of the earth. It was right
> here in this county that I was born and raised between two corn
> rows."

At that point a farmer out in the fringe of the crowd yelled,
"A punkin, By Gad!"

Many effective speakers do not believe in any kind of softening
up exercises. They contend that the minute you are introduced is
the minute you have everyone's attention. You should make hay

while the sun shines. This school of thought contends the speaker should immediately nail the attention of the audience onto the big idea of his speech. A speaker who was introduced to a national convention of women's clubs started out in this manner:

> I have just returned from France. I was there when the Gold Star mothers came over as guests of our government to visit the graves of their sons. I saw those mothers get down on their knees beside the graves and clasp the grass and soil in their hands in a pathetic effort to get closer to their boys. I resolved right then that I'm going to dedicate the rest of my life to preaching *peace*. I am going to do my level best to help make this world a place where there won't be any more Gold Star mothers.
>
> I think what I have to say today is so terribly important that I am going to start telling you about it right now. I am going to talk as fast as I can be followed, and I am going to keep firing away right up to the final gong. I didn't come here to entertain you or paint you a pretty picture. I came here to help prevent a pretty Gold Star from hanging in *your* window.

The above shows the objective of a speech may be stated dramatically and immediately. It is a first-class attention getter. However, in this case the speech started off like a rocket but it got weaker and weaker. The speaker maintained his terrific pace straight through to the final gong, just as he had predicted, but his audience tired. He would have had a standing ovation had he quit at the end of ten minutes. But at the end of fifty minutes the applause was scattered and unenthusiastic. It is the contention of this writer that the total effect of the speech would have been better if the speaker had started a little slower and finished stronger. There are dashes and there are distance runs. In this case the speaker dashed a mile, but the audience was not conditioned for it, and dropped by the wayside from sheer exhaustion. This type is sometimes known as a "ginger ale" speaker—he goes flat a few minutes after being uncorked.

Another good example of the fast start was made by a college president who was addressing a state convention of civic clubs. Here is his opening statement.

"I condemn progressive education. I charge it with everything that is evil. I credit it with nothing that is good."

### When *Should the Objective of the Speech Be Stated?*

It is not contended that the Preliminary part of the introduction should answer Dr. Pelsma's question and tell the audience what the speech is going to do. Stating the objective of the speech in a clear and interesting manner is still the main purpose of the Introduction, regardless of how it is achieved. How quickly the speaker gets to the statement of his objective must be determined in the light of the following factors:

1. *The nature of the speech.*

Stories should never be deliberately and awkwardly *dragged* in. The softening up exercises should be compatible with what follows.

2. *The nature of the occasion.*

Some speaking occasions demand the strictest dignity. To violate the spirit of the occasion would not be in good taste. Remember anything that is bad taste cannot be good speech technique.

3. *The nature of the speaker.*

Never attempt stories or humorous illustrations unless you *enjoy* telling them, and can tell them well. Do not try to change your character to fit a speech technique. Make the technique fit you.

4. *The nature of the circumstances that exist at the time.*

If the hour is late, or the time is short, one should forego most preliminaries and get to the point. Perhaps the chairman or previous speakers have related a number of stories prior to the introduction of the speaker. This is good and sufficient reason for reducing the number of warm-up items. Maybe group singing, or some other "crowd unifying" technique, has already welded the audience together before the speech starts. Such conditions leave less spade work for the speaker to do. On the other hand, there may be reasons for prolonging the preliminary comments beyond what may have been planned. Perhaps the meeting is in an auditorium, and late comers are still being seated in considerable numbers. Perhaps the banquet hall has not been completely cleared of waiters, or other distractions at the moment a speaker is introduced. There are numerous other types of circumstances which a speaker must assess before he can best judge when to set up his main objective.

### How *Should the Objective Be Stated?*

Regardless of whether the objective is stated earlier, or later, it should be *unmistakably clear*. Some speakers like to state their objectives affirmatively. Others will state them in problem form, or as a question. Sometimes it is deliberately provocative to increase interest. Witness this opening by a speaker before a state teachers meeting:

"Did it ever occur to you that a boy sometimes shows remarkably good judgment when he *quits school*?"

Note the way a sales manager started his sales meeting:

It is proverbial in sales work that "thin soles mean fat order books." But I say thin soles coupled with fat heads will still result in thin order books. The guy who wants to work solely with his feet should take up tap dancing. I don't want you to just *walk*—I want you to *think*. I don't want you to just work *hard*. I want you to work *smart*.

One of the poorest salesmen I ever had was always telling me how he "worked like a dog"—and he *did*. He *ran* all over the place with his nose to the ground, just like a dog works ahead of the guns. He never looked up. He never looked around. He would point the prospects and flush them out—but some smart guy always came along behind him, made the shots, and bagged the game. He actually did "work like a dog."

Today I want to tell you how you can quit working like a dog and start working like a man—and come in with a lot more game. I want to tell you how to make a complete shift in the emphasis—from the *feet* to the *head*.

With the above objective clearly stated the speaker can now set up several major points, place a few effective sub-topics and illustrations under each one, insert some change-of-pace items at the proper spots, come along at the close with a conclusion that clinches, and he has a good speech.

Let us consider a few more examples of arresting opening statements that lead to clearly stated objectives. An election was held in the city of Dallas to determine whether the voters would authorize the issuing of $40,000,000 in bonds to finance a variety of needed improvements. In order to sell this enormous package deal to the voters it had to be demonstrated that all of the items were *needed,* and that there was nothing to be gained by settling for goals that were piddling and penurious. One of the campaign speeches made in support of the bond issue started with this pertinent observation:

> Some folks are saying these days that our goal in this drive is "too big." When did *anything* ever get too big for *Dallas?* I believe these timid objectors must be newcomers. They don't talk like Texans.
> Now I ask you to think about this: If you deliberately play for peanuts and you win—*what* do you win?—Why, peanuts! You end up with peanuts because that's all you were even *trying for.*
> Remember this: You can't cross a chasm in two jumps.
> Let's face the facts. *The future of Dallas can't be paid for with peanuts.* I've come here today to tell you the kind of stakes *we* are playing for in this campaign.

With the above objective clearly and forcefully stated the speaker was ready for the main body of his presentation. It was an easy speech to build. The main points were the major items that were to be purchased with the bond money. Under each item the speaker could do as much amplifying as his time permitted, thus giving a desirable elasticity to the outline. Here and there he tossed in a humorous comment that kept the hearers in a "buying mood" and kept the speech advancing. Near the end of the address he told a walloping story that showed goals are never too big for those who won't play for peanuts, and he ended with this:

> You have been nice to me today, and I am grateful. Now, go out to those polls Tuesday and do something nice for *yourselves.* Go out there and vote this bond issue! Do it for yourselves! Do it for your kids! Do it for *today!* Do it for *tomorrow! Do it for Dallas!*

Here is another opener which quickly sets up the objective for an Informative speech:

> A prominent labor leader always loved to comment that "Labor has no problems that can't be solved by more pay in the envelope." A few weeks ago his sorrowing widow stood by his graveside. Her broken heart was burdened with a host of problems that cannot be

solved by more pay in the envelope. In all walks of American life today—from the janitor to the Board Chairman—in public affairs and in private endeavor—more and more people are assuming that spending more money is the answer to everything. Can the truth come only through tragedy? Or can we talk about it now, before the tragedy occurs? I want to talk to you today about some problems that can't be solved with cash, but only with *courage;* not with debts, but with *diligence;* not with spending, but with *spirit.*

The above Introduction was followed by a well-planned speech under clear cut headings, and concluded on an inspirational note.

One of the classic speech openings which comes directly to the point was that made by Franklin D. Roosevelt in addressing the United States Congress the day following the Pearl Harbor attack.

Yesterday, December 7, 1941—a date which will live in infamy— the United States of America was suddenly and deliberately attacked by naval and air forces of the Empire of Japan.

### Don't Bust Out With the Bromides

An important word of caution is in order here. Start your speech with some interest catching remarks or an attractive statement of your objective. Never start with a beaten up bromide or an accentuation of the obvious. Do not break the news to your crowd that "it is a fascinating age in which we live." The people know that. Or, at least they were finding life fascinating up until you started your talk.

When the late Dr. George Frasier was president of Colorado College of Education, he taught a summer session course in speech. The class was composed principally of school executives. In each session Dr. Frasier would emphasize some particular phase of speech making, and those who delivered practice speeches that day were supposed to lay particular stress on the feature point of the day.

One morning Dr. Frasier opened the class by discussing the deadly practice of starting discourses with hackneyed phrases, calloused clichés, and other warmed-over observations of various kinds. When he had finished his lecture, he called for the first student speaker. This turned out to be a midwestern school superintendent who opened his speech by saying,

"The child of today is the adult of tomorrow."

Frasier leaped to his feet and interrupted the speaker by exclaiming,

"You don't say! Now, there is a *remarkable* observation! I presume the way I just leaped to my feet would be the spontaneous reaction of most any audience that had just heard such an amazing revelation."

Last Christmas the writer received thirty-one Christmas letters which started like this:

"Another year has passed . . ."

"The Yule Season is with us again . . ."

"The Old Year is nearly gone . . ."

"Another New Year will soon be upon us . . ."

### *The Objective Should Be One with Which the Audience Can Identify Itself*

It should be clear by now that the introductory part of the speech *may* contain two elements, but *must* contain one. It may include some softening-up materials to establish an easy working relationship between the speaker and his audience. But it *must* contain a clearly stated *objective*. This objective should be one in which the audience has an obvious interest. The hearers should readily recognize the problem involved as *their* problem, and realize that any contribution the speech makes toward solving that problem is a *service to them*.

A prominent evangelist always said it takes about four weeks to put on a good evangelistic campaign. His formula was expressed this way,

"I spend the first two weeks preaching 'em *into* Hell, and the next two getting 'em *out*. After I get through showing the people the mess they're in, and where they are headed, they are mighty grateful for some help."

### PART 2—*THE BODY OF THE SPEECH*

Having set up the introductory phase of the speech, we are now ready to consider the main body of it—"the something in between" the introduction and the conclusion. This part of the speech is the *vehicle* that is going to "deliver the groceries," so to speak.

The first cardinal principal of guidance in preparing the speech is *do not attempt to cover too much*. Decide upon two, three, or four key points in support of your stated objective, and build your speech around them. Avoid topics that cannot be handled in this form, or else you will in all likelihood lose control of the vehicle and pile it up in confusion. Do not emulate the sixth grader who prepared a school discourse on "The Universe and What Is In It."

A colored minister loved to fill his sermons with big words—some of which are in the dictionary and many of which are not. The congregation finally decided to fire the preacher and the official committee called upon him to convey the decision. The preacher was both shocked and surprised.

"What is the mattah with ma sermonizin'?" he asked.

"Don't I expostulate and transmogificate sufficient?"

The committee chairman said "Yassah, ya-all expostulates and transmogificates sufficient, but ya-all don't tell *wherein*."

It is in the Body of the speech that the speaker must tell *wherein*. Remember: *It is better to drive home one point than to let three die on bases*.

You must know exactly how many main points you are going to use, *but do not tell your audience in advance*. Never say, "Today I am going to give you ten reasons why people fail in business." Do not entitle your speech "Seven Gates to Success." When you warn your audience ahead of time as to how many points you expect to make, the hearers immediately start a mental "count down." You have taken out the novelty and the anticipation of unexpected turns. There is nothing to do but march lock step straight down the road. Your speech will hold far more charm for your audience if it is a pleasant trip over a winding road with unexpected turns, rather than a straight turnpike with bold signs announcing the next exit is still 42 miles away.

As a beginning speaker, the writer had an address called "The Seven Fools." I realize now it should have been eight. I was the first one for thinking the crowd would stay with me while we counted off the other seven.

## Build Your Speeches in Topical Outlines

Your speech outline should contain subtopics under each of the main points. These subtopics can be words, phrases, sentences, or quotes. They represent the information, illustrations, and stories that you will use in support of that topic.

The topical outline plan has a number of excellent advantages:

*It gives the speech continuity, or coherence.* This plan permits your audience to see your speech develop. It should be obvious at all times that you are on course. Speakers are permitted to digress occasionally, and toss in a little of this and a "pinch" of that, but the main pot must be kept boiling. It is permissible to do some "zigging and zagging" so long as it is clear you are always moving in the right general direction. The audience should always be aware of your main theme, and conscious that all the off-shoots are attached to it. Never wander out on a limb and just keep going.

Again, the simple outline form *makes it easy for you to remember your speech plan.* In your mind you can literally see the topical headings, and while you are discussing one you can "visualize" what comes next. This permits your discourse to flow freely toward its goal without awkward and embarrassing pauses. If you speak from notes, your outline in condensed form will suffice.

A third advantage of the topical outline is that it *makes it easy for your audience to remember the highlights of your speech.*

More than thirty years ago I heard Dr. A. E. Winship deliver a magnificent address entitled "The Good Teacher." Because the speech was simply and powerfully constructed I still clearly remember its three main points:

> The good teacher is *informed.*
> The good teacher is *industrious.*
> The good teacher is *kind.*

Under each of these topics Dr. Winship used illustrations, incidents, stories, and statements of fact. But all the while he was building to his theme, and when he had finished we had a beautifully balanced picture of what constitutes a good teacher.

Again the topical outline permits the speaker *to put first things first.* He can weigh the relative merits of his "evidence," and determine what contributes more and what contributes less.

Finally, the biggest advantage of all—the simple topical outline is *completely flexible.* Suppose your topical outline consists of three major points with about three subtopics under each. You have designed the speech to be thirty minutes long. Now you arrive at the meeting and find other things on the program have taken a third of your time. If you had spent weeks *memorizing a fixed speech,* you would at this point be ready for the men in the white coats to come into the meeting and take you out. But with your speech built on a topical outline the news that you have just twenty minutes need be no shock. You had decided in advance what topics you would drop in such a situation. Maybe you will use your three big points and omit some of the supporting data. On the other hand, maybe you will use the first two points along with the supporting items and omit the third point entirely. You then proceed directly to your conclusion, as planned. Your speech is complete either way. The only way your audience would know any change was made would be for you to have made the mistake of telling them in advance that you were going to make three points, and then sit down at the end of the two topics, leaving your hearers waiting for the third.

The flexible plan also has the enormous advantage of permitting the speaker to take advantage of last-minute developments, or changes in "audience atmosphere."

On July 11, 1960, the Honorable Frank Church, the handsome and talented young Senator from Idaho, delivered the keynote address at the Democratic National Convention in Los Angeles. For several days in advance the newspapers had heralded the fact that Senator Church was a champion boy orator, had memorized his speech, and would fire it directly into the microphones. On the morning of July 11, Nikita Khrushchev announced in Moscow that the Russians had shot down an American bomber that had been missing for ten days prior. The delegates at the Los Angeles Convention were so concerned about this crucial development in international affairs that many of them listened to the world news on portable radios as the convention progressed.

The purpose of a political keynote address is to fire the convention and the country to action. Khrushchev's announcement of another American plane being shot down was a Godsend to the Democratic keynoter. It was a stupendous development, it was right-now news, it was on everyone's minds, and it fitted perfectly the pattern the Democrats were developing to oppose the Republican administration. But Church had memorized his speech. He had no flexibility. He did not take advantage of the windfall. He made no direct reference to the momentous news of the day. And his speech never struck fire as many keynoters have done.

Suppose when Senator Church was introduced at Los Angeles he had walked straight to the microphones and said,

"Mr. Chairman, and Fellow Americans:

Today Nikita Khrushchev announced the Russians have shot down another American plane. Two of its crew are held captive and the others must be presumed to be dead. These make a total of 80 Americans who have been shot down by Russia during the cold war. And where was the President of the United States when this earth-shaking announcement was made?—Out on the golf course at Cape Cod!"

The above opening, or something similar to it, would have instantly electrified the convention. This is but another example of the extreme importance of keeping speeches flexible.

### More Advantages of the "Fishing Pole" Speech

The writer always tries to build his speeches on what he calls the "fishing rod" plan. That is, they are built in *sections*. If the time permits, I can put in more sections and cast farther out. If the time is short, I take off some of the sections and fish closer to the bank. In either case you have the situation firmly in hand and under control at all times.

Each topic in the body of the speech should be virtually an *independent unit,* that fits in with the other topics but does *not lean on them.*

The flexibility of the topical outline also pays off in permitting you to freely substitute new materials in old outlines. You can always trade a newer and more potent illustration for an older and less pointed one. After you become adept at this technique you can even substitute points taken from the early part of the meeting you are addressing. This procedure permits you to "tailor" a more or less set speech to a special occasion, and makes a good speech render far wider service than would be possible otherwise.

An example of this, the writer has an over-all speech theme based upon the vital importance of the *human element* in business, vocations, professions, and careers in general. It represents the best refined materials off a mountain of data. This material can be presented in a wide variety of situations. The basic theme of the *human* element applies to any audience, since they all have the common denominator of being composed of *people*. This basic theme has been presented to one general type of audience under the title: *The "U" in EdUcation.* Obviously, this title features the human factors involved in success in the teaching profession, and most of the supporting illustrations are drawn from schools and teaching. For another whole classification of audiences the supporting data in the outline can be changed and the speech becomes *The "U" in IndUstry.* For a sales rally the main theme can easily be used when supported with sales techniques, devices, stories, and data. Then the speech becomes *The MAN in SalesMAN.* Again this important basic theme may be tailored in another direction and becomes the *MAN in MANagement,* or *The "U" in InsUrance.* The variations of a universal theme are almost limitless under the flexible outline system. There are limitations, however. For example, I have pointed out sometimes that it is significant that there is no "U" in "government."

## PART 3—*THE CONCLUSION*

Having discussed the Introduction and the main Body of the speech, let us now focus on that important third part, the Conclusion. This is the part where you *nail down your objective and clinch it.* If the speech is designed to entertain, then the Conclusion should give the people that big belly laugh that sends them out of the meeting to chuckle indefinitely as they recall the whole presentation. Or, for quick contrast, an entertaining speech can suddenly become serious for the last minute, and send the hearers away "glowing," and glad to be alive. For example, an expert humorous speaker recently built up the crescendo of a luncheon speech and told a climaxing story that would have shattered a laugh meter. The crowd was literally in the aisles with merriment. This time the speaker did not break through the laughter and hurry on to his next step. He let his audience have its laugh out,

and as it died down there was a pause. Then with a quiet voice
and a soft, kindly smile the speaker concluded:

God must truly love us or He would never have invented laughter.
With that one marvelous stroke of divine genius He lightened all our
loads. With that one Heaven-made device He rolls back the clouds
and lets His blessed sun shine through. I believe He was with us
here today. In this hour we kept every one of His commandments.
We have not stolen, killed, nor coveted; we have sinned against
neither God nor man. We have wished no one ill. If you leave here
with that spirit in your hearts, then surely our hour together was a
blessing.

We have seen how the Dallas bond campaign speech was concluded with a call to action. The action speech may end on a high
note of optimism, a plea, a promise, or a warning. Or, the action
speech may even end on a quiet note that commits the decision
entirely to the hearers.

Lincoln ended one of his campaign speeches by telling the
voters that if they elected him, he would serve their interests to the
best of his ability. But if they elected his opponent, then said
Lincoln, "I am too familiar with disappointment to be very much
chagrined."

For another type of conclusion on an action speech let us view
a paragraph from the famous criminal lawyer, Clarence Darrow.[1]
He is completing a plea to the court. He has entered a plea of
"guilty" for his clients Loeb and Leopold. He is striving only to
save the defendants' lives. He checks the horrible responsibility of
the decision straight to Judge Caverly:

We placed our fate in the hands of a trained court, thinking that
he would be more mindful and considerate than a jury. I cannot say
how people feel. I have stood here for three months as one might
stand at the ocean trying to sweep back the tide. I hope the seas are
subsiding and the wind is falling, and I believe they are, but I wish
to make no false pretense to this court. The easy thing and the popular thing to do is to hang my clients. I know it. Men and women who
do not think will applaud. The cruel and the thoughtless will approve.
It will be easy today; but in Chicago, and reaching out over the length
and breadth of the land, more and more fathers and mothers, the

---

[1] Charles Yale Harrison, *Clarence Darrow* (New York: Jonathan Cape and
Harrison Smith, 1931).

humane, the kind and the hopeful . . . these will join in no acclaim at the death of my clients. These would ask that the shedding of blood be stopped . . . I am pleading for life, understanding, charity, kindness, and the infinite mercy that considers all. I am pleading that we overcome cruelty with kindness and hatred with love . . . You may hang these boys; you may hang them by the neck until they are dead. But in doing it you will turn your face toward the past . . . I am pleading for the future; I am pleading for the time when hatred and cruelty will not control the hearts of men. When we learn by reason and judgment and understanding and faith that all life is worth saving, and that mercy is the highest attribute of man . . .

### Conclude With Something More Impressive Than a Summary

As a general policy, I do not recommend the summary type of conclusion. You do not flatter yourself nor your audience if you assume your main points and impressions cannot be kept in mind even until you have finished.

Furthermore, the summary type of conclusion may tend to nullify the flexibility advantage of the topical type of speech construction. It will be recommended later that your conclusion be virtually memorized. In the summary type of closing you may find yourself summarizing points which you have dropped from your speech. Thus, you will have confused an audience that you were trying to convince.

Some of the great speech conclusions of history have sounded the note of warning and defiance. In completing the magnetic address that electrified a national convention and nominated him for president, William Jennings Bryan shouted:

If they dare to come out in the open field and defend the gold standard as a good thing, we will fight them to the uttermost. Having behind us the producing masses of this nation and the world, supported by the commercial interests, the laboring interests and the toilers everywhere, we will answer their demand for a gold standard by saying to them: You shall not press down upon the brow of labor this crown of thorns; you shall not crucify mankind upon a cross of gold.

In finishing his defense at Worms in 1521, Martin Luther uttered his immortal conclusion:

I cannot and will not recant anything, for to go against my conscience is neither right nor safe. Here I stand, God help me. I cannot do otherwise.

As indicated previously, speeches are often combinations of the informative and the inspirational that call for action. In concluding an address to a national conference of his company managers, a corporation president said,

All of us laboring together, and thousands before us, have built this company, and it is truly a house built upon a rock. The Scriptures say "Unless the Lord buildeth the house, they labor in vain who build it." And it may be said with equal truth that they labor in vain who built our house unless we carry on to even greater honors and greater achievements. Tonight we stand with a proud past at our backs and a bright future before us. Hats off to the past! Coats off to the future!

One of the advantages of beginning your speech on an informal note, as this book advocates, is that you can end your remarks in the same informal, personal vein. Action speeches are usually most effective if they are concluded by a sharp call for the audience to take the desired action, or advocated stand. However, the informative and entertaining type speeches may well end as informally as they open. For example, the writer has found on occasion that such a closing as this is most effective:

You have been lovely to me and I shall long cherish the memory of this day. In closing, I should like to wish you something that is as nice as you are. What can it be?
        I might wish you wealth;
        Or, I might wish you health;
        Or, that good fortune would caress you.
        But wealth might bring sorrow,
        And health could fail—tomorrow;
        So, I'll simply say, *God bless you*! [2]

One of the classic speech conclusions will be found in Lincoln's Second Inaugural Address:

Fondly do we hope—fervently do we pray—that this mighty scourge of war may speedily pass away . . .
With malice toward none; with charity for all; with firmness in the

[2] Author unknown to me.

right, as God gives us to see the right; let us strive on to finish the work we are in; to bind up the nation's wounds; to care for him who shall have borne the battle, and for his widow and his orphan—to do all which may achieve and cherish a just and lasting peace among ourselves and with all nations.

Here is a conclusion of an action speech made by the general manager to an assemblage of the company's branch managers:

Our competitors are lean and hungry. They are trimmed for action and in a fighting mood. They are counting on us to do what leaders in nearly all successful businesses eventually do—and that is to grow fat and complacent. We expect you to make sure this never happens to us. Let's show our competitors and our customers that we are the biggest because we are the *best!* And that we are first because we *deserve to be first!*

The writer has some evidence for feeling that he rendered service to thousands of his fellow Americans through a speech entitled *Lamplighters.* That speech was sometimes concluded in this manner.

Sir Harry Lauder loved to tell of the old lamplighter of the village where he lived as a boy. Each evening as dusk came on, the old man would make his rounds with his ladder and his light. He would put the ladder against a light post, climb up and light the lamp, step back down, pick up the ladder, and proceed to the next lamp. "After awhile," said Sir Harry, "he would be out of sight down the street. But I could always tell which way he had gone *from the lamps he had lighted.*"

I believe that is about the greatest tribute any of us can eventually receive from our fellow citizens. With all my heart I hope some of the things I have said today lighted some lamps for you. I hope you will go out of here more resolved that as you go down this street we call Life, the people here in your home community can readily follow your course by the lamps that you have lighted.

An action speech, like an entertaining or informative speech may end with a story. In a kick-off speech for a fund-raising campaign a speaker reviewed all the elements the campaign workers had in their favor as they started their drive, and concluded with this story:

I remember so well as a boy, one of the churches in our little town brought an evangelist from the Deep South to hold a series of meetings. After this evangelist had won a number of converts he announced that on the following Sunday morning the congregation would assemble down at the river bank just as they sometimes do in the old South, and the preacher and the converts would wade right out into the stream and he would baptize them as they did in the days of John.

When Sunday morning came the congregation assembled at the river. In fact, the whole town was there, because word had gotten around that among the converts was old Efen Martin. Ef had been the town's worst reprobate for twenty years. And sure enough, there in the huddle of converts was old Ef, dressed in his best. He had on a white shirt and a tie, and his blue serge suit. Someone in the crowd said, "Efen, ain't you goin' to be baptized?" And Ef said, "Yep, I shore am. I'm goin' to wade right out there in the best duds I've got."

When the ceremonies started the minister selected Efen first and together they waded out into the stream. When Ef got in as deep as his trouser pockets, the Jack and ten of spades went floating out on the water. That created a slight ripple of laughter through the crowd, and greatly embarrassed Ef's poor old wife who was one of the "witnesses." But the minister and Efen proceeded on into the stream. When they got out to where the water reached Ef's vest pockets, the King and Queen of spades floated lazily out on the water. This brought forth a little stronger reaction from the crowd on the bank. But the minister and Ef were undaunted. When they got in as deep as Ef's inside coat pocket the Ace of spades floated proudly out upon the rippled surface and headed down stream. The assembled hosts on the bank could no longer contain their mirth and let out a great roar of laughter. This was too much for poor old Mrs. Martin, and she shouted out to the minister,

"Parson, there's no use foolin' with Efen! He's lost! Lost, I tell you, *lost!*"

The evangelist turned around in the stream, leveled a look of scorn at Mrs. Martin, and said, "I am ashamed of you, Sister Martin. How in the Hell could he be lost with a hand like that!"

That is my message to you as we open this campaign. We've got good cards in every pocket! We just can't lose with a hand like that!

## Churchill Was the Master of the Powerful Closing

Historians of the West will probably be almost unanimous in declaring that the world's greatest man for the first half of the Twentieth Century is Winston Churchill. They will probably be in equal agreement that his greatest single contribution was the speeches that steeled Britain and the world to stand against Hitler. In making this brief survey of how speeches may be effectively concluded, let us look at three of Churchill's classic examples. The first is from his address to Parliament after becoming Prime Minister in the spring of 1940:

> . . . I would say to the House, as I said to those who have joined this Government: "I have nothing to offer but blood, toil, tears, and sweat."
> We have before us an ordeal of the most grievous kind. We have before us many, many long months of struggle and suffering. You ask what is our policy? I will say: It is to wage war, by sea, land, and air, with all our might and with all the strength that God can give us: to wage war against a monstrous tyranny, never surpassed in the dark, lamentable catalogue of human crime. That is our policy. You ask, What is our aim? I can answer in one word: Victory—victory at all costs, victory in spite of terror, victory, however long and hard the road may be; for without victory there is no survival. Let that be realized; no survival for the British Empire; no survival for all that the British Empire has stood for, no survival for the urge and impulse of the ages, that mankind will move forward toward its goal. But I take up my task with buoyancy and hope. I feel sure that our cause will not be suffered to fail among men. At this time I feel entitled to claim the aid of all, and say, "Come then, let us go forward together with our united strength."

Following the evacuation of the British Army at Dunkirk, Churchill made his immortal speech to the Parliament and people of Britain. This is probably the greatest conclusion to an action speech that has ever been uttered.

> . . . We shall not flag nor fail. We shall go on to the end, we shall fight in France, we shall fight on the seas and oceans, we shall fight with growing confidence and strength in the air, we shall defend our island, whatever the cost may be, we shall fight on the beaches, we shall fight on the landing grounds, we shall fight in the fields and in the streets, we shall fight in the hills, *we shall never surrender* . . .

For a third classic example of Churchillian conclusions let us look at the clarion call with which the Prime Minister girded his people to begin the Battle of Britain:

> Let us therefore brace ourselves to our duties, and so bear ourselves that, if the British Empire and its Commonwealth last for a thousand years, men will say, "This was their finest hour."

# 8

# The Change of Pace

**W**e have seen there are three parts to a speech, and we have discussed the general principles that should govern the preparation of each part. We have also noted examples of how other speakers have opened and closed speeches. We shall now discuss one more vital part of a good speech—the change of pace. After that we shall see how *all* of these principles are incorporated into a whole speech. Then we shall discuss how *you* should go about using these principles in constructing *your* speech.

Right now let us focus our attention upon something which the writer feels is highly essential to successful speaking—the *all-important change of pace.* The object of this device is to keep your audience rested, refreshed, and always ready to go with you. A speaker can take his hearers to the heights with a flight of good oratory, but he cannot keep his crowd on the highest peaks all the time. The air is too thin up there. The smart speaker will lift up his hearers, but he does not try to hold them for the duration of his remarks. He lets them down and lets them rest—then they will cheerfully go with him on another thought excursion.

The change of pace is achieved in several ways. The first is achieved by a quick change in speech content. This is most usually done with a story, joke, or pointed remark. If the audience shows signs of restlessness or tiring under the "heavy bombardment" of the speech, a quick switch to a story or humorous incident will frequently get everyone back in the boat, and the cruise may be continued without loss. The story or incident should always be *related to the last thing said before the change of pace occurred*. Its nature can be in contrast with the previous remark, but it should never be incompatible with it. Most often it will be a story, or side remark, related to what has just been said. For example, a speaker was making a speech on the unemployment problem. In the midst of some rather heavy statistical data he said,

When Harry Truman was President of the United States he appointed a committee to study unemployment. He said he wanted to get the *facts*. Incidentally, that represented quite a departure for Harry.

The little sally above gave the audience a good chortle, and they were ready to hear what Truman's committee reported.

A speaker whose head is notable for its lack of hair was quoting a writer who described egg heads as "the boys with the thick glasses, thick brief cases, 14½-inch collars, and crew cuts." The speaker then interjected this change of pace.

"Now, understand, *I* am not criticizing crew cuts. I used to have a crew cut but the crew bailed out."

Note how a change of pace was interjected into the following heavy discussion on missiles:

This country was shocked and stunned when Sputnik No. 1 soared around the earth with its radio beeping the signal to all nations that the Soviets were ahead of us in the space race. Our first angry reaction was to look for whipping boys. Some chose the schools, some chose "capitalistic complacency," but most critics chose the federal administration. Of course, they told me down at Washington that it was not our government's fault that we got behind in the space race. They said that as long ago as September, 1958, President Eisenhower wanted to shoot a man into space—but Governor Faubus wouldn't go.

In the above illustration the speaker gave his audience momentary relief from some painful facts, and was then ready to proceed on with his theme. His audience had caught its breath and was ready to go on with him.

The following extract is from a speech on the theme of treating your problems professionally rather than personally. The listeners were amusingly assured that everyone has problems before the speaker undertook a discussion of theirs:

Administration is simply another word for problem solving. In the past few months I have addressed groups all over the country, ranging from the Live Wire Insurance Club in Michigan to the National Convention of Funeral Directors in Atlantic City. Believe me, they all have their problems. For example, the Funeral Directors devoted one session to the problem: "How do you look sad at a $10,000 funeral?"

Even speeches of a scientific and technical nature can occasionally interject a change of pace with profit, especially if it is addressed to audiences that are not so scientific and technical. Nothing is lost in this technique and much is gained. A naval officer giving a speech on the atomic submarine, Nautilus, provided a welcome break in some protracted data when he said,

People often ask me, "How long can the Nautilus remain submerged?" That is classified information. However, I *can* tell you this. It must come up once every three years so the crew can re-enlist.

There are other ways to inject a change of pace into a discourse besides stories, "cracks," or quick comments. For example, the speaker may direct a particular remark to some well-known individual in the audience. He may turn to the chairman, or someone else on the platform or head table, and direct a remark to him. Of course, the comment advances the speech and is for all to hear. But it provides variation. For example, a speaker is pounding over a discourse on labor negotiations and his audience has had some heavy going. He could continue in the same manner by saying, "We now have a new element in labor negotiations. It is called a *heat differential*." Or, for a change of pace he could turn to the chairman, and in a conversational tone say,

"Charley, did you ever hear of something in labor negotiations called a *heat differential?* As ridiculous as it sounds, we actually have some people who think their rate of pay should increase as the temperature in the plant rises."

## Occasionally Make Reference to Some Local Person Who Is in the Audience or Known by the Audience

Perhaps in one of his illustrations the speaker refers to a city or college. It is well known that one of the people in the audience, or the head table, is prominently associated with the place, institution, or organization mentioned. This connection can be easily recognized in a passing comment and the story moves on—refreshed by the personalized element that was injected. For example, a Fort Worth Chamber of Commerce speaker could begin an illustration by saying,

"I was in Kansas City the other day . . ." Or, he could say,

"The other day I was in Kansas City—where your fine City Manager, L. P. Cookingham, made such a great record before you brought him here . . ."

A third general technique for providing a change of pace is simply the lowering of the voice—in volume, or pitch, or both. Of course, the content of the material being presented must be in harmony with this variation.

Other changes of pace techniques are found in the use of visual aids and various types of audience-participation devices.

# Constructing the Speech

*"A speech well prepared is nine-tenths delivered."*
—Dale Carnegie

You now have in mind the general types of speeches and the component parts from which they are assembled. In this chapter we shall consider how *you*, as a speaker, should prepare your speech.

It is not for a moment contended that the plan I am going to give you for constructing a speech is the *only* plan, nor is it the only good plan. But this procedure is *tried* and *true*. It is a plan that *works*. If you are an inexperienced speaker, it will give you a definite procedure that will bring good results, and you can use it until you develop your own plan that you like better. If you are an experienced speaker, you may find you can profitably adopt some features of the procedure recommended here.

Before you are ever invited to do a speech you should be thinking of some things you feel are very important, but not sufficiently well known, or generally understood. You entertain certain *convictions* about some things. You find yourself talking to individuals about these things, or they are ideas you like to discuss in small groups. Furthermore, you note that you not only like to discuss these items, but others seem interested in what you have to say about them. Here, then, is the nucleus of a speech theme that is *yours*. You should begin thinking how you would develop these thoughts if you were to talk *to* one hundred people instead of talking *with* one person.

126

As your ideas take shape it is well to have a folder into which you can drop your own notations, or clippings, or data concerning your theme. Maybe an appropriate story is called to your attention that would clinch a point or provide a suitable change of pace. All of these things should go into the folder. All the while your ideas are beginning to jell. As you continue discussing them in private conversations you begin shaping the thoughts for your public presentation. You will discover this process clarifies and sharpens your own thinking. You already have two sides of the triangle that makes up a speech—you know the *speaker* and you know the *subject*. Then one day comes that invitation to speak. Now you know the third side of the triangle—the *audience*. Knowing yourself, your subject, and the nature of your audience—*you are now ready to construct your speech*. You are now ready to bring into action on your particular project the general principles we have been discussing.

As you undertake the actual construction of your speech, the first thing you do is to answer Dr. John Pelsma's question—What do you want the speech to *do?* Is it to entertain, to enlighten, or to motivate action? Or, is it a combination of these? When you have answered this question in your own mind, you have determined your *objective*. Next you test your objective. Is it one in which this particular audience would have an *inherent* or "selfish" interest? In other words, is the theme one with which the audience can readily *identify its own welfare?* Would it be of more vital interest if it were modified in form? Is this theme *worth* a half hour of this group's time? If not, could it be fully justified for half that much time?

When you have shaped up your objective in a way that passes your tests, you are then ready to build the first draft of your outline. You may begin with the Preliminary part of the Introduction, the softening-up exercises, or that may be the last part of the speech you prepare. Having decided this point, you move into the statement of your objective. These things done, you begin outlining the main part of the speech, the Body, or "subject matter"—the "part in between."

As you begin to outline the Body of your speech you ask yourself: What is the most important thing I am going to say in support of my objective? Next, you decide—Should I lead off with this point, or should I save it for the climax? After you have placed your best point in your outline, you will usually find your other big points will almost place themselves. There is usually a logical sequence, or order of steps, that is quite obvious.

*Remember,* in building your outline it is important to keep *each* of the major points as *topical* and *self-sufficient* as possible. This is the *sectional* or "fishing pole" technique. Build the speech in such a way that you can drop out any portion desired and the rest can be quickly adjusted to form a balanced whole.

### Build On a Few Strong Points

You have now decided upon the nature, number, and order of your main points. Remember the rule here is *"keep 'em few and make 'em good."* Now, you are ready to start filling in your sub-topics. If you could say just one thing in support of your best point, what would it be? That is item Number 1 under your climax point. If you had more time, what else would you say? Those are the other points—listed in order of their importance. Then you go through the same procedure for your other major points.

When you begin to fill in your outline you will be confronted with decisions as to what details should be included and which should be omitted. A simple test to apply to your items in question is this: If I were telling this story to *one* person—the average person in the audience I am to address—how much of this information would he have previously possessed? If he could interrupt me at will, would he say, "I *already know* that"? Try to determine to what topics in your outline he would point and say, "Now, *here* is where I want some more information."

You do not have the Body of your speech complete yet, but you do have the *skeleton*. You are now ready to think how you can wrap up the big idea into a small, attractive package that the people in your audience can conveniently carry out with them. This is your Conclusion. Will it be a story, or illustration, that nails down the whole objective? Will it be a call to action? Will it be a "soft sell," delayed-action charge? Will it be a short poem? Will it be a pleasant sign-off of the it's-good-to-be-alive variety?

### *Outline* Your *Speech* First—*Then Supplement With Research*

It is very important for you to note that I have not recommended that you begin your speech preparation by research on your subject. I have not suggested you go to the library and read everything you can find on the subject, taking copious notes and preparing reference cards. The first outline of your speech should be done *prior* to your reading and research. *Make it yours.* The first draft should be done as though you had to make the speech *with what you know right then.* If you do all your reading first, you are very likely to end up with a speech that is about 75% somebody else's, and you will not even know for sure whose ideas are whose. This is why so many speeches consist of little more than the moving of old bones from one graveyard to another. If you have not done enough thinking about your subject to prepare a first draft *without help,* then *select another subject* where you can start with more information and with firmer convictions.

It is obvious that the procedure recommended here for speech preparation will not function efficiently in instances where the subject of the speech is arbitrarily assigned to the speaker. A basic concept of this book is that a speaker should not attempt a discourse upon subjects concerning which he has no special interest or convictions. If the assigned subject rings no bells with the speaker, then he should not accept the assignment. Of course, there is a difference between agreeing to do a speech on an assigned subject, and merely "responding" for a minute or two on an assigned topic.

The danger of accepting assigned speech topics is that you do all your research first. Your speeches show you are suffering from encyclopediaitis. As Droke infers, they smell like the oil lamp under which you have been digging. It is true that too many speakers stay awake at night preparing speeches with which to put others to sleep the next day.

Should a committee ask you to speak on a specific subject in which you have no interest, you should tell the group frankly that your lack of interest disqualifies you from doing a good job. Under such circumstances a committee will often alter its request and give the proposed speaker a voice in deciding upon the subject. The result can be a suitable compromise, or a subject strictly of the speaker's choosing.

*Make Sure a "New" Idea Is Not Just New to You*

After you have prepared the first draft of your outline and made it *yours,* then you should do your additional reading and checking of facts. You may find that long ago someone blew up your pet theory. If such is the case, you must omit that point, or correct and amend it. There is very little that is completely new. You will probably render your greatest service by bringing age old truths to bear on present problems. One of the best uses of originality is to say common things in an uncommon way. If you announce a "discovery" to your audience, be sure it is not something your hearers have long since "discovered," or something that was discovered and prominently announced centuries before. As stated in another chapter in another connection, never label something as "new" if it is new only with you.

Some recent "pioneering studies" were made upon the sleep requirements of human beings. The findings announced that women need more sleep than men, and less intelligent people require more sleep than the more intelligent ones. Centuries ago, Aristotle made some studies on sleep. What did he discover? He described the amount of necessary sleep in this fashion, "six hours a night for men, seven hours for women, and eight hours for fools."

The reading and study you do *after* you have prepared the first outline of your speech will not only test your philosophy and facts, but will also provide *enrichment* for your finished product. You will find a few quotes that sharpen up your points, and some additional illustrations that demonstrate your ideas effectively. Perhaps a choice verse and some stories will emerge that seem tailor-made for spots in your outline. Then you will find some other items that are to be given lower spots in your subheads, to be used if time permits. Your thinking and reading may also unearth some choice bits that can be used for "sparklers," and change of pace items.

The process of checking on your outline and testing your ideas should include more than reading. *Talk* about your plan with some people whose opinions you respect. Make sure that poem or joke you discovered is not a worn out dud that apparently everyone but you has already heard. A beginning speaker came to my office to discuss his plans for a forthcoming engagement. His eyes fairly shone with enthusiasm as he told me of the poem he had found for his closing. He had already memorized and launched out with,

"A builder builded a temple . . ."

I hated to disillusion him. I do not know how he missed seeing the poem in his sixth grade reader. But I did him a service by heading him toward something else. The audience he was going to address was composed of teachers who could have repeated the poem in unison with him, like the Lord's Prayer. I saw a perfectly good speech torpedoed when the beginning speaker undertook to cap off the effort with a poem he "ran across recently." The audience leaned forward to receive the gem, but wilted with the time-worn first line:

"It takes a heap of livin' to make a house a home!"

As you prepare your speech, also check with *people* concerning your stories, and "quickie" comments. Only in this manner can you determine whether they have any life in them.

### How to Test Your Speech Before Writing It in Full

When you have completed the first draft of your outline, ask yourself this question: "What would I say from this outline if I had to make the speech *tonight* instead of two weeks from now, or a month from now?" Then, *with the full outline* before you, go over your speech in your own mind the way you would do it if you had to do it *now*. In this manner you will begin thinking of the speech in its *entirety*. You will begin phrasing your points and statements the way you will *say* them. This plan also provides you with increased learning motivation that comes with urgency.

When you have gone over the outline a number of times the way you would give it if you could look at the outline and talk, you will see where it is too "heavy," or where the theme seems to bog down in general. Brighten up these dead spots by dropping out the dull items, or perhaps injecting some change of pace items in between the heaviest charges. Check the whole speech for balance. Does it reach its peak too quickly and then fizzle out like a slow leak? If so, move your best points around to preserve logical sequence and still provide balanced power.

Now you have tested, enriched, and improved your outline until you are satisfied your objective is well stated, and you have a logical and attractive vehicle for reaching it. You feel you have a conclusion that wraps up the message in a neat package that the audience will want to carry home. You have "talked through" your speech in the informal manner you would use if you could hold the outline before you and tell the story to a few friends at the table. You find after talking through the outline that you are beginning to make the same points in the same words. *Now, you are ready to write your speech.*

### Beginning Speakers Should Write the "Final Drafts" of Their Speeches—But Not Memorize Them

There are many who contend that speeches need not be written in full, and I know many experienced speakers who do not prepare a complete manuscript of each new speech. However, this book is designed to give an inexperienced speaker a *sure-fire plan.* At no time have I said it would offer you the *easiest* plan. There is no easy way to become a good speaker any more than there are short cuts to medicine, law, or other attainments you may wish to achieve. If you want to speak *well,* you will have to *pay the price.* That means *work,* and *thought,* and *practice.*

In the beginning of your speaking experience, then, write out your speeches in complete detail. But, remember, you are writing the speech after you have *talked it through* a number of times. Write it as you will *say* it. Go over each sentence—not as you would *read* it—but as you would *speak* it. In preparing your manuscript, do not "write it down on paper," but *speak it down on paper.* You will find yourself becoming increasingly proficient in this technique as you gain experience from actually delivering what you have written.

After you have written your speech, check it for annoying repetitions. For example, I recently heard a speaker who said at least two dozen times, "I feel very definitely that . . ." Had he written his speech and read it, this boresome repetition would have been as obvious to him as it was to his audience. Again, the writing of a speech will reveal any glaring errors in grammar which might otherwise embarrass a speaker. If you are worried about such a possibility, your written copy is a good safeguard— simply have it read by someone who is more thoroughly grounded in English composition. Later in your speaking career you perhaps can take more liberties with the rules of grammar, like Booker T. Washington suggested, but in the beginning strive for correctness as well as clarity.

In the process of "speaking your speech down on paper," always keep your audience in mind. Are the words you are using going to mean the same things to the hearers as they mean to you? Make yourself clear, but do not assume you are talking to morons. *Never talk down to an audience.*

Someone has well said, "Never assume you are talking to people whose intelligence equals yours—they might have more." Of course, you must also avoid talking over your audience's heads as the old lady told the highfalutin' preacher, "Jesus said, 'Feed my lambs'—not, 'Feed my giraffes.'"

When you get too high in the stratosphere, your hearers find it uncomfortable to stay with you. A college president addressed an annual Chamber of Commerce banquet on a theme he called "Pastels in Prose." What he tried to do was depict the progress of man in three mythical stories. The result was deadly. In the crowd was a newspaper editor who was far more literary than the average person present for the event. After the adjournment finally took place, the editor confided to me,

"Either the good doctor or myself is nuts. I am going home and try to figure out which one it is."

With the manuscript of your speech completed you are now ready to prepare it for delivery. While the delivery of the speech is the subject of the next chapter, it should be said now that the speech should *not be memorized.* Read your speech aloud until you are familiar with it as a *whole*, and how your points *sound*, as well as how they *look*. Then begin "delivering" the speech from your outline with the manuscript beside it. If you find yourself stumbling on a point, you can check your manuscript to see how you *said* it there.  Presently you will find yourself saying the same thing in *about* the same way each time, and then *you are beginning to arrive.*

### Memorize Your Speaking Outline and Keep a Copy With You

Through the process of using your outline and going through your speech repeatedly, you will soon have it rolling along nicely. Now reduce the outline to a few key words under each point. This is your *speaking outline.*  It is not recommended that you use a speaking outline when you make your public speech, but it is recommended that you *have* one.  The chairman can put it on the rostrum for you, or it can be in your pocket, but you will derive some reassurance from the knowledge that it is near.  By condensing your complete outline to this highly abbreviated speaking outline you will find you can almost *visualize* it at will.  With a little experience you can drop some points out as you speak and still visualize what comes next on the outline.

### Now Let Us Look at a "Model" Speech Embodying the General Principles We Have Discussed

The speech which follows was prepared and delivered by a midwestern businessman Mr. E. J. Karnes, Sr., of Omaha, Nebraska.  His audience was a convention of retail grocers.  This speech was not selected because it is a model of perfection.  It was selected because it was constructed and delivered by a businessman, rather than a professional speaker.  It is the kind of speech any sincere, intelligent person can do if he will follow a few basic principles and apply himself.  Furthermore, this speech seems to follow most of the simple steps outlined in this chapter:

1. It begins with "softening up exercises."

2. It has a clearly stated objective to remind the hearers that democracy is supposed to protect the welfare of *majorities*.  This also serves to identify the welfare of the speaker with that of his audience.

3. It is built on the topical plan.  Each point is independent of the others.  Subtopics can be used, or dropped, at will.  It is completely flexible.

4. It provides changes of pace that break the "heavy thunder" in the body of the speech.

5. It concludes with a call to action, and wraps up the whole package neatly by effectively quoting the title again at the close.

After you have read this speech we can go over an outline, which reveals further how it conforms to the recommended pattern.

In reading the speech that follows, remember it is not at all necessary that you and I concur with all its points of view. This is how one good citizen expressed *his* views. If yours are different, you should learn to express yours equally well. If your views are essentially the same as this speaker's, then you should prepare yourself to answer the call he has issued, and help carry the banner with the groups you address. After you have read the speech, we shall break it down according to the principles advocated in this chapter; first a general outline, and then a speaking outline.

### PUT ONLY AMERICANS ON GUARD TONIGHT

Every once in a while my friends in business will ask me, "How do you have time to make speeches?" The answer is simple, "I don't." Frankly, I do not accept many speaking invitations, but I do take some of them for the same reason I go to church, or go to the polls to vote, or call on a friend in the hospital, or remember a loved one's birthday. You and I do not do any of these things because we "have the time." We *take* the time to do them *because they are important.* I am here this evening to do my best for you because I think *you* are important, and I sincerely feel there are some important things that very much need to be said these days.

I heard the other day of a hen and a pig that were looking at a restaurant sign that said, "Ham and Eggs Served Here." The hen said, "Doesn't it make you feel important to realize that we are the producers of the things that have become a good breakfast for people the world over?"

The pig said, "Well, with you hens—helping with this sort of thing is just a day-to-day occurrence. But you must remember that for us pigs it represents quite a sacrifice!"

Now, when it comes to making speeches, I find myself in the same corner with the pig—it may be an everyday occurrence for some, but for me it represents quite a sacrifice.

Someone told me recently of the two cows who were looking over the pasture fence, watching a milk truck going to town. On the side of the gleaming white truck it said,

"Pure Milk—Pasteurized—Homogenized—With Vitamin D Added."

One cow said to the other, "It makes one feel very inadequate, doesn't it?"

Believe me, facing a fine audience like this makes me feel inadequate. But remember, that truck would not be going to town if it were not for the *cows*. And I sincerely believe that business cannot "go to town" without people like you and me. We are the foot soldiers, so to speak. We are out on the firing line where the battle is fought every day, and I believe it is important that we do some of the talking.

No, I do not accept speaking engagements because I have *time*. I accept them because I feel you and I and others who sincerely want to preserve our freedom must have more people speaking up for our side of the story. I notice that when the left-wingers put a man up on the platform to speak for them he is always an able speaker. He is so good that he can make a phony argument sound plausible. The selfish interest groups seem to always have smooth talking boys to tell their story to important public meetings. I have heard various speakers sent out by socialistic groups. Without exception they have been polished and convincing speakers. I believe the time has come when you and I have got to do some of the talking. Maybe our rhetoric and our diction will not be so eloquent as some socialist or communist who is trying to destroy our American system, but remember, we do not have to be as smooth as they are—because we do not have anything to *smooth over*. We are standing on the *facts*. They have to *make* a case for their viewpoint. We do not have to *make* a case—we just have to *reveal* the case that is already made. But we *do* have to reveal it—it will not reveal itself. The truth does not necessarily *"will out."* Someone must *come out* for it. And that "someone" must be people like you and me, who will benefit from the truth—we cannot depend upon people who profit from suppressing the truth.

Some of the smooth talking boys try to make *anything* the left-wingers do sound good. Somebody told me the other day Adam and Eve must have been communists—they had little to eat and nothing to wear, but they still called the place where they lived "Paradise."

In one of the crucial stages of the Revolutionary War, our great American commander, George Washington found his army in a critical situation. There was real danger of being surrounded and destroyed by the enemy. Washington's little army was made up of a hard core of citizen soldiers who were fighting for their homes and their freedom. Then he had some various allied groups who were associated with him for causes that were less fundamental. So when faced with the really critical situation he issued his famous order, *"Put only Americans on guard tonight."*

General Washington knew that some of the professional soldiers who were allied with him might understand more military technique than his own native Americans. He knew that some of the full time scouts, Indian fighters, and foreign regulars might be able to shoot a little straighter than the farmers and craftsmen and small shop-keepers who made up his ranks. But he knew something else—the real Americans were *thinking straighter*. They had the most at stake and consequently had the most to lose. So he said, "Put only Americans on guard tonight." And he knew something else—if their hearts were in the right place—and if they believed in the right things—their shooting would *improve,* and they would eventually win.

I say to you the time has come again when we must put Americans on guard. Maybe we are just citizen soldiers instead of professionals, but if we really believe in the things for which we are fighting, then our marksmanship will improve.

I notice there is a movement now in the U. S. Chamber of Commerce and other groups for businessmen to get into politics. Personally, I do not believe businessmen should have ever gotten out of politics. But to me this does not mean every businessman should run for office or be a ward committeeman. Nor does it mean they should all be in one party either. Certainly it should not mean that businessmen should limit their interest in public life to the active campaigns that precede the periodic elections. I believe, and have always believed, that businessmen should be *citizens*—and should participate in their community life and in public affairs as *good citizens*—not as businessmen. And I think the same should apply to farmers, and labor groups, and all other groups. And because this fundamental concept is being violated by many other groups it becomes all the more important that it should be followed by responsible businessmen.

I am here merely because I am trying to do my part as a citizen. I feel it is a responsibility I cannot avoid. It is no longer a question of whether I have *time*.

Last summer I had to have a water line dug up at my home. One of the men doing the digging was an old colored man whom I know is a good deal older than I am. It was a terribly hot day and I said to him,

"Uncle John, I don't see how you can do this kind of work at your age. I used to be able to do this sort of thing, but I just couldn't take it now."

He said, "Sir, you could do it if you was in my situation. I does it because of *compellment*."

That is exactly why I am spending a good deal of time these days trying to help folks keep straight on some fundamental principles of Americanism. I am doing it because of *compellment*.

Now, the one great principle of our American system—about which

I want to talk with you for just a little while this evening—is one which we are fast losing sight of. That basic principle is that democracy—while protecting the rights of the individual—is supposed *to serve the welfare of the majority*. I am deeply concerned that the welfare of the majority is being pushed farther and farther into the background these days while the highly organized minority groups take over.

Let me say at this point that I have no quarrel with any minority group that I shall mention. I have friends in all of them. In fact, the viewpoints I shall bring you were crystallized by talking with these friends. I shall say nothing here today that I would not say if invited to speak before any minority group concerned. I believe my views would be well received by the rank and file of such groups, because it is with the *members,* rather than the *leaders,* that I have discussed these matters.

Of course, someone can take issue with *anything* one might say, if it is important at all. If it isn't important, there is little use saying it before a group whose time is as valuable as yours. As a writer pointed out recently, there are so many sore toes in the world these days, a person can scarcely move in any direction without stepping on one. If someone here this evening should have his sore toe protruding as I pass by, please be sure it gives me no pleasure to cause you pain.

The first majority group I want to mention tonight, whose interests are being supplanted by minority groups, is that great group known as the *voters*.

The line that separated the two major political parties in America used to be a *vertical* line that cut right through all economic groups. In both parties there were business people, professional people, farmers, and laboring people. Both parties had a good balance of "white collar people" and "workers." However, in the last twenty-five years the line that separates the two parties is becoming a *horizontal* line. More and more, the white shirts are above the line and the blue shirts are below it. Whereas people once affiliated with a political party because of their *beliefs,* they now vote more and more according to their *interests*. Certainly the change is not a healthy one for the democratic process. One of our great parties is being taken over increasingly and successfully by a combination of minority groups who use it as a medium to advance their own special interests. *Let's face it*. A great majority group known as the "voters" elected the President in 1952 and in 1956. But in 1952 special interests managed to elect a controlling majority in Congress and in 1956 they increased their control of Congress to what now amounts to a strangle hold. It is no secret that our present Congress is dominated by organized labor and that in certain circumstances a working majority of its members are obligated to put the welfare of labor *ahead of the welfare of the majority of all the people.* This makes it extremely difficult to get any legislation through the present Congress that really corrects any of the well publicized abuses of some union leaders. One of the big needs of labor legislation is to protect the rank and file union members against the abuses of the labor bosses. What happens to the rights of the majority of the voters under these circumstances? Why, they go out the window. And oddly enough, even the rights of the *majority of the minority* groups are lost. Bossism takes over. And that is the exact reverse of what we meant to accomplish by our democratic form of government. What is true of our national government in this regard is also true of numerous state and local governments.

Does this mean that all such sins are within one party? It certainly does not. The Republicans saw their party take a terrible licking in California and many other places in 1958, largely because of the highly organized and well financed power of labor. This is causing many Republicans to quake with fear and bow down to the pressure groups almost as completely as if they had also been elected by them. There has never before been so many "me too" Republicans as there are now. Many weak-kneed Republican politicians are shaking in their boots because of what happened to Bill Knowland in California and the Republican candidates in many other instances in the last election. They forget that the late Senator Taft won a much tougher fight in Ohio a few years ago because he stood up and battled all the way for the interests of the *majority of the voters—including the majority of the union members.* And he *won.* And he could not have won without the votes of a great many union members. This is enormously important. It means that *the right kind of leadership can still win the majority of the people.* It means when the proper appeal is made the *majority* can still rule—that they will think *first as American citizens* and secondly as members of the various groups to which they may belong.

There are many millions of fine citizens in both major political parties. We must somehow see to it that these great majorities take over the management of their parties again, and quit leaving the leadership to special interest groups.

We have too many people who think the only "workingmen" are men who wear overalls. The boss who never dreamed of a forty hour week for himself, is not a workingman. The doctor who cares for the sick at all hours of the day and night is not a workingman either. The school teacher who slaves the clock around to help the "workingman's" kids is not himself a workingman. The merchant who literally carries the community's load on his back is not a workingman. We must be done with this outrageous idea that only those who work with their hands, really work!

We have a somewhat similar problem in racial minorities. I do not have a single trace of racial prejudice in my system, and I defy any man to offer any evidence to the contrary. But I believe we have all become so concerned with guaranteeing minority groups their rights that we ignore the rights of the majorities. In Little Rock we all got so concerned with the rights of seven Negro students that we let the situation cheat 3500 white children out of a whole year of high school. The Supreme Court and thousands of local minority champions have been shouting to the house tops about the rights of the *seven,* and certainly the rights of the seven are very important. But who is speaking up for the rights of the 3500 which have been *completely ignored?* I say this is not the way democracy is supposed to work! I say that neither Governor Faubus nor the N.A.A.C.P., nor the white "citizens committees," nor anyone else should be permitted to deprive the *majority* of students of their rights.

I am concerned that we have too many people who make careers out of being identified with minorities. We have too many *full time* colored people who are aware of nothing except that they are colored. They have ceased counselling their people to *earn* equality, as did Booker T. Washington and other great Negro leaders. They are just *demanding* "equality." In too many cases these extremists have forgotten a higher obligation they have and that is to be *Americans.*

One of my dearest friends in the colored race said to me the other day, "It never seems to occur to some of our people that *they* can be guilty of racial prejudice. I remind them that when they demand a Negro be given a certain job just *because he is a Negro,* they are demanding that a white person be kept out of that job just *because he is white.* And that is racial prejudice. I keep reminding our people that a colored man doesn't deserve anything just because he is colored, any more than a white man deserves something because he is white."

We have too many *full time veterans.* They forget that they are just a minute minority of the millions of loyal and patriotic Americans who served their country in uniform. To this small minority our country is a cow whose pasture they helped to save one time, and in return for that service they should be privileged to milk the cow forever.

Yes, I think it is time we who represent the *majorities* do some of the thinking and some of the *talking.* We have listened to the ideas of the minorities and the results have too often been disastrous.

Down in Oklahoma they were telling me about a man who had a short leg and a stuttering son. One day the son said,

"Pa-pa-pa-papa, I th-th-, I think, I have thought of a way-a way, whereby you can wa-wa-walk down town and not be- and not be em-em-embarrassed by your sh-sh-sh-short leg."

The old man said, "That's good, son. What is your idea?"

The boy said, "You could wa-wa-walk with your sh-sh-sh-short leg up on the curb, and your long leg down—your long leg down in the gutter!"

The old man said, "That sounds good, son, I'll have to try it."

The next time he was down town the father tried the boy's idea and was getting along fine, but the new system put half of him out in the street—and a car struck him. He had been in the hospital a few days when the boy came to visit him. The boy said,

"Pa-pa-pa-papa, I sure—I sure—I sure am sorry you got h-h-hit."

The old man said, "That's all right, son. But, you know, I have been here in the hospital a few days and I have sorta had a chance to think. I think I have figured out a way whereby you can stop stuttering."

"Oh, have you, Pa-Pa-Papa?" the boy said. "Well, I'll sure-sure-sure be glad to try it!"

"All right, son," the old man said, "suppose you try just keepin' your damned mouth *shut*."

Now that is exactly the kind of advice we ordinary citizens should give to a lot of crackpots whose ideas are heading all of us for a precipice—and we had better do more of our own talking.

Another majority group that has fallen by the wayside in recent years is that great group that once was completely respected by the politicians and now is completely ignored—the *taxpayers*.

There was a time when a politician was proud to say that he was sensitive to the welfare of the taxpayer—that he had the taxpayer's interests constantly in mind. There was a time when that was the surest way to get elected and re-elected. But that was back in the days when the *majority ruled*. Paradoxically enough we have now reached a state where a politician is ruined if he is branded as "economy minded," or "budget conscious."

Every time the President speaks up for a balanced budget there are those who scream he is "putting dollars ahead of defense." Any politician who asks the simple question, "Where is the money coming from?"—is branded as a "Midas," a "tool of the special interests," a Scrooge who thinks only of the dollar and damns human welfare.

Now what one thing would do the *most good* for the *most people* of this country in an economic way? If we really wanted to help all the people, how could we do it at a single stroke? According to all the economic experts the answer is perfectly clear—*stop inflation*. Head off the downward plunge of the dollar. Give the average citizen the most purchasing power possible. Sustain the value of the fixed incomes upon which millions of our retired people are now living and many millions are destined to live. But this tremendous goal can only be achieved through *balancing our budgets and living within our incomes*. This, then is the only way the majority can be served, including again the *majority of the minority groups*. The taxpayer must come into his own again if our American system is to be saved. We must restore health to the rotting dollar. And the public leader who speaks up for the taxpayer must again become a champion instead of a cheap-screw.

Finally, the other majority group that must come into its own if our American system is to be saved is that great majority known as *customers*. I am amazed and shocked these days when I see how many minorities are conspiring and working overtime against the interests of the great democratic majority—the customers.

Under the American system of free enterprise the customer is supposed to be king. Theoretically he should reign supreme. Those individuals and firms who can serve the customer's interest best are what we call "successes." Those who cannot serve the customer's interests as well as the competition can do, are less successful, or are failures. This is the *basic doctrine* of free enterprise—this is the very *soul* of the system. Yet today, from Washington on down, new and higher barriers are constantly erected to keep the law of supply and demand from operating freely—to keep the customer from being *served* as the system *could* and *would* serve him without artificial and arbitrary restrictions.

Every conceivable kind of minority group wants protective duties for its products so they will not need to compete freely in the open market. Labor leaders pursue policies that constantly increase the price of the product by making it more and more expensive to produce. Some farm groups want the "government" to put artificial supports under their products and ignore the law of supply and demand. Right now the government has got nine and a half billion dollars invested in a "farm program." What does this really mean? It means the *majority* of the customers are having their taxes increased for the purpose of *increasing the cost of the food they buy*. Does that sound like democracy to you? Are you beginning to see what I mean when I say the customers are a great majority group whose interests are being bulldozed under by various minority interests? We are going to have to face up to reality and the time is *now*. The American Farm Bureau Federation has officially faced up to it and decided to do business according to the American tradition, and let the chips fall where they may. In its national convention in Boston the Farm Bureau adopted resolutions asking the government to get out of the farming business and let the law of supply and demand take over. But to date we have seen no similar action from a host of other minority groups who are pushing their special interests, regardless of what happens to that great majority group known as the *customers*.

When all the restrictions are removed, the customer will see to it that our system works fairly. He is going to buy from those firms and individuals who can pleasantly and efficiently deliver him *the most of the best for the least*. That is the very core of the American system. If your firm and my firm can do more for the customer than the competition can do *we should ourselves be successful*. And by serving our customers better we *will* be successful—*unless* minority groups use government power to throw a lot of arbitrary road blocks in our way. And every time the restrictions hamper us they prevent us from serving the welfare of that greatest of all majorities—the *customers*.

Why should the government now be trying to break up certain firms simply because they are large? Did they grow large by cheating their customers, or their competitors? No. They grew large by serving their customers better than the competition was doing. Under modern conditions that is the only way a firm *can* grow larger. Is this, then a crime? If *you* serve *your* customers better, do you not expect to grow larger as a result of it? Certainly you do not expect to grow smaller and weaker as the result of better service.

I say it is not for minority groups, acting through federal bureaucracy, to arbitrarily decide who shall grow larger and who shall grow smaller. I say let's get the government out of such matters and put the full authority and responsibility right where it is supposed to be—and that is in the hands of the *customer*. We do not need to put restraints on growth—what we need to do is to *remove* the restrictions. When is a firm too big? I say it is too big when it can no longer serve the customer as efficiently as its competitors. Does the government need to decide this? *No.* The customer will take care of all that *if you just let him alone.* Little David can always whip Goliath if Goliath *needs* a whipping.

The fact that you are ahead now doesn't mean you will stay there. You must *keep on* serving better if you want to stay on top.

Down in Georgia they told me about a couple of New Yorkers who came down to hunt quail. When they arrived at the plantation of their Georgia host, the New Yorkers opened the door of their station wagon and out bounced a couple of fine bird dogs.

The Georgian said, "What are the dogs for?"

"Why," said the New Yorkers, "we are going to hunt quail, aren't we? These are two of the finest pointers you ever saw."

"Oh," said the Georgian, "we always use grandpa for that." He motioned with his hand to indicate an old man sitting in a rocking chair on the porch. He had a long white beard that came to his waist. He seemed intensely interested in the conversation. "Yessir," said the Georgian, "grandpa is the greatest pointer you ever saw, and he just loves to do it. He gets his exercise that way and it all just works out fine."

Bright and early the next morning the hunters were in the field. Grandpa was working ahead of the guns when suddenly he stopped with one foot in the air, and his beard pointing straight out toward a clump of bushes. "There's your first covey!" said the Georgian. When given the signal, grandpa flushed the covey, the hunters brought down some birds, and the hunt continued. For all three days of the New Yorkers' stay in Georgia, grandpa worked perfectly and the hunters got their limit in no time.

The next year the New Yorkers returned to Georgia to hunt again. This time their host met them at the train. When the New Yorkers alighted on the station platform the Georgian said, "Where's your dogs?"

"Why," said the New Yorkers, "we didn't bring them. We just supposed we would be using grandpa again."

"Well, that is a very sad situation," said the Georgian. "I suppose I should have told you before. You remember how well grandpa was working when you were here last year? Well, it wasn't long after that he got to chasing rabbits, and we had to shoot him."

It just goes to show, the fact that you are on top this year doesn't necessarily mean you will be there next year. You have got *to keep on delivering.* As someone well said, even though you are on top of the heap you must remember you are still a *part of it.* That means it is always possible for you to get buried in the heap and then somebody else will be on top.

Friends, it has been *good* to be with you this evening and talk about some things we must *all* talk about—and *do* something about. We are the greatest people in the world—we are *grass roots people.* We are the kind of folks who have to do the dying to gain freedom—and we are the ones who have to *work* to save it. Our American way of life is a marvelous thing—but it is not foolproof. It will not operate itself. It has to be *operated by* the majority for the *good* of the majority, or the greedy guys will take over and take us all for a ride. If you want this meeting to be worth your while and mine—then go out of here tonight determined that you are going to put the business of *citizenship* above all other business, and you can be sure that is the only way there will be business enough for us all.

The time has come when we must issue a call to all sincere Americans in all minority groups and all walks of life. We must remind *everybody* that democracy means *the welfare of the majority comes first.* And the biggest majority of all—the one to which we *all* belong and to which we *all* owe our first allegiance—is the majority known as *Americans.* It is time to again issue the famous order—"Put only Americans on guard tonight!"

## *The Frame Work Around Which the "Model" Speech Was Built*

By reversing the usual process we can build an outline from the above speech, and see how readily it lends itself to the construction principles set forth in this chapter.

WORKING OUTLINE

SUBJECT

"Put Only Americans On Guard Tonight"

*Introduction*

*Preliminary*

   I. "How do you have time to make speeches?"
     A. I don't.
     B. *Take* time because important.
     C. Ham and eggs story.
     D. Cow story.

  II. Must have more speakers for "our side."
     A. Those who oppose our system are usually eloquent.
     B. We have advantage of truth.
       1. Adam and Eve.

 III. Washington's order.
     A. Conditions under which it was issued.
     B. *Why* it was issued.

 IV. U. S. Chamber of Commerce and others now leading movement for business people to become active in politics.
     A. Should never have gotten out of politics.
     B. Business people should participate in public life as *good* citizens rather than as "businessmen."
     C. "Compellment" story.

*Objective*

To reaffirm the basic principal that the first purpose of the American democratic system is *to serve the welfare of the majority.*

*Body*

   I. Highly organized minorities are subordinating the majorities' welfare to their own.
     A. This is not a condemnation of minority groups.
       1. I have friends in all the groups I have mentioned. They are chief source of my information. Find they resent policies of many leaders and extremists in their midst.
       2. Will not intentionally step on sore toes.

  II. First majority being ignored— the *voters.*
     A. Both major parties used to include all economic groups.
       1. Party lines use to be *vertical.* Now they are *horizontal.*

2. *Labor,* a minority group, now dominates U. S. Congress and numerous other units of government.
   A. This does not mean "rank and file." Average union member never "influences" congressman. "Labor" in politics means power concentrated in hands of "leaders" who *do* influence Congress, legislatures and other public officials.
   B. All the sins not in one party.
   C. We must battle the popular fallacy that no man is a "workingman" unless he works with his hands.
   D. Experience proves that when proper appeal is made, union members will think *as citizens—first.*

III. *Racial minorities* must prevent their leaders from subordinating *general* citizenship interest to *group* citizenship interest.
   A. I have *no* racial prejudice.
   B. My friends in racial groups concur in views.
   C. Welfare of majority completely submerged by all minority groups at Little Rock.
      1. Supreme Court
      2. N.A.A.C.P.
      3. White Citizens Councils
      4. Governor Faubus

IV. *"Veterans"* must not assume that because they served their country for a period of time that the country should serve them forever.

V. *Change of Pace*
   A. Story of short legged man and stuttering son.

VI. *Taxpayers* another majority group now in disrepute with law-makers.
   A. Once "ruled the roost" in legislative halls. Now the last group considered.

VII. *Customers* constitute final majority group whose interests are being trampled by selfish-interest minorities.
   A. The "customer-is-king" philosophy is basic to free enterprise.
   B. Customer constantly gouged now to provide benefits for minorities.
      1. "Built-in" raises for labor.
      2. "Protective" groups.
      3. Farm subsidies.
   C. Arbitrary restrictions imposed to prevent firms from growing who do serve customer better.

      1. Customer should determine size of a business enterprise —not the "government."

VIII. Change of pace.
    A. Quail hunting story.
      1. Hardest part about success is to keep on succeeding.

### Conclusion

I. Good to talk to *grass roots* people about basic problems.
    A. We are the ones who have to do the dying to gain freedom and we must be the ones who work to keep it.
    B. Meeting will be an important one if we all pledge first allegiance to that biggest majority of all—the one to which we all belong—that majority called Americans.
    C. Repeat Washington quote.

## How to Build the "Speaking Outline"

The foregoing outline could well have served for the one from which the speech was written, and it would suffice nicely as the outline for study and rehearsal. Once the speaker has the subject sufficiently in mind that it rolls along easily from the complete outline, he can shift to a highly abbreviated one. The following shows how the speaking outline can be reduced to six key "reminders" with some simple subheads. This is the outline the speaker should memorize until he can visualize it at will.

### SPEAKING OUTLINE

1. Friends ask *why*.
    Hen and Pig
    Cows

2. Must tell our side.
    Selfish interests speak smoothly
    Adam and Eve

3. Washington

4. U. S. Chamber
    Compellment

5. Democracy designed to serve *majority*.
    Majorities' welfare now subordinated.
    I have no quarrel with any minorities.

  A. *Voters*
    Labor
    Republicans
  B. *Racial*
    No prejudice
    Little Rock
    Stuttering story
  C. Veterans
  D. Taxpayers
  E. Customers
    Restraints to serve
    Bigness fallacy
    Quail hunters

6. *Conclusion*
  Good—grass roots
  Sound call
  Washington

It should be noted that this form of speech construction is entirely flexible and gives the speaker complete freedom. In this case, an effective short speech could be made by using the Introduction, the Objective, and any *one* of the majority groups from the Body of the speech. Or the speaker could discuss one majority group and merely name the others in passing. Another alternative would be to name one or more of the groups and mention only the first supporting items under each. The Conclusion will work equally well with any of these arrangements.

It should also be noted that any of the supporting points in the body of the speech can be deleted, and something substituted that is more recent or more potent. "Right-nowness" can be added by using an appropriate item from the latest issue of the paper, or even from a remark made in the portion of the meeting which preceded the speaker. The preliminary and change of pace stories can be used as they are, deleted completely, reduced in number, or substituted for. It cannot be over-emphasized that this style of speech construction has an enormous advantage in its complete flexibility.

*Steps In Building Your Speech*

A Brief Summary of Chapters 7, 8 and 9

1. Begin thinking about a subject or issue which you sincerely feel is truly important. Think what could be said about it that would help others whom it also concerns.
2. Discuss your ideas with people whose opinions you respect. This will test, clarify, and supplement your thinking. If you find small groups are interested in your ideas as you talk *with* them, begin to think how you would talk *to* larger groups about these same things.
3. Set up an idea folder for each speech theme you are developing. Drop into it ideas, suggestions, clippings, stories, references, and quotations that seem pertinent. Collect more ideas than you will need; thus your speech can be the cream off the top of many ideas.
4. Accept the first speaking invitation that will let you try out your ideas. Now you know all three sides of the "speech triangle"—the speaker, the speech, and the audience. You are ready to begin building your speech. Of course, you keep clearly in mind *how much time you have to speak.*
5. State your objective clearly and test it. If it is achieved, will it be a *service* to this particular audience?
6. Build an outline as though you had to make the speech *now,* with what you know and what you have collected in your folder. What is your most important point? Support it with some interesting data or illustrations—as though it were to be your *only* point. Make it so complete and independent that it could be a short speech by itself. Now do the same thing with one or two other good points that advance your objective. This is the first draft of your *topical outline.*
7. Prepare a strong conclusion that nails down your objective.
8. "Keep your main points few and make 'em good."
9. *Next do your research and reading* to test your points, and to supplement and refine your materials. Make sure your "new" ideas are not just new to you. But do not swap off

*your* original speech for a series of quotations by "authorities" and "experts"—keep it *yours*.

10. Insert some appropriate change of pace points where the going is too heavy or too long.

11. Prepare a few "softening up" remarks that will make an effective lead-off for the particular audience you are addressing. These remarks should reassure your hearers that you do not consider yourself the Oracle of Truth from whom all wisdom flows. Establish some "common denominators" with your audience if you can truthfully and appropriately do so.

12. Go over your speech with the full outline before you until you find yourself making the same points in about the same words.

13. If you are an inexperienced speaker, you should now *write the speech.* Write it as you were *saying it—"talk it down on paper."* If you feel insecure in your English, word usage, or sentence construction, you should have a competent person check your manuscript.

14. With your manuscript and your full outline before you, proceed to perfect your delivery. Do not memorize the speech.

15. Prepare an abbreviated Speaking Outline, and *memorize it.* Keep visualizing the outline as you rehearse your speech.

16. Practice what you would do if you found your speaking time reduced by a third or a half. Drop out some of the lesser points, cover the bigger ones, and go directly to your conclusion. Be prepared to do the same thing if you sense your audience is losing interest.

17. Remember: *Flexibility* is the keynote. Rigidity is deadly.

# 10

# Delivering the Speech

*"There are three kinds of speakers: those
you listen to, those you can't listen to,
and those you can't help listening to."*

—Archbishop Magee

This chapter and the next two deal with the various aspects of actually getting your ideas over the footlights and across the meeting tables.

In this chapter we find answers to such practical problems as:

1. What a speaker should do at a meeting *before* he is introduced, as well as what he should do *when* he is introduced.

2. How to "appear" before an audience.

3. How to improve your speaking voice and project it to your audience.

4. How to use a microphone.

5. How to determine *your* "style" of delivery.

6. How to master the basic techniques for holding an audience.

7. How to improve your *word power*.

"Preacher" Wilkes is one of the volunteer preachers who hold forth in the Blue Ridge Mountains. Brother Wilkes never studied any theology. In fact he never studied much of anything in school. He works the crops with his parishioners during the week and "exhorts" on Sunday. It must be admitted that his pulpit work is on the rough side, but there are several good reasons why the church members do not complain: First, they know Brother

Wilkes is sincere; secondly, they do not pay him anything, anyway; and third, they are a little rough themselves.

One Sunday morning Preacher Wilkes was holding forth on one of his favorite texts—the story of David and Goliath. He dramatically recounted how little David whirled the sling around his head and sent the stone unerringly to Goliath's forehead. As Brother Wilkes reached the climax of his sermon, his voice arose high with excitement,

"You see, folks, the point is this: It wasn't just that little rock that kilt that big bloke—it was the way that damned kid *throwed* it!"

In his own crude way Preacher Wilkes hit upon a mighty truth. Words are like rocks. In the hands of a David they hit the mark, but in less skilled hands they go wide of it. In facing an audience one finds that whether he "kills 'em or chills 'em" depends—not only upon what words are used—but also upon how they are "throwed."

It is true that there can never be any amount of charm, versatility, or personality that will substitute for solid preparation. You must have the goods on the shelves. But the pay-off is not in your "complete stock," but in the *sales*. It is the ability to *deliver the goods to the customer* that brings success. In this chapter we are assuming that you now know how to load the gun. Now let's discuss how to fire it effectively under combat conditions.

By way of general principles, Beveridge declares "the two indispensable requisites of speaking are, first, to have something to say, and second, to say it as though you mean it."

Leon K. Whitney puts it this way: "Effective delivery is that in which every action so definitely adds to the effectiveness of the ideas expressed that the hearer is not conscious of delivery at all."

The speaker should try to think of himself as a pleasant, attractive, and efficient *vehicle* for delivering important information and inspiration to his audience. He is there to *help* his hearers. The best delivery is the one that lets the audience concentrate exclusively upon *what* is being said, rather than *who* is saying it, or *how* it is being said. In other words, the keynote is naturalness. The question then is how *you* can be at *your best* in *delivering service* to other people through the medium of speech? To help you answer that question is the objective of this chapter.

## Your Speaking Engagement Starts Before You Are Introduced

I was recently scheduled to be the third and final speaker for the morning session of a national convention. When I reached the lobby of the convention hall someone yelled, "Hi, Ken!" It was the second speaker of the morning. He was having a short beer at the concession stand. I asked if he had already been "up to bat." He said "No, I don't start for ten minutes yet." In the conversation it developed he had not yet been in the main auditorium, he had not seen a program, he had not talked with the chairman, he had not heard the previous speaker, he did not know whether there was a convention "theme." He was calmly drinking beer and awaiting his turn.

To be sure there is merit in being relaxed before your speech, but the man in the above illustration was too relaxed. He was wrong when he said, "I am not supposed to start until 10 o'clock." That was the hour he was to be *introduced,* but he should have *started earlier*.

On the day you are to do a speech get in touch with the chairman of the meeting well ahead of the appointed hour. Tell him to mark you off his list of worries—you will be there. Check again on the time and place of the meeting, and where you are to report ahead of time. Ask again if there is anything *special* you should know about the audience or the occasion.

Try to get some rest before you go to your speaking engagement. If you can take a nap, you will find it rewarding in the extra energy it provides. Remember a thirty-minute speech uses up as much nervous energy as a half-day of manual labor. It is a great asset if a speaker can be refreshed when he gives his speech. The audience should be able to sense in both the speaker and the speech the quality of *vitality*.

It is my suggestion that you get to your meeting place on time, but not too early. For example, the convention meeting mentioned in the preceding paragraphs convened at 9:00 A.M. I was scheduled for 11:00 A.M. I should have been there by 10:00 or 10:30, but not at 9:00. There is nothing to be gained by a speaker sitting on a stage two hours before he is introduced, and there is much to be lost. Very few speakers look better lolling or fidgeting in a chair than they do standing. Do not suffer from "over-exposure" to your audience. Reach the platform in ample time to put your chairman and audience at ease, and in time to be respectful to the preceding speaker, or program; but do not make camp in front of your audience.

If your meeting is a dinner affair, you should join your head table group in advance and enter the banquet room with the others. It is not necessary to be "democratic" and jostle with the crowd in the foyer for half an hour before the dining room doors open. You will be in better shape to carry the ball if you haven't crashed the line for an hour before your signal is called.

## To Eat, or Not to Eat?

Perhaps we may as well dispose of another chronic question at this point: If the speech is for a dinner meeting, should the speaker eat with the others, or merely sit with them at the head table? This depends entirely upon the individual. If you do not feel like eating anything, don't do it. If you feel like a salad and coffee would be enjoyable—okay. If you feel like eating part, or all of what is being served, then proceed accordingly. If you want to order something special, do it. In any event, you might wisely trade your dessert for a half grapefruit, and finish with that.

One should never rise to speak so crammed with food that his breath is coming in gasps. Nor should he approach the microphone weak from hunger. The late Dr. Willis Sutton of Atlanta, one of the great orators the South has produced, told me years ago, "Don't let them tell you not to eat before you make a speech. I always eat a good steak just before the time I am to make an address. It gives me *powah!*"

Whatever Dr. Sutton did must have worked for him, because he certainly had power. Personally, when I am scheduled to address an audience at a breakfast, luncheon, or dinner meeting, I follow about the same eating habits I would follow if I were in the audience at the same event. Most everyone remembers the old gag about the preacher visiting in his parishioner's home. He declined to have dinner with the family prior to the evening service, saying, "I never eat before preaching a sermon."

The reader will remember that after the sermon that evening the little boy of the parishioner's household turned to his mother and said, "Mom, he might as well have et."

The writer belongs to the "might-as-well-have-et" school; but, to eat or not to eat is the individual's choice.

If there is a cocktail hour, or reception, preceding the evening meeting, the speaker can use his own judgment as to whether to attend all of it. A usually reliable rule is to be present for the latter part of the affair. If there is a reception line and the event is in honor of the speaker, then he must see it through from the first. The speaker's drinks, if any, should be rigidly limited. Some speakers say they get relaxed and do a better job if they can have a few drinks prior to the meeting. This may be true in cases where the individual is virtually embalmed from years of imbibing. But in most cases it cannot be true. Alcohol simply does not speed up the mental processes and shorten our reaction time. The speaker who believes he can think better when he is "crocked" had better avail himself of the sober judgment of his friends. He will then learn that whiskey doesn't make him think faster—it just makes him more impressed with a poor opinion.

A speaker's actions prior to his introduction, and his attitude toward his audience and other people on the program, should all reflect simple good manners.

Some authorities declare that a speaker's speech really starts from the time he comes on the platform, or the audience's attention is first shifted to a head table. Prior to being presented, a speaker can use his time advantageously to "size up" his audience, while the people are making a few mental calculations about him. His general manner needs to be that of neither a clown nor a prophet of doom.

The speaker should give respectful attention to his own introduction. He should not coyly indicate that the chairman is "just saying all those nice things because they are true." Nor should he nonchalantly disregard the introduction and carry on a conversation with someone else on the platform. He should respond with an attitude that is fundamentally gracious, and somewhere in his opening remarks he should reassure his audience that he is not overly impressed with himself—that he is not under the impression that he has personally brought down the Law of God from Mount Sinai. The audience will have ample opportunity to judge for itself whether the introduction was overdone.

A speaker should always be considerate of what is taking place on the program ahead of him. If the meeting is in progress when he arrives, he should avoid the "grand entry" technique, and make his entry as little noticed as possible. He should give his attention to what is being said by previous speakers. This is a courtesy that will not only be appreciated by the other speakers and the audience, but it will give the speaker an opportunity to sense the "tone" of the meeting. Perhaps he can pick up a few pointers upon which he can build in a way that will personalize his speech, and tailor it more specifically to the particular occasion at hand.

### What to Do When There Is More Than One Speaker on the Program

When two or more speakers appear on the same program session they should strive to correlate their efforts in a way that will give the audience the biggest, best-balanced *total* package to take home. For example, if two speakers are doing a sales rally, they should confer in advance to avoid duplication of materials. Perhaps one could develop the technique of selling—specific methods and devices. The second speaker could then come in with the importance of selling and the opportunities offered in the field. He could well make his best contribution by sending the crowd home convinced of the importance of its calling and inspired to do the particular things advocated by the first speaker. Two speakers on the same program can add to their mutual strength and success by commending one another before the audience. The second speaker can occasionally show how his points reinforce those of the first. When done within the bounds of good taste it demonstrates that they are there in a spirit of service rather than in competition.

One will occasionally encounter a situation where one or both speakers attempt to outshine the other. The writer was a "second speaker" at a sales rally where the first speaker was allotted 45 minutes. The first speaker actually consumed one hour and twenty minutes, and spent the last fifteen minutes in a series of unrelated stories and jokes. He stated later that he had set out to "get everything the audience had." He was attempting to guard a reputation which he mistakingly thought he possessed—that no one could follow him on a program. Of course, such an individual is much easier to follow than he supposes. He usually leaves the crowd with a mental attitude which says, "Let's get on with the program," and they welcome the appearance of the next speaker if he will do just that.

The writer also recalls a speaker who was to speak on the program ahead of him at a morning convention session. The printed program indicated the time allotment for each speaker. The first speaker was scheduled for 10:15 A.M. to 11:00, and the second speaker from 11:05 to 11:50. Both the speakers and the audience knew that the schedule must be adhered to, because an important luncheon session was set up for 12:00 noon. The first speaker was introduced at 10:20 and spoke until 11:35. He then left the hall without waiting to hear the second speaker even introduced. The second speaker had 12½ minutes in the clear, as well as the sympathetic good will of the audience who resented the discourtesy that had been shown. When caught in a situation of this kind, the second speaker can save the day by cheerfully accepting the limitations imposed upon him and using his time as effectively as possible.

Program committees sometimes defeat their own purpose when they have more than one speaker on their programs. The writer well remembers an occasion when his office had accepted an invitation for him to work with another speaker on a sales rally sponsored by a Sales Executives Club. When the advance publicity came out on the event, it was featured as "The Battle of the Speakers!" "Two Champions" had been brought together on the same platform to match their wits and vie for the audience's favor.

The writer promptly cancelled the above engagement and accepted an invitation for the same date from a committee that wanted *help* for its people—rather than to sell tickets to a gladiatorial contest.

*What to Do Between the Time Your "Engagement Starts" and the Time You Are Introduced*

Let us now suppose you are at the head table, or on the platform. In a sense your "delivery" has already started. You need not be on parade like Mrs. Astor's horse, but some of the people will be sizing you up. If you are a man who wears short sox, you are not going to increase your prestige sitting in a platform chair with your legs crossed, and your bare calf revealed. Remember, you are probably not Charles Atlas, and even if you were—the crowd did not come to see him.

Take advantage of the pre-program period to take out some insurance on your own performance. Survey your audience situation. Anticipate how conditions will be at the time you are introduced. Are the people *comfortable?* Is the room temperature conducive to concentration? If not, can it be corrected? Any suggestions you have for improving the physical set-up and facilities should be made solely through the chairman. Never "take over" the meeting until you have the floor. Any announcements the chairman makes at your request should be done in *his* name— not yours. *He* should ask the people standing in the rear of the hall to move down front, rather than to say, "Our speaker requests that those in the back of the house please fill up the vacant seats in the front rows." The speaker should never be forced to "discipline" a crowd. That is the chairman's job. Of course, the speaker should be prepared to meet such situations, especially if working with an inexperienced chairman.

Before you are introduced pay particular attention to the microphone and acoustical conditions. Are the people readily hearing everything the chairman and previous speakers are saying? If not, maybe the microphone is being used incorrectly; or maybe the volume needs to be adjusted.

Pleasantly enlist the chairman's cooperation in making sure your audience is comfortable. Before a banquet program begins the chairman should have everyone turn their chairs, if necessary, to face the front of the room. If you are doing an auditorium meeting and find your crowd badly scattered, the chairman can get the people into one section and give you the advantage of dealing with an *audience,* rather than a series of isolated, mental islands.

A simple rule for a speaker is that you should never have to compete with anything but yourself in holding the attention of the audience. If at all possible, avoid starting your speech before the waiters have left the banquet hall, or before the ushers have seated the auditorium crowd. The problem of handling interruptions after you have started your speech is a different matter and will be treated later in this chapter.

Perhaps there is some point that could be included in the chairman's introduction of you that would give you a "running start" with your speech. If so, do not hesitate to mention it in a courteous way. The introducer will be grateful for the idea. After all, it is his job to get the meeting air-borne, and he will welcome anything that serves as a booster rocket.

Your contacts with the meeting prior to your own introduction should give you a chance to sample something of its general flavor. Is there any big, overshadowing issue on the minds of this particular organization or group? Is business good? Or, are your hearers pessimistic at the moment? What is this group's biggest problem as a group, or as members of this particular business or profession? If the setting of the meeting is not your own community, then find out about general conditions locally. It is surprising how quickly head table guests can acquaint a speaker with helpful background information.

You should know the general facts about your audience as you prepare your speech, but you can also pick up some significant special facts at the time and place of the meeting. It can be safely assumed the elected officers of the organization, or presiding officers of the meetings, know their people. At least they must have known them well enough to get elected as their leaders.

A young minister from Ohio accepted an assignment to fill a pulpit in an Ozark Mountain community. He joined the local civic club and was told it was customary for each new member of the club to serve a term as "hog caller." The young minister protested that he did not feel such a title was "compatible with the cloth," but his fellow club members were insistent that he take his turn in the office. Finally, the minister relented, and said,

"If you think it is best, I shall serve as hog caller. I came here to be the shepherd of the flock—but, after all, *you know your people*."

If you plan to use some stories, check them with someone who has heard the group's previous programs to be sure they have not been used with this same group recently. Repeating a recently told story is an unpleasant hole in which a speaker need not find himself.

Professor Micken [1] tells of a professor who addressed a college chapel. He told a joke that fell flat. After the assembly one of the honest little coeds went up to him and said, "Professor, the reason your story didn't go over this morning is that another speaker told it here last week, and told it better."

> Black Moment [2]
> I tell this joke so cleverly;
> How beautifully I word it.
> How clearly stares convey to me
> That everyone has heard it.
> —Curtis Heath

Prior to the time you are introduced it is also well to get a gist of recent programs, or earlier speakers. All of these items are helpful to a speaker, yet people will occasionally ask me, "What *does* one talk about at a head table?"

## Make Sure Your Remarks Blend With the "Local Color"

One more caution is in order. If you are away from home to do a speech in another city, and you plan to refer specifically to something that has made news in that city—*check your facts with some local person*. Get the "local color" which surrounds the story and which was not in the news stories. Even in your own city make sure you are not embarrassing anyone by referring to events connected with local people.

To illustrate the need of the above precaution, let us note one

---

[1] Micken, *Speaking for Results* (Boston: Houghton Mifflin), 1958.
[2] *Look*, February 16, 1960.

example. A District Governor of a civic club was guest speaker for the annual ladies night banquet staged by a club in his district. In his speech the District Governor spent ten minutes describing how a building and loan employee in a Virginia city had systematically looted the institution's funds over a period of some two decades. His big point was the need of "internal integrity." The illustration would have been good under normal circumstances, but the circumstances that particular evening were anything but normal. Seated directly in front of the head table was the widow of a bank official who had committed suicide upon the revelation that he had been bilking his depositors for some fifteen years. The bank officer had been a member of that civic club. His wife, who was a truly lovely person, had gone into seclusion following the disgrace. Her friends had finally persuaded her to come to the civic club dinner which was her first social engagement since the tragedy. The District Governor was at a complete loss to know why his speech suddenly died. It was a set speech he had memorized to give all the clubs during the year. It had no flexibility. He could not go immediately to his conclusion. The poor devil staggered on blindly to the bitter end. The terrible failure of his speech could have easily been avoided if he had but asked a few questions at the head table, or at the cocktail hour that preceded the banquet.

Your affiliation with the meeting prior to your own part in it will also let you hear what is said by others. If you have prepared your speech on the flexible, logical plan recommended in the previous chapter, you will in all probability pick up some pointers that will help you *personalize* the speech for the audience and the occasion. This technique never fails to enhance a speaker's appeal. Sometimes the speaker can refer to these prior items in his own preliminary remarks. An extremely clever device is to save a good point from the earlier part of the program and use it in the body or conclusion of your speech. A good example of this, which I have heard, was used by a humorous speaker, who heard the chairman quote two well-known lines of verse by Ella Wheeler Wilcox:

> Laugh and the world laughs with you
> Weep, and you weep alone.

After giving the crowd a delightful evening, the speaker capped off his remarks by perfectly fitting on the *other* two lines of the Ella Wheeler Wilcox stanza:

> For the sad old earth must borrow its mirth,
> But has trouble enough of its own.

The effect on the crowd was tremendous. Personally, I was so impressed that I later inquired as a matter of "professional information" whether the first two lines had been "planted" with the chairman by the speaker. They had not. The chairman expressed his admiration by saying, "He caught my pass forty-five minutes after I threw it—and ran for a touchdown."

It is in the preliminary part of the program that the speaker is often able to pick up some little "common denominator" items that help him get with his crowd quicker.

An observant speaker can determine whether the things that have been said and done in the meeting prior to his introduction have *unified* the audience. Have the people laughed together, sang together, or participated in anything that made them a collective audience, rather than a room full of individuals. If little of the "oneness" spirit has been achieved prior to his introduction, then the speaker will need to spend more time on his "softening-up exercises." If numerous stories have already been told, or if a skillful chairman has already unified the audience, then the speaker can get going with his main theme that much quicker.

### How to Get Your Speech Started

*Now you are being introduced.* Listen carefully to the introduction. A man may have lost the Presidency of the United States because he did not listen to his own introduction. When James G. Blaine was campaigning for President, he made a campaign speech in New York City. Being tired from his strenuous schedule, he paid no attention to the chairman's introduction. He did not hear the chairman say, "We are fighting the party of Rum, Romanism, and Rebellion."

Because he did not hear it, Blaine did not refute the statement in his speech. The opposition seized upon it as a hammer with which to hit Blaine throughout the balance of the campaign and the results were disastrous.

When the microphone is turned over to you, rise *easily* from your chair. Some speakers feel they must bounce to their feet to register animation, and fairly race to the front of the stage, or to the head table podium. I have known sales rally speakers who ran out on the stage and yelled, "How are ya, gang!" You do not need to shoot out of your chair, but you should get out of it without a struggle. Don't push yourself up with your arms, but stand easily. Walk *naturally* to the microphone, and address the chairman. You do not need to recognize a half dozen others by name. If the governor, or some distinguished official of the church or government should be present, he should appropriately be acknowledged. Perhaps the names of some other officers of the group being addressed may be woven into the preliminary remarks.

*Do not hurry into your speech.* Catch your breath. Start a little on the slow side, but make your first sentences count. If you are using some warming up remarks, do not start in on a long story first. Give your audience a "quickie." If you are going to have them laugh, do it immediately. Get a punch line in there early.

Witness the example of the speaker who responded immediately to a flowery introduction before a sophisticated audience by saying, "I rise from the coffin of exaggeration to protest my canonization."

Your opening manner should be *congenial.* Let your opening demeanor be such that individuals in the audience can say to themselves, "I don't know yet whether this guy is smart, but he is pleasant."

Louis Nizer says:

An audience is a heavy mass. It cannot be moved easily. That is why a speech cannot start at high speed. The first and second gears are necessary to create momentum. A graceful beginning, without jolt, obtains the confidence of the audience and befriends it.[3]

[3] Louis Nizer, *Thinking on Your Feet* (New York: Liveright Publishing Corporation), 1940.

It is recommended that the opening part of your regular speech —the statement of the objective—be memorized. There are several valid reasons for this recommendation. First, it insures this important part of your speech will be well stated. Secondly, you *know* you will always use that part of your speech regardless of what other portions may be deleted. Finally, if you find yourself nervous or near-panicked at the beginning, you can still state the proposition well, and gain time to collect yourself and your thoughts.

As suggested in a previous chapter, it is also a wise precaution for speakers to virtually memorize their concluding statements. This is the other part of the speech that will always be used, regardless. It is the final clincher of your whole effort, and you should make sure it will be as well worded as you can make it.

When you have been introduced, *speak out* clearly. Do not force your voice, but *project* it. Talk to the man on the back row. Look at him and project your voice to him. If you tell an opening story, check to see if the response comes back to you from all over the house. Did the man on the back row laugh? Did the folks in the balcony laugh? What about those under the balcony? What about those at the banquet tables that were set up in the foyer because the crowd overflowed the room?

Someone has pointed out that the story-telling test does not always inform a speaker as to whether all of his crowd is hearing him. You may tell a story and the man on the back row may not laugh. This does not necessarily mean he did not hear it. You must allow for the possibility that he had already heard it. Therefore, your preliminary "testing" should be complete enough to be sure your stuff is getting through.

Our discussion at this point illustrates another advantage of having a Preliminary section in your Introduction. You can do your testing and get your crowd with you, and adjusted to you, before you start serving the real meat of your speech. Softening-up exercises should not be considered as time wasted. The express train can leave the station later than the freight train and still reach the common destination earlier. *Express* your ideas. It is faster, it's more comfortable for the passengers, and you do not need to start so early, nor continue so late.

A good speaking voice is essential to success in public speaking, but there is not much general agreement as to what constitutes a good voice, nor exactly how it can be developed. The good speaking voice is one that can be clearly and easily understood, and which does not have unpleasant qualities that detract from what is being said. Some good voices are high in pitch, some are medium ranged, and some are low. In the main, the medium and higher registers have better carrying power.

## How to Use the Microphone

The problems of the speaking voice were enormously reduced with the development of the public address system and the microphone. For centuries the number one problem of speakers was to develop clear, powerful speaking voices that would reach out to the uttermost fringes of a crowd. William Jennings Bryan could not address any more people at one time than Demosthenes could. Mechanical amplification of sound has changed all this. Since the microphone is so universally in use, let us pause here to discuss the important technique of using it.

A speaker should rarely decline the use of a microphone. The only exceptions would be in cases where the audience is too small, or the mechanics of the public address unit are faulty. With the use of the microphone a speaker can do a better job and do it easier. He can be all times master of the situation. He can break through laughter or applause and keep the speech moving. He can use tone shadings and voice inflections that would not be possible if the volume were the prime consideration in producing every syllable. A basic rule is to let the microphone do as much of your work for you as you can. Your voice "will be heard in the land" for years longer with this method, and it will be of better quality.

*Never* start a speech by indicating you are uneasy or unfamiliar with microphones. Nothing stamps the amateur any quicker than to have him approach the microphone by saying, "I don't know much about these gadgets," or "I've never used one of these things." No reference should be made to the microphone unless it is something of a humorous or "patter" nature, like,

"I am glad we have this mike, and you should be, too. My voice is something like my face—it looks like it ought to hurt me —but it doesn't."

Let the crowd *forget* the microphone. That is possible only when the speaker apparently forgets it. Actually, the speaker should never forget the microphone unless he is so experienced that its correct use is automatic. As indicated earlier, the speaker should observe the microphone carefully before he is introduced. While it is being used by the chairman and others the speaker can note its characteristics. Is the chairman standing the right distance from it for the best results? Even when the chairman speaks out clearly is the volume too low? Or does the system roar because of excess volume? Is there an operator handling the system, or does the speaker need to make his own allowances for change of volume?

When you are introduced, make whatever adjustments you want in the microphone as you make your preliminary remarks. Then keep your hands off the microphone the rest of the way. If the microphone is of the stand type that comes up from the floor, do not "wrestle" it. A standard trademark of some third rate masters of ceremonies is their eternal preoccupation with tilting the microphone stand from one side to the other.

Avoid standing too close to the microphone. This habit of drooling on the microphone is called "mike-eatus." Some beginning speakers, and others who are short of breath, stand close to the microphone and breathe heavily into it. The general effect is the same as James Watt got with his first steam engine. This is also a common fault with radio speakers. The audience hears a sucking in of air between every two sentences, or phrases. Have you ever heard the long distance telephone operator breathing while you waited for your call to come through? Maybe some day an alert inventor will devise a method for screening out such noises; meanwhile, you must do your own screening.

In using the stationary type of microphone the fundamental rule is to *always keep the microphone between you and your audience*. No matter what position you may assume in relationship to the microphone, always be *looking across it as you speak*. If you move around to the right, then turn your head to the left and continue talking into the microphone. If you address a side remark to someone on the stage or at the head table, then move around to the opposite side of the microphone in order that the audience may be in on it, too.

A lapel microphone should be used when a lecture involves visual aids, or the speaker for any reason desires freedom of movement. Here again the "professional" technique is to minimize the microphone. I have heard a speaker who races around on the platform with fifty yards of wire from the lapel microphone trailing from under his coat tail. The general effect is that of a monkey on a string. This particular speaker is a good one—he has to be to overcome that handicap. Other lapel microphone users stroll around the stage with a coil of wire in their hand giving the general impression of a telephone lineman, or a cowboy stalking a calf. Of course, the newest type of lapel microphone needs no wires attached.

In general, remember the microphone is your *friend*. Let it help you. *Relax* and let it do the work. It will let your throat relax and produce much better tone quality than would be possible otherwise, and it will carry those better tones to every hearer present. Do not keep straining to be your own microphone. I know some men who rush to make airplanes, and then keep on rushing after they are aboard. They would live longer if they would relax on board and be content to let the plane do the rushing. The same principle applies to speakers and public address systems.

A caller in a New York office was told by the secretary that her boss was talking to Chicago at the moment. As the boss's voice came crashing through the door the caller asked politely, "Why doesn't he use the telephone?"

## Suggestions for Improving Your Speaking Voice

Has the public address system solved all the problems of the speaking voice? As useful as the sound system is, it can obviously amplify only such sounds as go into it. The speaker's voice quality will always be an exceedingly important factor in his success or failure. This is not a textbook, and it will not attempt to provide rules and exercises for voice training. The writer quite agrees with Freeman on this point:

I have never been able to believe that the inexperienced, frequently terrified orator is likely to derive either inspiration or encouragement from scientifically labelled pictures of the larynx, glottis, tonsils, and respiratory apparatus in general.

Here are some practical suggestions for improving your speaking voice:

1. *Relearn to breathe.* By "relearn," I mean learn to breathe as you did when an infant and a child. Learn to breathe *naturally*. Watch a baby breathe when he is asleep, or watch the family cat breathe. It is the *stomach* that moves. Relearn to breathe *deeply*. Relearn to breathe *often,* so you always have an ample *reserve* of air *behind* the vocal cords. This is what prevents the last words of your sentences from thinning out into nothingness like the final notes of a bagpipe.

2. *Relearn to use your vocal cords.* Have you ever wondered why the baby can cry all night and still be in good voice the next day? The reason is that he has not had any "training" as yet. He has not been taught by his elders how to make those pear-shaped tones that come along with "culture." Animals never receive this "training." That is why an adult dog can bay at the moon all night just like he could when a pup. To achieve a good speaking voice you must relearn the *natural* way of speaking, that starts the action below the vocal cords. Let the throat relax and quit gargling your words.

3. *Learn to project your voice. Think* your voice out to the point where you want it to go and then *project* it out there. An excellent exercise to perfect this technique is to read selected portions of addresses as though you were making the speech in the setting in which it actually was given. Read Lincoln's Gettysburg Address as though you were standing before the great crowd at Gettysburg, and you want the man on the back row to hear every word. There are a number of good single volumes of speeches that describe the conditions under which each speech was given. Put yourself into a variety of these situations and read the speech for all who were present to hear. One writer recommends that you get a picture taken of a large meeting from the vantage point of the platform or head table. There you stand with the people looking at you. Pick out this one and that one and talk to him. Project your voice to the degree which you think is necessary for him to hear at the distance he is away from you.

4. *While you are learning to project your voice without restricting your throat, strive to improve your enunciation.* Even

people who themselves annihilate the King's English will criticize
a speaker who slurs and slights his syllables. A western rancher
attended a football banquet at the district high school and heard
the coach make a speech on the season's prospects. After the
meeting the rancher accosted the coach with this,

"Young feller, you don't talk good. Ain't nobody ever learnt
you to enunciate clear? Now, I ain't no good talker myself—but
I wasn't on the program."

Sloppy diction usually indicates a "slouchy" personality. It is
one kind of indolence. It is a symptom of a total personality that
needs to pull up its sox. Here again we need to relearn the mental
and physical alertness that are *natural* to people until "trained"
out of them by "civilization."

When I was a public school executive, I used to watch the
bright-eyed youngsters as they enrolled in the kindergarten. Their
little backs were straight, their expressions were pleasant, they
were alert to everything about them, and their little voices were as
clear and musical as Swiss bells. Thirteen years later they would
come shuffling across a commencement platform to get their di-
plomas. In many cases their eyes had lost their snap, their general expressions had deteriorated, their voices were unpleasant,
their sentences were half slang, and—as a doctor friend of mine
said—their postures had "gone to hell in a hand basket." And I
would sometimes ask myself, *"What have we done to these people
in the thirteen years we had them?* Have we done as much *for*
them as we have done *to* them?"

To develop the speaking voice, and improve our diction, we
must go back to nature's way. We must recapture the personality's natural buoyancy and vitality. We must go back to the
philosophy of an earlier chapter, and learn to speak out with *enthusiasm* because we have something *very important to say*.
Proceed in a way that says, "I am sending this message out to
you—and you—and you—because it is terribly important that
you have it. It will *help* you. I will make it clear *because I want
you to hear!*" This is the kind of *thinking* that *recaptures* vivid
awareness, personal power, and the other attributes which good
speakers possess.

I believe businessman John A. Bush of St. Louis was the first to tell of the man who won the hog calling contest in Nebraska. When asked the secret of his success the victor explained, "Your voice must have more than power. It must have *appeal.* You must make the hogs feel *you have something for them."*

5. *Another helpful device in improving voice quality and enunciation is to listen to yourself.* The tape recorder is a wonderful device for both the beginning speaker and the experienced one. While you are practicing the projecting of your voice, make a tape of it. You were talking to that man on the back row. Now you can *become* the man on the back row. Did the speaker get through to you? Could you hear every word without strain? If not, *why* not. Now you are objectively diagnosing your own speech deficiencies and that is a sure-fire device for improvement.

6. *Remember to improve the quality of YOUR voice and YOUR enunciation. Never try to adopt someone else's.* When I was a graduate student at Columbia University, I used to stand in line on Sunday mornings to get into the Riverside Church and hear Dr. Harry Emerson Fosdick preach. Presently I realized I was aping Fosdick's style in my own meager speech efforts. I was *overly* emphasizing every syllable of every word in a subconscious effort to out-Fosdick Fosdick. Of course, the results were pitiful. Finally, one day a dear friend took me aside and said, "If you are going to make an ass of yourself, at least try to be original."

I have always been grateful for his advice.

7. *For extreme and persistent speech difficulties one should consult a logopediast, or perhaps take voice lessons under a competent instructor.*

8. *Finally, if you sing, you have an advantage which should be pursued.* Keep on singing, even if it is merely bathroom tenor. Try for improved head resonance and more purity of tone.

One of the standard jokes in Hollywood concerns the number of actors who became successful, and could then afford dramatic lessons. After going overboard on the dramatics, they lost their originality and naturalness which had accounted for their success in the first place. Then they had nothing. Under competent instructors there is no doubt that private lessons and class lessons help. But these media are *guidance* techniques, which means no one can develop the speech arts *for* you. Whether it is Demos-

thenes speaking over the roar of the waves, whether it is Abraham
Lincoln speaking from a stump in the pasture, or Richard Crooks
singing above the drone of his fighter plane—the individual must
*will* his way to success. There are so many different kinds of good
speakers. Most anyone can achieve the goal and emerge with his
individuality *at its best*. Someone has said, "You should be extremely careful in deciding what you want the most in this world,
because you are so likely to get it."

Robert Benchley said, "It took me fifteen years to discover that
I had no talent for writing, but I couldn't give it up because by
that time I was too famous."

*Things You Can Do to Improve Breath Control and
Tone Quality*

1. Remember there is an amazingly close connection between
   how you *feel* about a point and how you *say* it. If you are
   vibrant and alive with the importance of what you are saying, your voice will also be vibrant and alive. *Let yourself
   go* when you speak.
2. Relearn to breathe with exercises that fill the bottom of
   your lungs with air. Stand erect and mentally count five
   as you inhale. Hold the air in your lungs for a count of
   five, and exhale on a five count. Empty the lungs as completely as possible before repeating the exercise. (If you
   become dizzy, delay exercise until recovered. Any tendency toward dizziness will disappear with regular practice.)
3. Remember tone quality and volume is not determined so
   much by the amount of air coming through the vocal cords
   as by the amount *behind* them. Practice relaxing your
   throat muscles and speaking from "down under." This is
   relearning nature's way to make tones.
4. Practice reading aloud until you find yourself *automatically* breathing frequently enough and deeply enough to
   insure an adequate reserve of air for finishing phrases with
   good tone quality.
5. Go to your speaking engagements with the confidence that
   comes with being *thoroughly prepared*. This will avoid

your "tensing up" and becoming "breathless" through nervousness or fear.

6. Sing when you can—in the choir, in the bath tub, on the job, driving your car, or anywhere that it is appropriate. This will improve your breath control, your tone quality, and your ability to sustain tones. Keep your tones coming from "down under" your vocal cords. Keep your throat muscles relaxed.

7. Listen to yourself on a tape recording. Diagnose your own difficulties. Record the same passages again and improve.

8. Consult your physician if you think some physical obstruction is preventing you from achieving proper resonance, tone quality, or breath control.

9. Take some speech and voice training if you feel you are not making sufficient progress on your own.

10. Determine through practice the pitch and speed at which you are most easily heard and understood. This is the correct altitude and speed for you to "cruise."

11. Practice saying things as you *naturally* say them *when you are anxious to be heard, understood, and believed.*

## Determine Your Own Style of Speech

Earlier in this chapter we left you at the microphone. You responded to the chairman's introduction and you started your speech slowly and easily. You looked at that man on the back row, and using your microphone, you projected your voice out to him. Now you have shifted out of low and out of second. You have the speech and the audience moving along together. What is to be your *style* of speech?

The "modern" school of speech training contends that a speech is merely "heightened conversation." This school of thought has many exponents and a few good examples. One could turn on the radio most any Sunday morning and hear this style at its best in the voice of Dr. Ralph Sockman, of New York.

## The "Conversationalists" Seem to Admire the Non-conversationalists. Dale Carnegie's Idol Was Abraham Lincoln

Most modern speech teachers advocate the conversational style of address. They advocate "public talking" rather than public speaking. Dale Carnegie used to say a modern speaker would no more want to use the style of Webster or Ingersoll than he would want his wife to wear Mrs. Webster's or Mrs. Ingersoll's hat. I once addressed the Founders Banquet of the national convention of Dale Carnegie Clubs, and the Founder was at the head table. I had a delightful visit with him in which I raised the question of the hat illustration. To get his reaction I said, "Your fine book on speech repeatedly uses Abraham Lincoln as Exhibit A in the display of platform artists. Surely you wouldn't want your lovely wife appearing in Mrs. Lincoln's hat, would you?"

Dale laughed and said, "I'd be proud for my wife to wear Mary Lincoln's hat if I could speak like Abe."

Certainly Lincoln was no "heightened conversationalist." How did he proceed with a speech? Contemporaries reported that Lincoln almost invariably started in the same manner. He would walk to the front of the platform and stand there with his feet together and his hands behind him, with "the back of his left hand in the palm of his right, the thumb and fingers of his right hand clasped around the left arm at the wrist." It was not a graceful pose. Let Mildred Freburg Berry [4] tell us how he proceeded:

As he began to speak, his face . . . seemed dull and lifeless . . . As he warmed up to his subject the dull, listless features dropped like a mask. His face lighted up with an inward fire. The eye began to sparkle, the mouth to smile, the whole countenance was wreathed in animation. His body began to move in unison with his thought. He straightened up; his form expanded . . . a splendid and imposing figure . . .

To keep harmony with his growing warmth his hands relaxed their grip and fell to his side . . . He did not gesticulate as much with his hands as he did with his head. He used the latter frequently, throwing it with him this way and that. This movement was a significant one when he sought to enforce a statement. It sometimes came with a quick jerk, as if throwing off electric sparks into combustible material . . .

He had, however, certain typical gestures that the audiences were want to recall with delight. When Lincoln dropped into explanation, he "frequently caught hold with his left hand, of the lapel of his coat, keeping his thumb upright and leaving his right hand free to gesticulate." At moments of great intensity his arms swung into action.

4 Mildred Freburg Berry in Brigance, *History and Criticism of American Public Address* (New York: McGraw-Hill Company, Inc.), Vol. II, 1943.

When he cried out, "The advocates of the extension of slavery into the new states will soon find themselves squelched!" he "raised his right arm to the right, bringing his hand down almost to his feet." This sweeping gesture he used often, "stooping forward almost to the ground to enforce some point . . ." At other times, "to dot the ideas in the minds of his hearers," he extended the long, bony index finger of his right hand. When he wanted to show thorough detestation of an idea, he would throw both hands upward, with fists clenched in determination. At other times . . . his clenched hand came down as if he were a blacksmith striking an anvil . . . They were jackknife gestures, quick, concise, unpredictable in their suddenness, accompanied often by a "quick turn of the body to the right or left as he drove home a red-hot rivet of appeal."

As Lincoln grew in political stature his method of delivery became more restrained, but it was never anything that could be called "conversationalist." Lincoln told a friend that he did not like preachers who stood still with their hands at their sides, as they delivered their sermons. He said he wanted his preacher "to look like he was fighting a swarm of bees."

What of Lincoln's voice? It was "high-pitched, with a nasal tenor quality." But he developed it by his own persistent practice until it was later described as a "clear trumpet tone that can be heard at an immense distance." The *New York Times* reported that thirty thousand people heard every word he said at his first inaugural—and that with no amplifying equipment! If this is "conversational" style, then it is most assuredly *"heightened!"* Berry's research documents the fact that Lincoln "not only could be heard; he could be understood at great distances. A slow rate, a peculiar emphasis, and a perfect enunciation conspired to produce the effect." Lincoln had learned his lesson well. As a boy he studied Scott's *Lessons in Elocution* which said,

> "Learn to speak slow. All other graces
> Will follow in their proper places."

I have developed the Lincoln example at some length to indicate how a man took the equipment God gave him and developed it to do the job *he wanted to do.* He was homely, he was awkward, his voice was unmusical, and he started most of his speeches frozen with stage fright. But he was one of the greatest speakers of all time because he had a *message in which he believed with all his heart and soul,* and he was determined to *deliver it* as a *service to his fellow men.*

"But," you may ask, "suppose a speaker is *not* handicapped by appearance, voice, timidity, background, or anything else? Suppose he has everything—what could the effect be then?" Daniel Webster was a speaker who did have everything. When he arose to speak one of his colleagues said, "No man could be as good as Webster *looks*." He was handsome, immaculate, dynamic, highly intelligent, well educated, and possessed a voice of rich, musical quality. How did *he* affect his hearers when he was at his best. George Tichnor heard Webster deliver one of his finest examples of flawless eloquence. The occasion was the bi-centennial celebration of the landing of the Pilgrims at Plymouth. Tichnor gives this account of his reaction to Webster: [5]

"I was never so excited by public speaking before in my life. Three or four times I thought my temples would burst with the gush of blood . . . When I came out I was almost afraid to come near to him. It seemed to me as if he was like the mount that might not be touched and that burned with fire. I was beside myself, and am so still."

## Don't Automatically Conform to a "School of Thought"— Set Your Own Style

What should be *your* style? Start speaking and find out what you want to do to get your message over. If you want to raise your voice and gesture for emphasis as you drive home a point— then *do* it. Do not keep your voice in a listless monotone and your arms in a straight jacket in order to be "in style." *You* set the style—*your style*.

A speaker has the same problem as a murderer—what to do with the body? As Alfred Hitchcock would say, the solution is also much the same—dispose of it and go about your business.

Shakespeare gave us the perfect formula for determining style when he said, ". . . suit the action to the word, the word to the action." Keep your thought, your feeling, your voice, and your

---

[5] *Encyclopaedia Britannica,* Volume 23, p. 471.

gestures *coordinated*. Genuine enthusiasm is not something you can *turn on* and *turn off* like a spigot. Even a child can see through such a shoddy performance. Do you remember the lad who said, "Our minister preaches the same sermon every Sunday—he just yells in different places"?

I have seen sales rally speakers, evangelists, and others who bounded around the stage in kangeroo fashion, and then dashed through the orchestra pit and out into the crowd. Some of them were sincerely practicing violent change-of-pace tactics, in an effort to set the crowd on fire by touching fagots to as many areas as possible. But most of them do not strike fire with their hearers. The reason for this will be found in the fact that what they are *saying* is not making the *listeners* enthusiastic. Too often the audience does not feel the speaker's ideas are "anything to shout about." His message is not good enough to make his hearers excited—and therefore they do not believe his enthusiasm is *genuine*. Go anywhere you want to with flights of oratory *if you can take your crowd with you,* but be sure you do not soar "into the wild blue yonder" all alone. *Give the people an airplane ride instead of an aerial show.*

I hope it is obvious by now that whether your style is to be classified as "conversationalist," or something more forceful, depends entirely upon your own experience in getting your message across. Remember, you are free to be your own individualistic variation of *any* style, so long as it is natural, sincere, and effective.

### What Gestures Should You Use?

James Gheen, for many years a popular after-dinner speaker in America, loves to tell the story of the country preacher who used just two gestures, regardless of his sermon's content. One gesture was up, and the other was down, and the second always followed the first. One day he was expounding from his pulpit. Pointing upward with his characteristic gesture he exclaimed,

"When the roll is called up yonder" . . . then pointing downward with a majestic sweep of his arm, he shouted ". . . I'll be *there!*"

When you have developed the style of speech delivery that seems to get your message over the most effectively, *study* what you are doing. Are any of your gestures ungainly? Could you get a better effect with a more graceful and meaningful gesture, or with no gesture at all? Do not let yourself get to be a windmill speaker who constantly fans the air regardless of whether he is pumping any water into the tank. Ask your friends to give you the benefit of their candid advice. Do not relax into a self-satisfied sleep if your friends respond by saying they "liked" your speech. Perhaps with a few improvements here and there they would have *loved* it. Always be your own severest critic. However, your friends will give you constructive advice if you will tell them frankly that you are trying *to do a job,* and you would greatly appreciate their help. Assure them you are not going to be offended personally. You merely want them to help you tune up the delivery wagon in a way that will permit it to deliver the maximum load for its horsepower and design.

*Use "Attention Getters" If They Help Advance Your Theme, But Be Sure They Are Not "Confusion Creators"*

Some speakers have adopted styles in which they use "attention arresters." For example, Gene Flack, for many years a popular sales speaker, has developed a "trade mark" by pitching cigars to the audience. He will tell a story and then toss some cigars into that section of the crowd where the response seemed best. At the same time he will whistle. "Red" Motley occasionally scores a point by pulling a police whistle from his pocket and blowing it. Herb True uses visual aid charts, aisle-walking, and sleight-of-hand tricks to keep his audiences following him. The rule is simple. Most anything is good if it works, and if it is appropriate to the crowd and subject matter.

If you go in for the gymnastics, be sure you know your people and be sure the devices are *yours.* The writer saw another sales convention speaker try to ape Gene Flack. Instead of pitching cigars immediately following a story, this man pitched rubber balls out into the crowd at any time things seemed to be getting dull. The result was not attention-getting in nature, but was completely distracting. His hearers stayed alert to dodge—not to listen.

## At What Speed Should You Talk?

Your rate of speech should be tailored to your ability to enunciate clearly, to the nature of the material being presented, to the size of the crowd, to the quality of the amplifying equipment, and to the nature of the occasion. In spite of the advice given by Lincoln's old elocution author and others of the same school, the modern rule is not to "speak slow." *You should speak as rapidly as you can be clearly and comfortably understood.*

The average conversational speed is 125 to 150 words per minute, but many speech teachers urge their students to slow down to 100 words per minute. Yet Professor Ralph Nichols of Minnesota and others have recently made studies on the "listening rate," and they have discovered *an average audience can take in ideas at the rate of 400 words per minute.* A highly intelligent audience can drink in thoughts at a rate of 600 to 800 words per minute! Thus, a speaker who can fire words into the microphone at 200 words per minute still has a serious time lag between his ability to put out, and his audience's ability to take in. The bigger this lag the more likely is the audience to become side-tracked from the speaker's thoughts and start doing some wool-gathering on its own. With all other things equal, this means the speaker who slows down to hold his crowd's attention is probably increasing his chances of losing it.

Learning to speak is like learning to drive—you should never push your car into high speed until you have thoroughly mastered it at a slower rate. Speaking and driving are also similar in the fact that the speed must, in a measure, be determined by the load being hauled. Soper [6] states a commonly accepted principle in determining the rate of speaking—the heavier the material, the slower the rate. He qualifies this by saying one should never drop below 100 words per minute. Of course, what is a safe speed is not alone determined by the load, but also by the road—and whether you are driving a Hupmobile or a Cadillac. It should

[6] Paul L. Soper, *Basic Public Speaking* (New York: Oxford University Press), 1956.

also be added that the speaker should vary his own rate of speed. For example, he can set up relatively unimportant details rapidly and then slow down to accent every word of the clincher point.

### Basic Factors in "Holding an Audience"

Earlier in this discussion we left you at the microphone. You had shifted from low through second and you were in "high." You had the speech moving and the audience moving with it. Without forcing your voice, you were projecting your words in a way that all could hear. Your gestures were your natural and spontaneous physical reactions to give emphasis to the things you were saying. You have passed through both stages of the Introduction section of your speech outline. You got acquainted with your audience through some informal "softening-up exercises," and you moved smoothly into the purpose of your speech. Now you are into the Body of your speech outline. Are you "holding" your audience satisfactorily? Let us devote some thought to that technique.

### 1. *Your physical manner.*

Your speaking posture is a factor in holding an audience. There is no set rule about posture, even though the old "elocutionist stance" was formerly declared to be the only way. Are you standing on your feet, or are you slouched over the microphone and literally leaning on the rostrum? Stand on both feet. Too many speakers lean upon the speaker's stand with one foot hooked around the other like a droopy dray horse. Relax—but don't *collapse*. Nor, as one writer points out, should you emulate the pose of a wading bird. The important thing in posture is the same factor we have discussed in both content and voice—it is *vitality*. Never let your audience get the impression that your resources of material and delivery power are getting low. The hearers should feel, that although you are rolling along at a good clip, there is plenty of unused power in reserve. Remember the rule: Never put your audience under the psychological strain that comes with the impression you are using everything you have on the level road, and have nothing left for the hills ahead.

Speakers occasionally arrive at the meeting place in an exhausted condition, and promptly announce to the committee that they are in no shape to do a good job. Everything about this procedure is wrong. Although it will be too polite to do so, the committee has a right to ask, "Did you not consider our meeting as important as the other things into which you poured all your energy?" The speaker, who may have intended to emerge as the hero who succeeded in spite of great difficulties, has actually put himself on the defensive. He lost the advantage of good will and good wishes. He is not now *expected* to do as well as he formerly was. The committee will look for evidences of his fatigue and will anticipate a below-par performance. *Never* announce to a committee or an audience how tired you are or how badly you feel. If you do feel badly, give yourself a break by not mentioning it— otherwise you are deliberately stacking the cards against yourself. The people will be much easier to please if they are expecting a good performance.

If you are capable of doing things well and saying things well, it is almost certain that you are a busy person. The dispatching of your total responsibilities may often result in your feeling below par as you go into a conference, an important appointment, or a speaking engagement. You must learn to deliberately *marshal your resources* to meet the demands of the occasion. Someone asked Babe Ruth one time why he was always able to swing with such power, day in and day out, and regardless of circumstances. He said, "Because I am a 'pro,' and a 'pro' can hit *whether he feels like it or not.*"

Remember artistry is making the difficult look easy. Delivering a good speech is not easy any time. If you are below your norm physically and mentally, it is still more difficult. But if you want to perform like a "pro"; if you want to be an artist in the field of speech; then you must learn to "hit 'em, whether you feel like it or not." A special merit of this plan is that if you *begin* as though you felt good, you will find yourself picking up power, and soon you will feel good. Wait until after the speech is over before you tell the committee you are not feeling well, and by that time there will usually be no point in it.

Never let an audience know you are uncomfortable, or ill at ease, while speaking. Do not mop your brow, frown with annoyance, or sigh with fatigue. *Be a trooper. The show must go on.* And the responsibility for keeping it going is *yours.* Make it easy on yourself by getting the help from the crowd that it accords only to *success* and to *winners.*

Occasionally a speaker can capitalize upon the fact that he had a rough time getting to the meeting, was up all night, and virtually has the blind staggers. The writer has been able to score that point with the following approach:

It is *good* to see you! Of course, I know it is customary for speakers to be glad to see people. In fact, you could hardly be a speaker and not see people. And here is a coincidence—the speakers are apparently always "glad to be" wherever the meeting is being held at the time.

Did you hear about the golfer who was having a terrible afternoon? Finally he blew up completely, cussed out the caddy, and said, "You are the *world's worst* caddy!"

The caddy said, "Oh, no, Sir. That just *couldn't be,* Sir. That would be just too much of a *coincidence!*"

It is quite a coincidence that speakers are *always* glad to see people, and *always* glad to be wherever the meeting is being held. But I doubt if they are usually as glad to see people as *I* am to see *you.* If you knew how I live, you would know what I mean. This business of keeping a full-time job going *in* the office, and another full-time job going *outside* the office, is *something.* In order to be here I flew all night on Flight 105. They call it "105" because that is the number of times it stops between Kansas City and here. There actually aren't that many airports but it stops at some of the places several times. That 105 is the original yo-yo flite.

I mention all this *only* to let you know that when you live like that, and you say to folks, "I am glad to see you," it has that extra ring of sincerity that comes with being glad you can see *anything!* To reach this convention, I had to be up all night, but I can truthfully say that I already feel just like one of you. I don't know, of course, which one of you it is that I feel like, but I do know that whoever it is—*he should go to his room and rest!*

The kind of approach indicated above lets the crowd know in a humorous way that the speaker made some effort to be present for the occasion, but it asks for no sympathy, and sets the stage for some good punch lines. It is especially effective with convention groups where some of the hearers are likely to have been up all night.

## 2. *Eye-to-eye contact.*

Eye-to-eye contact with the audience is an immensely important item as a speaker's ability to hold a crowd. If your audience is small enough that you can actually look each person in the eye, you have an advantage which it is folly not to use. Keep your eyes moving around over your audience pausing momentarily to look straight into the eyes of *individual* listeners. To your utmost extent you should give *each* of your hearers the feeling that this matter is "just between the two of us." As previously stated, the ideal situation has been achieved when each listener feels that *he* is the one who is hearing you, and the others are overhearing.

To accomplish eye contact with your crowd it is not necessary to keep your head spinning on its axis like a pin wheel. In fact, this defeats the purpose. To borrow an expression from the Western thrillers, "keep 'em *covered.*" Your head moves slowly around as you talk, with your eyes making many just-for-an-instant contacts with individuals, and with spot sections of your audience.

There is a special technique required for handling very large crowds. You start slower than with the smaller groups. You stay in "low" and "second" longer. You gradually proceed to pull your crowd together. The response to your opening story will ripple and roll to the back wall and up in the balconies. You must take time to make *all* of the people feel they are in the meeting. Those that are a half block away must be reassured that you know they are there.

When I addressed 13,000 Ohio teachers in the Coliseum at Columbus, I was completely surrounded by the audience. There were several thousand people behind me. In my preliminary remarks I told the audience of the man who took a job with a traveling carnival in the South. It was not a good job, but it was all he could get. His duties called for him to bend over and put his head through a hole in some canvas. For ten cents the customers could throw three balls at him. If it looked as though a ball were going to connect, he was to duck, or quickly turn his face down and let the ball hit a thick helmet he wore on top of his head.

In discussing his job with him someone asked, "Doesn't it keep you pretty busy—bent over there—dodging all those fast balls they pitch at you from out front?"

The man said, "Yes, it does. But the people out front don't

bother me as much as those guys who are throwing the darts from *behind*."

This is simply an illustration of the kind of device you can use for getting everyone "on the bus" before you shift into high.

In holding the large audiences the matter of eye contact is just as important as with the smaller ones. Use direct eye contact with all those who are near enough to you, and let everyone know you are looking straight at them a good portion of the time.

*3. Check your "audience barometers" and change your content if necessary.*

A helpful device for a speaker is to select several individuals in various sections of the crowd to be used as "barometers." With a little experience you will find yourself automatically picking out a few people who have particularly expressive faces. You can easily read their reactions at a glance. Use some of them as your barometers, or special check points. If their eyes quit meeting yours, it means the attention of your audience is straying. This is the signal to *change pace* before the crowd becomes visibly restless. Maybe your hearers are getting tired because you have kept them up on the mountain peak too long. Let the folks back down awhile and let them relax from the more rigorous climbs of your message. If you think they have taken about as much climbing as they can comfortably stand for that session, then eliminate the rest of the peaks from your tour.

When a pack of wolves would start following a sleigh in the harsh winter of Siberia, the Russian drivers would whip up the horses and stay ahead as long as they could. However, if the savage pack gave evidence that it was going to over-run the vehicle, then it sometimes became necessary to "toss" one of the passengers "to the wolves." This process was called "lightening the sleigh." It was a hard decision to make, but the Russians figured it sometimes had to be done, and done quickly. Similarly, a speaker may occasionally find it necessary to lighten the sleigh. If so, he should do it with dispatch, even though it means tossing out some of his choicest points. When such decisions are necessary the speaker should do it cheerfully, and be glad he has mastered the *topical* plan of speech construction that permits him to operate the remainder of the speech as a balanced whole.

A favorite story the writer used for some years concerned the speaker who was scheduled to address some cattlemen. A terrible sleet storm struck on the day of the meeting. When the speaker arrived at the meeting place there were just three men present. The three were seated on the front row of seats—two younger cowmen with an old man between them. After waiting in vain for more people to arrive the speaker said,

"Frankly, gentlemen, I am somewhat at loss as to what I should do. I went to some effort to prepare a speech, and even more effort to get to this meeting place. But, now I find just the three of you here, and apparently no more are coming. Even the chairman did not make it. Do you have any suggestions as to what we should do?"

The old man, seated between the other two, said,

"Well, I sure ain't no orator myself. All I know about is cattle. But I'll say this: If I went down to feed a herd of cattle and only three critters showed up—I would sure feed 'em."

"That settles it," the speaker said. "You asked for it."

He thereupon proceeded to deliver the entire speech, just as he had prepared it for an expected audience of 300. After talking an hour and ten minutes, the speaker concluded his prepared effort, and remarked to his audience of three, "*Now,* what do you say?"

The old man was again the spokesman, "Well, as I was sayin', I don't know nothin' about speakin'. Cattle is my business. But, it's like I said. If'n I was to go down to feed a bunch of steers and only three head showed up—why, I would feed 'em—but I don't think I would give 'em the *whole damn load!*"

Remember, in public speaking there is no law that says you must give 'em the whole load—whether they are hungry for it, or not.


4. *Keep your speech on a constructive note.*

If you wish to hold an audience, never be guilty of "scolding" or "nagging." If you have a criticism to make—make it and be done with it. People do not mind a speaker legitimately stepping on their toes occasionally, but they have every right to resent his *staying* on their sore toes, and grinding around for an hour with hob nail boots.

Lincoln said, "Always preach hope; never despair." Keep your messages on a positive note. Even when you are setting up the problem your hearers should have the feeling that it is *their* problem and *you are going to help them solve* it. Then, by all means, do help them. Jonathan Edwards could preach for two hours on the fact that a person's chances for getting into Heaven were about as good as those of a spider on a web suspended over a blast furnace. But very few present-day crowds would hold still for that kind of a speech. This is not Puritan New England. Furthermore, it was their rugged faith that kept the Puritans in their pews—not their preachers. The Puritans knew their Scripture so thoroughly that they would catch a single misquote the minister might make in a two-hour sermon.

## How to Improve the Language of Your Speech

Many books on public speaking contain a special chapter, or section, on language, word usage, vocabulary, and sentence construction. The fact that no special section of this book is set aside for such a treatment does not mean the author does not fully appreciate its importance. There are three general reasons why the language of the speaker is not given extensive, separate consideration in this volume:

(1) As previously stressed, it is not a textbook, and cannot undertake to include a course in English composition.

(2) The vocabulary of the speaker is considered throughout the work. For example, the chapter on Simplicity deals largely with expressing ideas in words that are most effective. All through the book the reader will find *examples* of using the language to achieve the objective.

(3) It is assumed most readers of this book have amassed a vocabulary sufficient to express most of their ideas to individuals, or in group conversation. A prime purpose of this volume is to help the reader become a speaker, or a better speaker, *by beginning where he is now.*

There is nothing in the foregoing that precludes the reader from *improving* his vocabulary and his use of language. On the contrary, it is highly recommended that every effort be made to increase one's word power.

A basic rule in speaking is to *never use a word unless you know you are pronouncing it correctly and that it means what you think it means.* The writer recently heard a county agent make a speech on the problems of the farm surplus. A dozen times in his discourse he spoke of the "dearth of wheat" and the "dearth of corn." At first his audience was bewildered but eventually it became obvious to most of the hearers that the speaker thought dearth meant abundance or surplus. The misuse of this one word killed the effect of what could have been a good speech.

Do not let your speech get saddled with standard phrases. Have the man you are describing be busier than something besides a one-armed paper hanger, as bald as something other than a billiard ball, or blinder than something besides a bat. Two partners were giving their local civic club a report on their recent safari in Africa. One said the chief gun bearer was "black as the ace of spades," but the other said he was "so black the lightning bugs followed him around in the daytime." One said the cook was as "dumb as a door nail." But the second man said the cook was "so stupid he couldn't find his hat with both hands." From these small samplings you can see which speaker was the sparkler and which was the drone.

Be loyal to your own section of the country. Do not try to hide your section's accent or avoid using its colloquialisms. If you are a Texan addressing a Boston audience, do not say "I have bean to the pawk." Just tell 'em where you've "bin," like you would in Amarillo. The audience will respect you for that, but they will never forgive you for saying,

"I haven't never bin in Boston before."

Dwight Eisenhower's midwestern enunciation is understood by all. Franklin Roosevelt won votes in all sections of the nation without forsaking his Harvard accent. Billy Graham has saved souls all over the world without ever dropping his pleasant and distinctive Carolina language. President Kennedy is always the Bostonian.

*Ways of Increasing Your Word Power*

 1. If you are unsure of your English usage, have a competent
    person read the manuscript of your speech. If he discovers

mistakes, ascertain whether they are "regular" ones with you. In any event, find out *why* they are errors and correct them in your manuscript *and in your mind*.

2. Buy a good dictionary and *use it*. Words are the tools of the speaker's trade. Keep yours sharp.

3. Buy a dictionary of synonyms. When you find you are wearing out a word with repetition, replace it with a better one. Then make the synonyms a part of your working vocabulary.

4. Diligently practice to avoid sloppy syllables. Do not say, "The guvmunt agent was in Kans City." Constantly strive to improve your word usage and enunciation in all private conversations—then correct English will not be an uncomfortable "Sunday suit" which you "put on" for public meetings. The general goal is to reduce both the size and number of your words and still make your meaning perfectly clear.

5. Avoid hackneyed phrases and beaten up bromides.

6. Study lines that particularly impress you and determine *why* they are good. Listen to successful speakers and analyze *why* they are good. Do not ape their style but apply their successful principles to your own style.

7. *Read orally*. Go over a given exercise until you know the meaning of every word, until you are correctly enunciating every syllable, and until you are confident each word is receiving the tone quality it should have to convey the meaning intended.

# 11

# Techniques for Holding
# An Audience

$T$his chapter is a continuation of the section of this book dealing with speech delivery. Among other things, it tells you:

1. How to deal with interruptions and unexpected developments.
2. How to approach an unfriendly audience.
3. How to capitalize on distinguishing physical characteristics.
4. What to do when you pull a "blooper."
5. How to memorize poems and quotations.
6. How to conduct a question-and-answer period.
7. How to handle visual aids.
8. How to read a speech—if it *must* be read.
9. How to prepare and deliver radio and television speeches.

One would not need to learn the art of "thinking on his feet" if he could always be assured that when he planned a good speech he could unfailingly execute the plan. But sometimes the conditions under which a speaker delivers his speech are different than he anticipated; and sometimes things happen that no one could have anticipated. It is well, then, that we should give some thought to the matter of handling interruptions and unexpected developments. If we are caught totally unaware of such possibilities, the results may be disastrous.

In a small southern community a colored parishioner, named

Charm Gibbons, was going to church one morning when a huge opossum ran across his path. Old Charm swung his cane and hit the opossum on the head, stunning the animal. As the opossum lay at his feet, Charm had to make a decision. He knew the creature was "playing possum" and could not be left there until after church. It was too late to take him back home, and Charm did not want to miss the morning services. And he certainly was not going to be deprived of such a delectable dish as he had just captured. There was no alternative. He would have to take it to church with him. Accordingly, he picked up the opossum by the tail, carried it to the church, and deposited it in the aisle next to the end pew where he always sat.

The services had already started when Charm arrived. Presently Parson "Coop" Clay arose to begin his sermon. He was just speaking his opening sentence when he saw the huge opossum in the aisle. The interruption came at an unfortunate point. Parson Clay said,

"Brothahs and Sistahs, we is all chillun of God—*damn, what a rat!*"

A Kentucky preacher was annoyed by someone humming a hymn as he was preaching his sermon. Stopping a moment, he glared at the back of the church and said,

"Whosoever that is hummin' Lead Kindly Light through your nose—*quit it!*"

### Three Ways to Deal With Interruptions

When interruptions occur, the speaker has three choices of action, depending upon the conditions: He can pause until the matter clears itself; he can recognize the situation and help clarify it; or, he can capitalize upon the interruption.

Speakers may as well resign themselves to the fact that people in an audience, even when interested in a speech, will let their eyes and interest follow some new element that has been introduced into the situation. An usher going slowly down the aisle trying to locate someone keeps a part of the audience distracted until the person is located. If the search is a short one, the speaker best ignore it. If it continues, he should probably pick an easy place to break his line of thought and ask who is wanted. One speaker turns such circumstances into a laugh by stopping and asking the individual in the aisle if he is "looking for the information booth." (If the chairman is sharp, he will probably send word to the door keeper to prevent a recurrence.) At any rate the speech is resumed without damage.

I was once addressing a morning session of the National Sales Executives in their annual convention in the Grand Ballroom of the Waldorf-Astoria. One of the hotel employees, a laborer who was apparently setting up properties in another room, needed to go from one side of the Ballroom to the other. He chose to walk deliberately across, between the audience and myself. I lifted my eyebrows a little and gave the man a glance, there was a chortle in the crowd, and the incident was over—for the time being. But presently the man came back through, as unconcerned as if he were picking daisies in Central Park. This time something had to be done. The chairman was horrified and the crowd did not know whether it was a gag, or just incredible stupidity. I stopped my speech, called to the man, and told him to stop and look at me. This he did, standing dead center in front of the crowd. Showing him my hands, I said,

"If you stick your neck in this room again while I am speaking, so help me, I will take these bare hands and *choke you to death!*"

The man literally *vanished* out the door and the audience rewarded the effort with tremendous applause. In this case I could *capitalize* upon a serious interruption because of the nature of the crowd, the unpardonable stupidity of the individual concerned, and the fact that the psychological situation was one which the crowd felt demanded action. Under different circumstances the above incident should better be ignored.

An eastern minister was preaching a sermon which he had prepared with great care. He was just reaching his climaxing point and was reciting in soft tones a sad poem. In the midst of his recitation the church janitor decided to raise the window nearest the pulpit. With his shoes squeaking loudly the janitor walked the length of the church, and had just reached the window when the minister's wrath exploded. Shouting at the janitor he said, "Will you please sit down!"

The outburst was obviously uncharitable, un-Christian like, and inappropriate. In this case the congregation's sympathies were completely with the janitor, although he had obviously manifested poor judgment. The minister had not only permitted the interruption to wreck his sermon and his morning service, but it hastened the conclusion of his ministry in that church.

A speaker was in the midst of developing a point when a loud crashing noise came from backstage somewhere. The stir which swept through the audience could have seriously disrupted a speaker who had memorized his remarks and who possessed no flexibility, or change-of-pace devices. But the speaker turned the loss into a gain by saying,

"There must be mice in here!"

The crowd laughed. The hearers were relaxed again because they knew the speaker was undisturbed. The speech threads were picked up and put together with no harm done.

Speakers are sometimes disturbed by news photographers and amateur photographers who are taking pictures during the meeting. It is quite appropriate for a speaker to request in advance that the chairman arrange for the picture taking to be done during his preliminary remarks. Little harm can be done to the speech at that time because the speaker has not picked up speed as yet. Photographer's interruptions can also occasionally be turned into gains. I have successfully used a device for occasions when a photographer flashes a bulb in my face while I am speaking. I will stop, smile at him, and say, "I can *still* see a little out of this other eye, if you would like to take one more picture."

The crowd loves it, and the speech moves on.

Photographers can become a real menace to a speech when they interrupt after it is well under way. It is when the speaker's train of thought is in high gear that it can be most easily wrecked. Especially vicious to the speaker's welfare is the photographer who comes forward, monopolizes the crowd's attention, gets set, and *waits* for exactly the right gesture or pose. I have found it advantageous in such situations to stop, address the photographer in a smiling and friendly manner, and say something like this,

"Why don't you come up here, boy, and make this speech—

and let me take the picture. I want to trade places with you because I believe you have more people's attention than I have."

While the crowd laughs about this development, the speaker can smile sweetly while he quietly tells the chairman to "have somebody get this stupe out of here."

A photographer once came out on the stage where I was speaking, and, to the amazement of everyone, stood with a flash bulb attachment held high above his head. I stopped and told him he looked very much like the Statue of Liberty. I then had him remain standing in the same position while I recited the following well-known lines from the inscription on the statue:

> "Give me your tired, your poor,
> Your huddled masses yearning to breathe free,
> The wretched refuse of your teeming shore.
> Send these, the homeless, tempest-tost to me,
> I lift my lamp beside the golden door."

This device not only saved the speech, but it also taught a photographer to be more considerate.

What should the speaker do about crying babies and children who romp through the balcony or down the aisles? One is likely to occasionally encounter such conditions in meetings that are made up of broad cross-sections of the populous. Commencement exercises and farm gatherings are the types of occasions where such interruptions are most likely to occur.

Josh Lee, of Oklahoma, used to include in his preliminary remarks a device for solving the crying baby problem. After telling a story or two, and establishing good will, he would compliment his audience—and then say something like this:

I see most everyone has turned out for this occasion tonight. And I see some of you have brought your babies with you, and that is fine. Folks used to think they couldn't go anywhere if they had small babies, and they would stay at home and miss everything. Then about the time *that* baby got old enough to go somewhere—well, you know what happened! My! You can't stay home *forever,* you know. So, I'm glad you came and I am glad you brought your babies. And I want you to know now, that if the baby should start crying while I am speaking—it won't bother me—*if you take it out.*

The above device is a good one because it is offered *before* any baby cries, and no one is being scolded. Also, it brings a laugh from the crowd, and occasionally some applause. This fact serves notice on the mothers with babies that the crowd approves what the speaker said, and under the force of public opinion the crying babies are usually withdrawn promptly.

Jeff Williams likes to recount the story of the mountain preacher whose voice volume mounted higher and higher as his sermon progressed. A young mountain mother sat on the front pew with a sleeping baby in her lap. As the preacher's voice grew louder, the baby grew increasingly restless, finally awakened, and began to cry. The young mother had started toward the door with her baby when the preacher stopped and said, "Sister Smith, you don't need to take the baby out. He ain't botherin' me none."

She said, "Maybe he ain't, Parson, but you are sure botherin' hell out of him."

In cases where older children are disturbing a meeting, it is a problem for the chairman and the committee. The speaker should remember that whenever it is at all possible, the chairman should not only "call the meeting to order," but it is his responsibility to *keep it in order*.

### The Disturbing Drunk Is a Special Problem

A serious problem that sometimes occurs in certain types of groups is the problem of interruptions by people who are intoxicated. Sometimes the offenders are "influential" members of the organization concerned, and neither the chairman, the paid secretary, nor any of the other members are anxious to intervene. There is one rule a speaker should religiously follow in such cases: Give the chairman or committee a reasonable length of time to correct the disturbance, and if it is not done the speech should be terminated forthwith. A speaker should *never* attempt to continue indefinitely competing with drunks or hoodlums.

Occasionally during the progress of a dinner meeting a trouble spot can be seen developing where a concentration of heavy drinkers is forming. Perhaps they came into the banquet hall "polluted" from too many drinks at the cocktail hour which preceded it, and perhaps from "hospitality rooms" prior to that. If these people will stop drinking and eat their dinners, they may be in reasonably good shape by the time the program starts. But if they have bottles on the table, or drinks brought in during the meal, then the warning flag is up for the committee to see. Steps should be taken to insure the ninety-nine per cent of the crowd do not have their evening spoiled by an inconsiderate few. Those in charge of the event should act with dispatch—either the drinking stops or the offenders should leave the room before the program gets under way. This is not a matter of "blue nose" morality. It is a matter of simple good manners, good taste, and common decency.

Occasionally a good-natured and "harmless" drunk can toss a bombshell into a meeting. Also to be feared is the "sober" or "sincere" drunk. Witness the classic example of the drunk who stumbled into a funeral home while a funeral service was in progress. He sat down in the back of the crowd and became tremendously impressed with what the minister was saying. Eventually he became literally carried away with the preacher's message. At the peak of his sermon the preacher said, "The Lord giveth and the Lord taketh away!"

That clinched the argument in the mind of the drunk. He struggled to his feet, looked at the crowd, and said, "Folks, if that ain't a fair deal, I ain't never heard of one!"

A master of ceremonies was introducing his head table guests. One of them proved to be a beautiful blond with an unusual hair-do. As the lady stood, the M. C. commented upon her hair-do, and asked the crowd, "Would you like me to turn her around?"

A drunk in the back of the house said, "Turn her around, hell! —*Pass* her around!"

*When Addressing Unfriendly Audiences Play Up Your*
*Areas of Agreement and Play Down Your Differences*

The art of handling a hostile audience is a special one of its own, and should usually not be attempted by amateurs. For masterful examples of this technique one should read such things as the life of Henry Ward Beecher, and follow his experiences as an anti-slavery speaker. How great political speakers have handled hecklers is also enlightening. Mark Anthony's oration is a classic example of success in meeting this problem. In the main, the speaker addressing an audience known in advance to be hostile can well follow this general procedure: He can open his remarks by expressing his appreciation for being invited when his views were known to be different from the majority of the audience. This approach stresses the fact that he *was invited,* and gives him opportunity to commend the "American way" which permits us to "disagree without being disagreeable." If this point can be established, it labels the heckler as undemocratic, unsporting, unfair, and un-American. Yet the point can be made in a way that does not excite more hostility.

It is also good strategy to commend your opponents on something that the crowd knows to be true. Remember, "It is difficult for a man to keep a chip on his shoulder while he is taking a bow."

The speaker addressing a hostile audience should open the body of his speech by reviewing the points upon which he is in general agreement with his audience. He should then reach and state clearly the "point of law," or the exact nature of the difference of opinion. Following this he should briefly state why he supports his view, thank his audience again, and quit while he is ahead.

If an unfriendly audience tends to be noisy, the speaker should not keep raising his voice to be heard. He can never win such a contest. The better approach under such circumstances is to lower the voice. The crowd will then either quiet down in order to hear, or it will make it plain that it does not want to hear, regardless. In the latter case, the speech is over. More often the lowered voice will achieve the desired effect. It is human nature for people to want to hear what even their enemies are saying.

Speeches made to hostile audiences should never be personalized. The more objective they are the more likely they are to succeed.

*Capitalize Upon Distinguishing Physical Characteristics—Your Own or Those of the Meeting Place*

Speakers can frequently help their deliveries by taking advantage of their own distinguishing physical characteristics. Maybe the speaker is very large, or unusually small, or bald, or possesses a peculiar accent. Most any distinguishing characteristic can be capitalized upon.

H. Roe Bartle, Mayor of Kansas City, Missouri, tips the scales at around 270 pounds. His voice is as strong as a lion's. When he is first introduced, he will sometimes simply stand at the microphone a moment to let the crowd see how big he is. Then pushing the microphone to one side he will let his mighty voice roll out across the auditorium as he asks, "Can you folks hear me back on that back row?"

Of course, the back row and all the other rows are literally vibrating with sound waves, and the mayor's approach shot is usually good for a big response.

Again, Bartle will capitalize upon his size with a story like this:

I was waiting in the airport at Toronto the other day when I discovered they had an unusual kind of scales there. Whenever a person stepped on the scales, a voice came out of a mechanical speaker and *told* the individual his weight.

I decided to try it. There was a little girl ahead of me. She stepped on the scales and the voice said, "Forty-four pounds, please." A lady was next, and the voice said, "One hundred twenty-one pounds, please." Then I stepped on the scales, and the voice said, *"One at a time, please!"*

Dr. No-Young Park is a popular lecturer who speaks with a pronounced Chinese accent, but can be easily understood. He gets his audience adjusted to his accent by telling how he addressed a university assembly. At the close of the session a freshman rushed up to him, beaming with pleasure and said,

"Why, Dr. Park. I understood *everything* you said! I had no idea the English and the Chinese were so much alike!"

A very short man was elected to the national board of his organization in its annual meeting in Chicago. When his election was announced he was called to the platform to respond. His head could scarcely be seen above the speaker's stand. He recognized that something concerning his size needed to be said to put the crowd at ease and he responded as follows:

"For the benefit of those in the rear of the room I wish to announce that I am *standing*. I am an all right guy. I just got a late start in life. My father was an old Indian fighter. My mother was an old Indian."

A bald man responded to an introduction in this manner.

"It is true, as the chairman said, that I arrived late on the day they were passing out the hair. But the chairman was not correct in saying there was no hair left when I got there. As a matter of fact, they had some stringy, yellow hair—like *his*—but I wouldn't take that. . . . I do not enjoy being bald, but you must admit it is *neat*."

Sometimes a speaker can use an over-powering personality and great experience to literally *command* respect. The late Dr. Willis Sutton, of Atlanta, Georgia, is an excellent example of this type. He was a venerable gentleman who has done his "three score and ten." His imposing figure was crowned with a heavy shock of snow white hair. After warming up a college commencement crowd with several wonderful stories, Dr. Sutton turned his attention directly to the class. As he stood impressively in his black velvet Doctorate robe, the crowd grew quiet with expectation. Dr. Sutton in a clear, even voice said,

A few more years—ten at the most—and I shall rest beneath the soil of my beloved native State of Georgia. I have come down life's road a long way. I know where the rough spots are. I've seen a lot of wrecks, and I have also been passed by many who were wiser travelers than I. Now *you* are beginning *your* trip, and I have come up here from Atlanta to tell you some things—some things that will save your time, your money, your happiness, and maybe your lives. This, then, will be your "commencement" address. You're commencing your trip by listening to an old man who has made his journey. Surely that will be appropriate for the occasion, and I am going to try awfully hard to make it interesting for you.

The above approach set the stage psychologically for one of the most effective commencement addresses ever given. How much more appropriate it was than if Doctor Sutton had approached the class with an "I-want-to-be-one-of-you" pitch. He chose to be his own magnificent self—and the class loved him for it.

Sometimes a speaker can capitalize upon a physical feature of the meeting place, or a development that occurs in the meeting arrangements. A banquet meeting I was to address overflowed the hotel ballroom and one table had to be set up in the balcony. The side of the table facing the rest of the audience was covered with a white tablecloth that came to the floor and about a dozen men were seated behind it, and there were two at each end. The crowd was very much aware of this special table but no comment about it was made by the chairman. As I was getting under way with my speech I made some relatively minor point, then suddenly turned to the special table group in the balcony and said, "And the same goes for you guys up there attending the Last Supper."

The little group's similarity with Leonardo da Vinci's painting was so obvious that the point went over with a bang. Not only that, but the special table scene continued to provide amusement throughout the evening. It was one of those "naturals" that fall into a speaker's lap occasionally.

### Make Your "Bloopers" Pay Dividends

It is well for the beginning speaker, as well as the experienced one, to think out in advance what he will do when he pulls a "blooper," because it is almost inevitable that he will eventually find himself needing a device for such an emergency.

The first thing to understand about "bloopers" is that if you pull one you *are not ruined*. They are regular occurrences with all kinds of speakers—the veterans and the beginners. Few men have more speaking experience under their belts than an old political war horse like Senator Everett Dirksen, of Illinois. In a Senate debate over the confirmation of Claire Booth Luce as Ambassador to Brazil, Senator Dirksen attempted to tell the Senators that they should quit dragging in earlier statements by Mrs. Luce. He said, "Why keep thrashing old straw? Why keep beating an old bag of bones?"

The writer was addressing a banquet meeting which closed a District Rotary Conference in South Dakota. It is customary at the closing banquet to present the out-going District Governor with a gift. On this occasion the gift was a beautiful silver service, and the District Governor was genuinely overcome with gratitude and emotion. He arose and responded in this manner:

"Fellow Rotarians and Rotary Anns, I am simply overwhelmed. I do not know what to say. I just want you to know that I thank you from my very bottom!"

The chairman took over from there and declared this was truly a "deep-seated emotion." Later speakers carried the theme still farther. The poor, retiring District Governor thought he was ruined forevermore, but he wasn't. He just set the stage for a rollickingly successful evening. His blooper broke the log jam, and the meeting rolled from that point on.

I was present at a West Coast convention held in San Francisco when an ultra-serious retiring president made his annual report. He started to tell the crowd that his administration was the most successful year in the history of the organization, but what he actually said was, "This has been the most sexual year in our history."

His remark was greeted with a roar of laughter. The befuddled speaker did not know whether to wind his watch or go blind. What he had done was to make an unintentional sacrifice hit that saved the game. The dinner meeting, which had been dull and listless up to that point, instantly caught fire. Succeeding "toasters" threw away their notes and took off from the new launching pad that the retiring president had provided. They told such stories as the one about the credit bureau that was trying to locate the man named, "Sexower." The bureau called the business house where it was understood the man worked. When the telephone girl answered, the credit bureau caller asked, "Do you have a Sexower down there?"

The telephone girl said, "Oh, my, no. We don't even get a coffee break."

When you pull a boner, do not try to ignore it. Let the crowd enjoy it. The entertainment is already *charged to you* and you may as well be a congenial host. The question is, how do you get going again? It is recommended that you have another and bigger blooper in your reserve arsenal of stories that you can relate upon an instant's notice. Then, after the crowd has had its laugh, you can say, "I am in *good* form tonight. But I was in even *better* form a few weeks ago when I . . ." Then comes your blooper story.

This recommended approach is completely disarming. It makes no attempt to "cover up." You are not hurt because the audience laughed at you. You are even glad to give the people another laugh on you, which you do with your story. It sets you up to take off again with your speech and with your audience. After all, your crowd will not condemn you for being human— and "to err is human."

### Always Overlearn Anything You Plan to Quote

There is a special technique involved in a speech delivery that includes quoting materials verbatim. The secret comes not in merely memorizing such materials, poems, and quotations; but their successful use requires that you *over-learn* them. If you plan to quote some stanza from memory, do not be satisfied when you can quote it readily in your office or home. Facing an audience is a different deal than facing your desk or your mirror.

The "westerns" in movies and television frequently feature a young punk who practices the draw until he can shoot a half dozen target bottles with lightning speed. Then he goes forth to the town bar to test his new skill on a rival. But when he faces another man, the inexperienced gunman often freezes, and cannot get off the shot in time. A similar situation exists in speaking. Lincoln used to practice his speeches out in the countryside, but, as he said later, "facing rows of people is different than facing rows of corn."

If you are going to quote materials from memory, then you should know them so well you could quote them standing on your head in a graveyard at midnight. The writer has found the best way to memorize materials is to work on them just before going to sleep at night. Go over your poem or other quotes the last thing before you drop off, and let your subconscious mind get the materials fixed in order while you sleep. If you have never used this device, you will be delighted how it works for you. A poem or quote that you were recalling with great difficulty the last thing at night, will roll along without a hitch the next morning. Then try quoting the piece several times during the day—suddenly, and without warning. You can run through it while you are going to lunch, or driving to an appointment. Get it so thoroughly in mind that it just cannot take you by surprise—then no amount of tension can make the words freeze on your lips.

### *Any Question-and-Answer Period Should Be Well Organized and Be Brief*

Some speakers like to follow their formal presentations with a question-and-answer period. Whether or not this procedure is desirable depends upon the subject, the speaker, and the time available. The answering of questions should probably not be attempted by the speaker who has not yet acquired a reasonable amount of platform composure. Furthermore, the speaker who answers questions should be so absolutely *loaded* with his subject that he will have little concern as to what phase of it the questions will turn.

If your speech is one which finishes on a "high note"—is inspirational, or ends with a call to action—then it is usually undesirable to permit the "let down" that would accompany a question-and-answer period. If your speech is in the nature of a travelogue, current affairs, a hobby, or anything of an "explanational" nature—then the question-and-answer period may be a most useful device for making sure you touched upon the points your audience wanted discussed.

It is recommended that in conducting a question period the questions be written on pieces of paper furnished the audience by ushers *after* you have finished. These can be quickly collected and given to the chairman. The chairman can ask you one representative question to get you going, then he *groups* the rest of the questions into classifications. It will be found most of them are centered around a few *key* points and the chairman can classify them into four or five questions. The chairman can then represent the audience in asking you these key questions from the platform. In no case should the question period be prolonged.

The question-and-answer plan recommended here avoids duplication. It also throttles the character in the audience who likes to hear his own voice. This type loves to stand and take over the audience that came to hear someone else. As pointed out in another chapter, he begins by saying, "I want to ask you a question." What he usually means is, "I want to make a speech." And he

As Droke [1] points out, an audience cannot anticipate a pleasurable message when a "speaker" begins by producing a "stack of notes that would founder a billy goat." Trying to read a paper and also look at your audience is a process which Droke describes in the words of a colored woman who said of her new minister,

"His sermonizin' puts me in mind of a crow in a corn field—two dabs and a look-up."

> The room was hushed
> The speaker mute,
> He'd left his speech
> In his other suit.

Bishop Fulton J. Sheen says, "Anyone who does not have it in his head to do 30 minutes extemporaneous speaking is not entitled to be heard."

Sometimes it is justifiable to read highly technical discourses before technical audiences. Even on these occasions one should consider that the specialized audience could probably read as well as the speaker. There is no justification for reading a speech in order that the press will report it accurately. Abstracts, summaries, or press copies can be prepared for that purpose. Of course, important messages of state must ordinarily be read to avoid any possibility of misinterpretation, and to conform strictly to advance releases for press, radio, and television.

If a speech *must* be read before an audience, the "speaker" should be so thoroughly familiar with it that he could almost complete any sentence from memory if he glanced at the first few words. Only in this manner can he show awareness of his audience and use any eye-to-eye contact at all. I have seen "speakers" bury their heads in manuscripts and never look up as their gargled words reverberate around their own pages. They make me think of a parrot that is owned by a friend of mine. The parrot loves to bury his head in his feed dish and do his talking in that position. In this manner he can amuse himself indefinitely, but no one knows what he is saying.

[1] Maxwell Droke, *Encyclopedia of Creative Thought* (New York: Maxwell Droke), 1941.

*Special Considerations for Delivering Speeches Via*
*Radio and Television*

Just as it is seldom justifiable for speakers to read their discourses in public meetings, so it is equally unwise not to read
them in the radio and television studios. Let us first examine a
few elementary principles of radio technique.

Radio speaking usually means the speech is read in its entirety.
The result of such a presentation is much less stilted for the
speaker who has learned to "speak his thoughts down on paper,"
than for the usual manuscript reading. Make your softening-up
remarks brief. Get to your objective quickly and with an attention-getting statement. Leading off with a question is good radio
technique, and questions can profitably be inserted at other spots
in the speech. Keep your hearers alert and expecting something
every minute.

You should space your high points and change-of-pace items
with special care. Remember, your listeners can turn you off any
time with no embarrassment. You are competing with professionals all around the dial. In radio speaking make your sentences short. Emphasize the important points by repetition.
Make the whole presentation as short as possible.

It is well to remember the radio and television are open to all.
Unless you are speaking on a closed circuit anyone can tune you
in, even though your remarks are directed to a particular group.
Check your copy carefully that you do not inadvertently offend
any of the multitude of groups and individuals who compose the
"listening public."

Your manuscript should be marked for two things—emphasis
and timing. Inject into it the maximum amount of naturalness.
Read it aloud to yourself and others until there are no surprise
turns for you in the copy or the thought. Insert check marks to
indicate pauses. Underline words to be emphasized.

Although you will not need nearly so much flexibility in your
radio manuscript as in regular speaking, you will need to mark
some sentences or paragraphs that can be eliminated if time runs
short. It is important that you not let the red light come on with

your conclusion still unread.  In radio and television you cannot "beg indulgence" and continue past the closing minute.  If you are reading from the usual double-spaced copy, at the normal rate of speed, you should not be more than two pages from your ending when the studio clock indicates five minutes remain.  This will give you a comfortable margin and give the announcer a few seconds to close out your program.  The next-to-the-last page should contain a paragraph or two that can be by-passed if you are running short of time.  This plan assures you the full amount of time for your conclusion.  You will also find it helpful to mark time allotments on your total copy after you have read the speech aloud several times and injected your note of naturalness.  You can then mark where you should be at the end of the first five minutes, and so on to the last five.  If you find early in the speech that you are falling behind your scheduled speed, you can drop out some "expendable" sentences you have marked for that purpose, and "increase the beat" on the remainder.

Television speaking embodies the characteristics of both the platform manner and the radio.  Unless you are highly experienced you should not attempt to televise any impromptu or informal speeches.  This means your speech will be read either from manuscript, cue-cards, q-prompter, or "teleprompters."  (Technically, "Teleprompter" is a brand name that has come into common usage to indicate any type of device where the copy moves forward at the rate the speaker reads.)  If reading from manuscript, observe the techniques of reading to an audience.  Glance up as often as possible and be so familiar with your material that you can read in sweeping phrases.

When reading from a teleprompter or q-cards, the speaker should look toward the taking lens as much as possible.  One of the newest and best of the "teleprompters," is a device that has the trade name of TV Lens-Line.  By using a two-way mirror system, TV Lens-Line permits the speaker to see his copy clearly by looking straight into the taking lens.

When you make a radio or television appearance do not be too proud to tell the studio officials of your inexperience and enlist their help.  They can give you a few explicit directions that will make the difference between a smooth performance and something less. Even experienced radio and television speakers should welcome suggestions from station personnel, especially when making appearances in studios that are new to them. In the case of telecasts, it is well to consult with the studio in advance as to how you should dress, whether make-up is to be used, and other details.

### A Powerful, All-embracing Speech Formula From a Simple Mountaineer

The late Jess Blackmore was serving with the Chevrolet Division of General Motors during the great depression of the Thirties. It was discovered that a small dealer in the hills of West Virginia was setting a remarkable sales record. He regularly exceeded his dealer quota despite the general depression, and despite the fact that his particular territory was an extreme depression area. It was decided Mr. Blackmore would call on the dealer personally, learn his secret, and pass it along to others in the Chevrolet organization.

Arriving in the West Virginia community, Jess Blackmore got his first surprise when he walked in the dealer's plainly furnished little office. The dealer was talking on the telephone, and he motioned Jess to a chair. This gave Jess a chance to study the man's appearance, as well as to see him in action. The man wore no coat nor tie. His shirt and slacks were plain, but clean. He smoked a cigar. ("Gotta use our own products," he explained later.) But, Jess was most fascinated by what the dealer was saying on the telephone. It went like this:

"Hello, Charley. This is Hank, down at Chevrolet. This is the day to sell them hogs of yours. Yeh, the market is as high as it's gonna git. Yeh, bring 'em all in today. I've got everything arranged. And after you git 'em all in the railroad car, bring that old truck over here and pick up your new one. It's all ready for ya. Contract is just like we made it when you was in here before. Jest needs you to sign it, that's all.

"And, Charley . . . tell the rest of the boys up the valley there I'll be callin' them when its time to sell their stuff."

Blackmore asked, "Do these people simply take your word as to when they should sell their produce?"

Hank said, "*Sure.* I've been helpin' 'em for years. Kinda hard for hill folks to keep a finger on markets and things like that. I don't know how things are done in Detroit and the big cities, but us country boys find a feller will buy sumthin' a little quicker if you can help him get the money to pay for it!"

Blackmore had a most enlightening visit with Hank and came away with Hank's parting statement in his heart,

"Mr. Blackmore, it has been wonderful to have you come down here to see me, but I didn't put on no dog, nor change nuthin', to get ready. I figured you meant what you said—that you wanted to see *me,* and how *I* sell. *I believe in order to succeed, a feller's got to learn to deliver the most to his people, in the way that him and them understands best.*"

You can find a more grammatical rule for public speaking, but I doubt that you will ever find a more effective one.

# 12

# Speaking to Youth Groups

$T$his chapter completes the three-chapter section 10, 11, and 12) on the general subject of speech delivery.

There is a special technique required in holding audiences of children and youth. Most speakers consider these to be the most difficult of all audiences. The speaker will save himself much grief if he approaches his audiences of children and youth with this understanding: Young people are *genuine*. They are not naturally crude, but they do not feel it is necessary to *pretend*. If they do not like what you are saying, they do not feel it is necessary to *act* like they do. Although their hearts are as big as all-out-of-doors when properly appealed to, they are often inclined to be uncharitable toward those who do not appeal to them.

In addressing young audiences the following general rules should be observed:

## 1. *Make it short.*

Unless you are thoroughly accustomed and experienced with youth groups, hold your first speaking effort to ten or fifteen minutes. High school audiences can be successfully held for thirty minutes by a good speaker with an appealing subject, but shorter speeches are better. There are certain great youth speakers who can hold such audiences for an hour or more, but their numbers are few indeed.

## 2. *Make it snappy.*

Let the young folks know quickly that you are not "Holy Joe" who has come over to tell them all the things they shouldn't be doing. For this event you don't spare the horse for the stretch; come out of the starting gate fast and keep the horse under the whip all the way. Use your best and most appropriate story first, and be sure it is one in which you reach the punch line quickly.

3. *In addressing youth groups do not try to be "one of them."*

Youths understand the processes of biology. They know the only way an adult can become a child again is to become *senile*, and enter his second childhood. Young folks know senility is not a desirable quality in a speaker. Don't be a child with the children—try to be the kind of an *adult* that *they want to become*.

A speaker of the jolly-good-fellow type was introduced to a midwestern high school assembly. Rushing to the front of the platform he shouted, "What's the word, gang?"

One boy in the back of the house said, "Nuts!"

The speaker had his answer, and for all practical purposes his speech was over.

4. *Avoid topics, illustrations, and stories that your young audience will label as "corn."*

Modern day youth is sharp. The speaker who would succeed with youth groups should keep his stories and illustrations as clean as a whistle, but more on the sophisticated side. Never tell a joke out of the current issue of *The Reader's Digest*. Never labor the old clichés like telling an assembly of students that you know they are "anxious to get back to class." Don't give them too many Horatio Alger illustrations. After a speaker had used five or six "halo" stories, a youth in the audience turned to his seat mate and said, "Take the roof off the greenhouse, Mother—the corn is getting taller."

A speaker for a preparatory school group thought he would make his hearers more appreciative of their modern-day advantages by recounting the struggles of his own youth. As he got into his heart-rending account, one student turned to another and said, "Get ready, boy. He is going to make with the early hardships."

A temperance speaker was addressing a 4-H Rally on Frances Willard Day. He portrayed a distraught mother at home with her baby while her drunken husband squandered the family's meager means at the corner saloon. Said the speaker to his youthful audience,

"Picture this poor mother, if you will—rocking the cradle with one foot and wiping away her tears with the other!"

The audience of kids did what the speaker asked. They "pictured" the scene as he described, and the result was a near riot.

5. *Never talk down to youth groups.*

A speaker should remember the average group of high school age lacks the wisdom and judgment that can come only with maturity; but such a group is better *informed* than the average adult audience. Both the teenager and the college age resent *condescending* approaches. They encounter so much of that in their daily routines that they will rise up and bless the speaker who gives them a respite.

6. *While modern youth groups are blasé on the surface,* they are really idealistic and easily moved emotionally.

Never misinterpret the seemingly blasé attitude of modern youth as shallowness, insincerity, or callousness. It is none of these things. Once a speaker wins the confidence and respect of a youth group he can hammer over a tremendous message. *Young people are inherently fair and tolerant.* They can be deeply stirred by illustrations with human and emotional appeal. They will rally around basic ideals faster than adult audiences, and are grateful for leaders who help them plant their feet on higher ground. Never under-estimate the sterling qualities of the average young person.

7. *Some audience participation is an effective device with younger groups.*

Intelligently directed audience participation will help hold the attention of young audiences, and the younger the audience the more important the device becomes. When a kindergarten teacher wants to get all the children's attention she does not begin with a discourse on Rousseau's reasons why children learn. She is more likely to say,

"How many of you have cats at home?"

All those who have cats excitedly hold up their hands. The rest look around to see how many have cats, and become intensely interested in what is going to develop. After some of the children have told the rest about their cats, then the teacher is ready to tell them all a story about a cat. Her "speech" is certain to be a hit.

### A Sample Approach to a High School Audience

The following is the "softening up" section of a speech the writer successfully delivered to a high school assembly. Read it, and then go over the check list which follows it, noting how it incorporates principles promulgated in this book.

Thank you for that kind introduction. It made me feel welcome, and that is what an introduction should do. It's like the man who saw his picture on the post office wall. He said, "It's good to know you are wanted." Confucius said, "It is good to be among friends—even if they aren't yours." After spending twenty-four years in the school business, if I am not among friends with student groups, I don't know where I would fit in.

I want you to all relax now, because I didn't come here to tell you how to run your lives. This school was doing fine before I got to town, and I am sure you will go right on after I leave. Your football team seems to be doing especially well without any help from me.

Do you know that I once played high school football against one of your teams here? Back in 1923 you had a great team and the star fullback was named Rock Williams. Does anyone here remember Rock Williams? Well, look at the hands go up! No doubt some of the faculty saw Rock play and evidently a lot of you students know of him. Well, I played against Rock. In those days the football fields were not as good as they are now. In the second quarter of that game, Rock stepped on a pipe and twisted his ankle. They had to take him out of the game, and they took me out at the same time because it was my windpipe that he stepped on.

I was surprised over how many of your faculty *remember* old Rock. Some of you teachers must have been around here for quite a spell. But you look like youngsters compared with some of these college faculties. Did you read how that girl in Texas defined a college? She said, "A college is a bunch of old buildings, standing well back from the street, with the ivy creeping around the outside, and the faculty creeping around the inside."

Well, I have been around quite awhile myself. And I can remember when we once understood some fundamental principles that we seemed to be losing sight of in recent years.

At this point the stage is set for some serious points.

How the above approach incorporates sound principles for "softening up" audiences in general, and youth groups in particular:

1. It gets to a humorous point quickly.
2. It identifies the speaker with the audience—the "common denominator."
3. It compliments the football team of which the school is proud.
4. The speaker makes it clear he is not appearing as a beacon of truth and light.
5. The story about Rock Williams injects local color, provides audience participation by a show of hands, and ends with a laugh *on the speaker*.
6. The definition of a college gives the students a laugh on the faculty—a sure-fire technique. But the faculty is appeased by knowing the speaker was "one of them" for 24 years.

# 13

# Using Humor

*"Oh rippling river of laughter—thou art
the blessed boundary line between beasts
and men."*
　　　　　　　　　　　—Ingersoll

A young man who had recently completed a correspondence school course in public speaking wrote this testimonial:
　"They laughed when I said I was going to tell a joke—but
they stopped when I told it."

This young man is just another to join the legions who have
learned that jokes do not always bring the desired results.

Jokes, humorous stories, and witty remarks constitute such
important weapons in the arsenals of a substantial percentage of
successful public speakers that a book purporting to give practical
aid to public speakers could scarcely omit a discussion of this
most significant aspect of oratory. In discussing this phase of
speech we shall try to avoid the criticism that "too many such
discussions in the past have been tainted by the stale breath of
the joke collector." There are numerous attractive volumes of
classified stories, witticisms, and anecdotes. A good example of
such collections is Braude's *Handbook of Humor for All Occasions.*[1] It is not the purpose of this chapter to rival any of these
books. The objective of this chapter is indicated in its title. It
will attempt to show how humor is *used* to illustrate ideas, provide changes-of-pace, to clinch ideas, and advance speech themes

---

[1] Prentice Hall, New York, 1958.

generally. Humor should help the speaker clinch ideas, but should not be substituted for them. As Hazlett said, "Wit is the salt of the conversation, not the food."

Perhaps a classification of terms will be in order at the outset. Mark Twain [2] has described how to distinguish the three standard forms of laughter-getting devices that are used in speaking:

"The humorous story may be spun out to great length, and may wander around as much as it pleases, and arrive nowhere in particular; but the comic and witty story must be brief and end with a point. The humorous story bubbles gently along, the others burst."

## Earlier Speakers Feared Humor Branded Them as Frivolous

Most speakers of an earlier day were afraid to use humor in their public utterances. They feared the practice would cause the public to discount their serious points; and that people would tend to take them lightly on all matters. Senator Tom Corwin always felt it was his reputation as a witty speaker that cost him the Presidential nomination. However, historians disagree with him on this. Most seem to think his Presidential hopes were blasted by what is agreed was the greatest speech of his career —his Senate address against the Mexican War. In any event, Corwin was so embittered by his belief that in an address for a law school he said, "Young men, if you desire a reputation for wisdom, never joke; be as solemn as an ass!"

Champ Clark once declared that many persons who never had a bright idea in their heads nor a generous sentiment in their hearts . . . "assume an air of disdain toward wit and humor and like to think themselves superior to the practitioners thereof . . ." But King Solomon, whose name is synonymous with wisdom, assured u; there is a time for everything—"a time to weep and a time to l ugh."

Although one of the greatest private story tellers of all time, Lincoln was slow to use humor in a public address lest he be thought frivolous. The fact that some of this sentiment still persists to plague those who seek high public office has been

[2] Mark Twain in Max Eastman, *Enjoyment of Laughter* (New York: Simon and Schuster), 1936.

demonstrated in the reaction to the campaigns of Adlai Stevenson. He was criticized because some of his campaign speeches and press conferences pointed up certain problems in a humorous vein. One reporter on Stevenson's campaign train wrote:

"After listening to this man's speeches I can't figure whether his objective is the Presidency, or a six-weeks contract at the Roxy."

On the other hand, some of the world's most successful public figures in modern times have used humor in public addresses with great effect. Sir Winston Churchill used a practical technique of inserting clever "asides" in his prepared manuscripts. These do not appear in the "record." For example, when he addressed the combined houses of the United States Congress, December 26, 1941, following America's entry into World War II, the record shows he pointed out that in a single day Japan had declared war upon the world's most powerful republic and the world's greatest empire. At this point in his speech, Churchill paused, took off his glasses and held them momentarily in his hand. With a Puckish smile he remarked, "To say the least, this is considerable of an undertaking!"

The remark brought forth a roar of laughter and applause, but it is not included in the recorded copies of his addresses.

President Roosevelt took time on a national radio hookup to tell about the old man who went to see his doctor because his hearing was failing. When he returned home he reported the doctor had told him he would lose his hearing entirely unless he stopped drinking alcoholic beverages. The family asked what he had decided to do about the doctor's advice, and the old man answered, "Well, I've thought it all over. I've decided that I like what I've been drinkin' so much better than I like what I've been hearin', that I reckon I'll just keep on a-gittin' deef."

*A Sense of Humor Does Not Mean You Lack Depth or Sincerity*

Modern day thinking seems to be increasingly lining up behind the fact that *there need not be any conflict between humor and sincerity*. When skillfully used, humor can be a mighty aid "to float a heavy speech and give wings to solid argument."

We have seen in previous pages how humor can be used to condition an audience for weightier things to follow. We have seen how humor can be used for the essential purpose of changing pace to hold audience interest. We have seen how humor can be used to clinch points and under-score illustrations, and it has been pointed out that humor can be used as a summarizing technique for closing speeches or inspiring action.

In closing a moving speech for Civilian Defense a speaker demonstrated how one anecdote can package a whole discourse. The story (which was new at the time) was the classic account of the dub golfer whose ball landed on an ant hill. As the dub swung at the ball and missed it, his club plowed through one side of the ant hill—maiming and killing several hundred ants. In his next swing he duplicated the death and destruction on the other side of the ant hill. Still the ball remained untouched. Finally one ant said to the others who remained,

"Fellows! If we want to save our lives, *we had better get on the ball!*"

## Test Yourself Before Telling Stories

Before you incorporate story-telling as a part of your public speaking technique you should subject yourself to a few important test questions. Do you *genuinely enjoy* a good story? Do you *enjoy* telling stories to others—singly, or in groups? Do you successfully tell stories to others? Do they respond to what you think is funny and at the points you think are funny? Do you find stories easy to remember, with the punch lines falling readily into place? If your response to all the questions is in the affirmative, there is no reason why you cannot bolster your speeches with the various types of humor.

If your answers to this "humor test" are mostly negatives, or luke-warm affirmatives, you should not be in the least discouraged. Humor is simply not your device. Do not attempt to ignore the test results and be a humorous speaker anyway. You will be courting disaster. Here we get back to the basic concept again—be *yourself* and perfect *your own style*.

*Humor Not Essential. It Is an Aid*
*for Those Who Know How to Use It*

One of America's most dynamic and successful platform speakers is Dr. Walter Judd, Congressman from Minnesota, the 1960 Republican Convention Keynoter. He served as a medical missionary in China and became an authority on the Far East. Dr. Judd's success as a speaker is the result of being on fire with the importance of the Far East in world affairs and he is driven by the terrible urgency of awakening his fellow countrymen to the situation. He sticks to his field and plays to his strengths. I recently heard him do a masterful address that held his audience spellbound for seventy minutes. From the beginning to the end, not a single story or witty remark did he use. His change-of-pace was done with voice modulation, varying speeds in the word count, diversification of subtopics, and with meaningful gestures.

On an eastern convention program I heard a speech by a prominent engineer. With precision that only an engineer could have planned, he dragged in a story every five minutes. The stories were completely unrelated to the speech theme and to one another. They were old chestnuts that had been cracked so many times they were pulverized. The poor man *read* the "jokes," along with the balance of his copy, and without ever looking up from his manuscript. Each time he waited for the laughter which never came, and each time he broke the stony silence himself by saying, *"Seriously,* though I . . . ."

The total effect of this effort was so bad that the audience was embarrassed. The question everyone asked afterward was, *"Why did he do it?* He had some good thoughts if he would only have permitted us to follow them."

A minister friend of mine, who could not smile without cracking his naturally somber face, reached the single-handed decision that he should demonstrate to his congregation that he was in reality a "hail fellow well met." Consequently he preached a sermon on "Humor." The result of his sermon beggars description. Ebenezer Scrooge or Simon Legree could have handled the subject better. He began by saying, "No one loves jollity

more than I . . . ." Then he followed with the revelation that
there are seven basic kinds of humorous stories and that he
would analyze them all in order, providing illustrations of each
as he proceeded. Periodically he paused to reassure his hearers
that "it is no sin to laugh." If it had of been a sin to laugh,
nothing happened that morning that caused a single parishioner
to leave the church with even one black mark against his record.

It is hoped we have now established our first important principle concerning the use of humor in public speaking—it is a life
line in the hands of those who can use it—but it is both suicide
and homicide in the hands of those who can't.

### Let Humor Inject Itself Easily into the Speech

Max Eastman lists "Ten Commandments of the Comic Arts."
High on the list is this one: "Be Effortless." Never run down a
joke, bulldog it, tie it, and drag it in. Remember the "old
faithful" concerning the boy scout who came in exhausted from
doing his good deed for the day. He had taken an old lady across
the street. The punch line came in the fact that she hadn't
wanted to go. Do not force your jokes to go in places where
they do not want to go. Let the stories come in easily, naturally,
and because they want to help you. If a suitable joke doesn't
suggest itself and "volunteer" for a particular assignment, then
do not draft one.

### Humor Must Fit Your Audience as Well as Your Material

The second principle to observe in using humor is that it not
only be appropriate to the background of your subject matter,
but also to the background of the audience. Take the example
of the old man who was on his death bed when the preacher came
to see him. The preacher said, "Brother Wilkins, are you willing
to renounce the Devil?"

The old man said, "No, I ain't. I don't figure I am in any position to be makin' enemies!"

This story would obviously go over better with a college assembly than it would before the Senior Citizens Club.

The teenagers like the slap-stick better. For example, the

disc jockey who announced, "The new cars are now rolling off the assembly lines. If they can start keeping them *on* there, you will soon be seeing them at the dealers."

The junior high school assembly would like this next one better than an adult audience:

The police of Baltimore were waging a campaign to collect dog taxes. A policeman stops a driver who has a dog sitting in the front seat of the car beside him. The policeman asks, "Does your dog have a license?"

The man answers, "No. He doesn't need one. I do all the driving."

If you want your adult audience to have a dog story, it would prefer one of the more sophisticated caliber:

A man goes in the movie theater while the feature is in progress, and locates a vacant seat. When his eyes become better adjusted to the darkness he discovers the seat beside him is occupied by a dog. He then becomes aware that the owner is in the next seat beyond the dog. The man is enthralled by the great interest the dog takes in the picture. When there is something sad, the dog cries; with each amusing incident the dog yips with glee. Finally, the man taps the dog's owner on the shoulder and says, "I think it is amazing that your dog is so interested in this picture!"

The owner says, "This surprises me, too. He didn't care a thing for the book."

A speaker likes the crack about having an "old-fashioned girl —she never drinks anything else." Obviously this is better for the country club ladies' night dinner than it is at the Epworth League.

A doctor's convention liked the following one, but the League of Women Voters didn't:

A colored minister called for all the virgins in the congregation to stand. In the back of the house a "tall yaller" gal stood with a baby in her arms. The preacher said, "Sister Washington, perhaps ya-all didn't heah the announcement right. I wants only da *virgins* to stan'."

The "tall yaller" gal said, "Lan' sake, Parson, you don' think this little bitty ole baby can *stan' by herself*, does ya?"

In one of his sparkling after-dinner speeches Jimmy Gheen demonstrates that nothing can be funny unless the experience of the audience can fill in the missing elements. For example, he tells a story that falls flat because the point depends upon the audience knowing how many players there are on a cricket team. It would have gone great in England, but it was a dud in Eureka Springs.

In the parlance of horse fanciers the term "easy keeper" means a horse will stay fat on almost any diet. A speaker told a story at the Round-Up Club concerning a prospective buyer who asked an owner if his horse was an "easy keeper." The owner said, "Oh, yes! In fact, you are the first fellow who ever wanted to buy him."

The story got over so well at the Round-Up Club, that the speaker tried it on the local Kiwanis Club the next Thursday noon. This time the result was such that the speaker asked the chairman if the public address system had failed.

## Humor Should Be Kind

A third basic principle representing the successful use of humor as a device in public speaking is: *never be unkind*.

To be funny, things must be said in fun. This is often the difference between the humorous story and wit. As Mark Twain said, the former is soft and bubbly, but the latter can be cruel and cutting. Cervantes said, "Jests that slap the face are not good jests."

When asked what humor is, Will Rogers responded, ". . . Almost anything . . . you happen to hit . . . just right." Then he added, "But there's one thing I'm proud of—I ain't got it in for anybody. I don't like to make jokes that hurt anybody."

Take a page from the notebook of a master like Will Rogers. If you must hurt someone to get a laugh, forget it. It isn't worth it. There are too many better ways of doing it. Some time ago I was at a meeting where a rather blustering, but well-meaning citizen was admonishing his fellow citizens in a civic club concerning some local conditions. At the conclusion of his remarks he apologized for his bluntness by saying, "It's the only way I know how to do it. I always speak straight from the shoulder."

A second speaker on the same program transfixed the first one with a single shaft of wit, by saying, "John must be right when he says he speaks straight from the shoulder. So far as I could tell, none of his ideas originated any *higher* than that."

The crowd laughed at this remark, but it was a nervous, uncomfortable laugh. The speaker who uses wit and humor to hurt people soon becomes *feared,* rather than admired and loved. He is the professional gunman who is too quick on the draw for the average God-fearing citizen. You find yourself uncomfortable because you have a feeling the next person he guns down may be you.

If you do tell a story on someone in the audience, precede it, or follow it, with a compliment. Let the audience know you intended nothing personal. When A. E. Winship was a schoolmaster, there was one back country lad whom he had to discipline frequently. After one such session Winship told the boy that making students mind was a part of a teacher's job, and that he bore no personal grudge. The tough-edged but kind-hearted boy said, "I know you are okay. You jaw me a lot, but I always notice your eyes ain't mad."

Do you remember the Scot whose Christmas gift to his wife was an X-ray picture of his own chest? He said, "I can't spend my money on her gift this year but I want her to know my heart is in the right place." A speaker will do well to keep his audience periodically reminded that his heart is in the right place.

### Go Easy with Jokes on Race or Religion

As a general rule jokes that have to do with race and religion are risky. However, the taboo on these classifications has been carried to such an extreme recently that the pendulum is swinging back somewhat. Common sense is coming back into the picture again, and it is being learned that *judgment* can be applied in these matters, as in all others. For example, the most lovable single characteristic of the colored race is its magnificent sense of humor. It is silly to arbitrarily eliminate all the wonderful stories that have eminated from that boundlessly rich source. Yet these stories should be told in ways that are not in any sense degrading to the race, and they should be told only in settings where no one will be hurt, or even slightly embarrassed.

Similarly, stories pertaining to religious and denominational groups must be handled with care. This, by no means, negates their usefulness. For example, the writer addressed a dinner meeting of a hospital association in Minneapolis, at which a Catholic Sister presided. She brought the house down with a priceless story of a little old Irish lady who came to America on a ship. The Irish lady brought along some of her native brandy, and while enroute she took a nip occasionally to keep herself in good cheer. She still had about two-thirds of one bottle left when she went through customs in New York. When the inspector inquired what was in the bottle she answered, "Holy water." The inspector removed the cork, sniffed the contents, and said, "It smells to me like good Irish brandy."

The little old lady seized the bottle, smelled it, and shouted, "Praise the Lord! It's a *miracle!*"

This story, told by the Catholic sister, was a block-buster. The story could be safely told by anyone who *would attribute it to her*. This plan gives the speaker the added precaution of identifying the *source* of his story as someone in the religious group concerned.

### Dialect Stories Are Risky

Another general rule which is proved by its exceptions is the one which says: *never tell dialect stories*. This rule was set up by public speaking authorities to protect the public from one of the most murderous devices to which meeting-going mammals are exposed. I recently heard a speaker nauseate a crowd with some Swedish dialect stories that were as lengthy as they were pointless and unintelligible. The only single adjective that could describe it was moronic. Another recent occasion brought out a "Scot" complete with the kilt and bagpipes. He had made a two-week tour of Scotland and developed this program to "entertain" his "friends" for the rest of his life—which they now fervently hope will be short. He put "bur-r-rs" in places that my own native clan in Scotland never heard of, and the general effect of his dialogue was to put a "burr" in the chair of every listener. If a general law could be passed that would put this type of character out of business, it would be worthwhile, no matter how many really funny dialect artists were barred by the same legislation.

In spite of the prejudice which the ham dialecticians have built up in the public mind, there are certain types of these stories that are terrific when properly told. Without the dialect they lose their flavor completely. Anyone will understand this point who has heard Sam Cohen say, "Piece goods on earth, good wool toward men!"

A good rule on the dialect story is to undertake it with fear and trembling. Try it on your friends first. Then ask them frankly if it is better without the dialect than with it. Finally, ask them in all kindness to tell you whether it is any good *either way*. If it passes their test, then check it against the back drop of your audience. If you sincerely think this particular audience will like it, and you are confident it will not offend anyone, then blaze away.

It is also well to handle with special care any stories that pertain to physical afflictions. For example, the story of the short-legged man with the stuttering son (page 140) would hardly be appropriate in a meeting where the chairman, or some other prominent personality, had a speech impediment, or was physically crippled.

### Don't Fly Off the Nest if You Lay an Egg

Let us suppose you select a story with loving care. It fits naturally into the speech, like a friend who wants to help you put over your theme. You put the story through all the tests, you work it smoothly into the presentation, you check with the chairman the day of the meeting to be sure it has not been previously used for his group, you get the punch line off just right—and blop!—it hits the ground with a sickening thud like a dying duck in a hail storm. There isn't even a ripple of response. What do you do?

When you discover you have "laid an egg" instead of giving the people an intended laugh, the thing to do is to *move on* to the next point. Don't try any salvage operations on the sunken point. Let it go. *Never wait for a laugh*. And do not emphasize the fact that your joke flopped by continuing in the vein of the engineer previously mentioned who resumed in his discourse, after each period of silence, by saying, "Seriously, I . . ."

Some professional masters of ceremonies, entertainers, and after-dinner speakers can almost pull a laugh out of a crowd by refusing to let a joke die. This is dangerous business for an amateur to attempt, and is not too productive for the seasoned veteran. For example, when Louis Nizer tells a story that falls flat, he will sometimes pause and say, "I think I'll try that one on the other side of the house—this side is *dead*."

Other speakers will say, "You may as well laugh *now*, because this isn't going to get any funnier."

A typical M. C. response to a dead joke is to peer out from under the spotlight and say to the audience, "I know you are out there because I can hear you breathing."

The speaker should also be cautioned on how to handle an unexpected laugh. Do not appear startled. If you have already started your next sentence when the laughter breaks, then smilingly wait for the folks to enjoy themselves, but do not wait too long. As the laughter subsides, break through it and start your next point over again.

### If You Use Humor—Make It Yours

Speakers can learn to develop their own distinctive styles and techniques in using humor. Tom Collins, of Kansas City, is the "dead pan," sad-voiced type. Hamilton Moses, of Arkansas Power and Light, has developed a delightful device of telling several stories in succession but withholding the punch lines. Then he gives his audience all the punch lines at once, and there are continued bursts of laughter as his hearers fit the points to the stories.

Chick Sale used to tell of the small town depot agent who was a one-man show. His railroad did not believe in "feather-bedding." The agent sold tickets, served as telegrapher, hustled baggage, ran the concession stand, and cared for a flower garden beside the station house. One morning his waiting room was full of passengers and the agent was receiving a telegraph message.

Complete with green visor and black sleeve protectors he listened
intently as he wrote down the message, and at the same time he
was caring for his customers.

One man looked through the grill on the ticket window and
asked, "When is the next west bound?"

The agent replied, "Just a minute, please," and kept on taking
down the message.

Another passenger asked, "When is the Rochester Express due
in?"

Without looking up from his keyboard and pad the agent said,
"Just a moment, sir."

An anxious mother said, "My little daughter is playing near
that fish pool in the flower garden—how deep is it?"

"Just a moment, madam," said the agent.

Picking up some individualized super-king-size cigarettes off
the concession stand, a waiting passenger yelled to the agent,
"How much are these?"

"I'll be with you right away," the agent said. Then finishing
his message, he tapped out his sign off, turned to the people who
had made the inquires and pointed to each as he answered them
in the order of their questions:

"Half past eight."

"Quarter to nine."

"Up to her neck."

"Three for a dime."

### The Genius of Story Telling—
### Have a Good Point and Get to It

The other "must" for using modern humor is that it *must be
snappy*. The expensive time element involved in television shows
has been a contributing factor in the necessity for making humor
move faster than it once did. In the days of Mark Twain, Irvin
Cobb, and Governor Bob Taylor, a crowd would let a speaker
take five minutes in leisurely building up to one good punch line.
Those days are gone forever. If your story cannot be contained
in a few sentences, then you have the alternative of either aban-
doning it, or else giving the people a few chortles as you proceed
to your main point. For example, note how a few by-product
points keep the following story alive while it moves ahead.

I am not here to tell you how to run your business. I have learned not to "take over"—even in small groups—in fact, even if there is just one other person involved. Some years ago I was going down Twelfth Street in Kansas City, Missouri, when I was stopped by a bum. You see, this was several years ago. *Now* he would be a "poor unfortunate victim of adverse economic circumstances," and he would need several highly paid social workers to analyze his case. But everyone used to know that guys like that were bums. This one knew it, himself—in fact, he was the one who told me. He said,

"I'm hungry. Now, wait—I see that look on your face . . . ."

I said, "What look?"

He said, "You're goin' to tell me that I am a lazy no-good, and that I ought to get a job and quit panhandlin'—I *know* that. But there's no time to discuss it right now. I wish you would believe me when I tell you that at this moment I am hungrier than I have ever been in my life before."

I said, "I do believe you, and I am going to buy you a good meal."

Actually, I enjoy opportunities to talk to those boys once in a while. It is easy to find out what the boys in the jet airliners are thinking, but I also want to hear occasionally from the boys under the water tank. These gentlemen of the road are pretty sharp sometimes. For example, there was the bum who was sleeping behind the bunker on the golf course one sunny morning when he was discovered by the club manager. The manager gave the bum a kick amidships, and the bum leaped to his feet and said, "Who are *you*?"

The manager said, "I am the *manager* of this golf club!"

"Well," the bum said, "this is a hell of a way to get new members!"

Yes, these lads are honed by adversities and they get pretty sharp. But to return to my Kansas City bum—I took him into a small restaurant on Twelfth Street. I made up my mind that if I were going to buy him a meal I would buy him a good one, and I would eat with him. When a waitress came to our table, I said,

"I want to order *two* of the biggest Kansas City steaks in the house, and *everything* that goes with them."

The bum's face beamed with pleasure as he turned to the waitress and said,

"And I'll take the same!"

## How to Determine Whether a Story is "Proper"

One of the most significant factors for success in public speaking comes in the individual's ability to accurately assess what is *proper* to say, and what should be avoided. Nothing devastates a speaker's effectiveness any quicker than to have him exceed the bounds of decency and good taste in either his stories or his general remarks. Since most of the transgressions in this important category come in the story-telling department, it is appropriate that we devote some straight thinking to the issue right here.

How do we determine whether a particular story, statement, or word is suitable for a particular audience? The answer to this is powerful in its simplicity. If there is *any question* as to whether you should use it—then *there is no question*—you do *not* use it. Here is a fine place to make your mistakes on the conservative side. Even though the joke is perfect for your point, even though you heard it used for a similar group somewhere else, if its use would push you close to the border line of impropriety, then ruthlessly prune it from your outline. If you feel rather confident that the point is fully acceptable, but still have some slight misgivings, you will be wise to test it with friends whose judgment you respect. You may say, "Everyone laughed when they heard the story in Jersey City," but you are now talking to another audience, in another city, and under different circumstances. Furthermore, while the people in the Jersey City audience may have laughed, they may also have made some post-meeting comments which were not flattering to the speaker's judgment.

There is no worthwhile market for crudity. If there are "no ladies present," there should be gentlemen present. If there are no gentlemen present, what are *you* doing there? Abraham Lincoln, Franklin Roosevelt, and many other great speakers loved a snappy story in private, and recounted tales to small groups and individuals that were on the "salty" side. The fact that a story makes lively head table conversation does not necessarily mean it should go over the footlights.

I recently heard a convention speaker whose stories, statements and vocabulary kept his audience in a state of nervous and restrained laughter. His hearers were constantly turning to look at others and study the effect the stories were having on the crowd. Many of the speaker's remarks were "borderline" in nature, and others were definitely over the line. His hearers were alert but uneasy. The question on many minds was "What will he say *next*? When will he become *impossible*?" Of course, the audience was in no state to receive any real ideas or to be inspired

by anything. After the meeting one member of the audience
made this acid appraisal of the speaker,

"Every story he told had to do with sex or bodily eliminations.
I don't believe the guy ever gets his mind above his waistline."

Before you risk exceeding the bounds of good taste in speech,
you should ask yourself whether you would be proud to have such
an appraisal made of you and your speech? This is a good point
to dwell upon before you start running roughshod across the
lines of conventional standards, good manners, sound judgment,
and basic morality. Leave the gutter stories in the gutters—
never bring them into the meeting places.

### There Is a Choice Between the "Low Brow" and the "Blue Nose"

While there is always danger in playing too close to the "loose
lipped low brows," there is another danger—though much less
lethal—in permitting yourself to be paced by the "blue noses."
Some sad souls go through this world like the man with the limburger cheese on his nose, and to them *everything smells bad."*
To cater to them is also folly.

I know a superintendent of schools who constantly expects
to be shocked and is rarely disappointed. He personally clips
all "offensive" ads and articles from the new magazines before
they are put in the school library. He got his degree in a "hard
shell" college where he must have majored in monotony. His
friends say he is so modest he won't write an improper fraction
on the blackboard. He confided in me that he never attends
"modern movies."

I asked, "Why? Haven't you got the money?"

He said, "Oh, yes. It isn't a question of finance. It is just that
they are *all* so *suggestive.* After I have seen one of them I want
to go home and literally *fumigate* my mind!"

I finally asked this man if it had ever occurred to him that if
*everything* is suggestive, there must be something wrong with *him.*
After all, these things do not tell him the point—they apparently
just *suggest* things that he *already knows.* I told him of the girl
who had a date with a soldier. When she came home, she told
her mother she was *never* going out with that boy again because
he knew a "whole lot of naughty songs."

Her mother asked, "Did he sing such songs in your presence?"

The girl said, "Oh, no. He doesn't sing any of the words. He just whistles the tunes."

The late Reverend William Alexander, of Oklahoma City, lead his congregation in the building of a futuristic "church of tomorrow." Bill's followers were devoted, but a few of his church members dragged their feet in going along with some of his modern innovations. The Youth Center of the beautiful new church was referred to by some of the ultra-conservatives as "Alexander's Pool Hall." All of this made Bill particularly attentive as he listened to a fellow minister preach a sermon entitled, "Why Youth Should Not Dance."

"After the conservative divine had listed all his reasons," Bill reported later, "I'll admit I was *confused*. After listening to him, I didn't know whether young people should dance, or not. But I was sure of one thing—*he* shouldn't!"

Dr. Alexander declared that if a long face is a prerequisite for piety, then a mule should be the noblest of all creatures.

I delivered an after-dinner address for the annual banquet meeting of a bankers association in a southern city. At the head table was a member of the local clergy who had been invited to deliver the invocation and be a guest at the dinner. The speech effort that evening rolled along nicely from the first, and picked up power as it went. At the close it was rewarded with a standing ovation that was both genuine and prolonged. I went home feeling good. I had the genuine satisfaction that comes with being confident one has rendered a real service to his fellow men, and that it is appreciated. In the days that followed the mail contained numerous letters from people who had attended the meeting, and their general tone perpetuated the glow of satisfaction I felt—until I got a letter from the minister. He said nothing whatever about the service the speech had rendered, nor how it had been received by the crowd. He simply felt "constrained" to tell me the message would have been stronger had I omitted from one of my stories the word "damn."

It apparently did not occur to this man that he was an *invited guest,* who was "taking over the party" and thus subjecting to serious question his own sense of what is proper. It apparently did not occur to him that "everyone was out of step" but himself. The limburger had been on his blue nose too long, and had caused him to lose his perspective.

One minister friend of mine declares that after living forty years among the "good" people he understood better "why Christ chose to spend His time among the sinners."

Regardless of whether we endorse or decry the trend, the public is becoming more realistic as to what words may be used in polite society. The movies and television have had to break out of certain codes that made some of their efforts juvenile to the point of being ridiculous.

Movie directors reached a point where they simply could not stomach the process of watering down their scripts until all the fire was completely extinguished. They knew, and the public knew, that when an Indian's arrow drove into the chest of a cavalryman and sent him crashing off his horse, the tough old sergeant in command of the patrol wasn't going to turn around, spit out his chewing tobacco, and say, "Gee whiz! What will those red rascals think of next?"

In a recent movie Anthony Quinn plays the part of a tough rancher. At one point he exclaims to a cow hand, "You know damn well what I am talking about! Now, you get your butt off this place! And if you ever come back, I'll kill ya!"

That still is not what the rancher probably said, but it begins to convey a more accurate impression of the spirit of the occasion. Furthermore, the vast majority of people who watch westerns these days would probably rule that this script is acceptable.

If a man steps in an empty clothes basket in the darkness at the head of the basement stairs—and goes all the way, hitting every step—it just doesn't make sense that he is going to announce his arrival at the bottom by saying, "Oh, Fudge!"

The speaker must learn to *sense* the appropriate. He should make his mistakes on the conservative side without robbing his illustrations of their *virility*. On the one hand he must not risk legitimate offense; on the other hand he must not be Casper

Milquetoast. I do not know of a single great speaker who could be characterized as "gutless." To be a gentleman one must be gentle, but he can also be a *man*.

Whether a story or a general approach is appropriate must be weighed in the light of the occasion, the speaker, and the audience.

### A *"Good"* Story May Not Be Good *for* You

Stories, terminology, and illustrations that would be entirely inappropriate in one setting may be commendable and effective in another. For example, the writer heard Bob Longtoft, a hard-hitting sales manager, open a meeting of his sales staff. Personally, I would not use Bob's approach, because it is not my style. Yet I would not be critical of Bob and say he was too rough—because the humor was *his* style. It was natural and easy, his hearers understood it and genuinely liked it, and it *achieved its purpose*. Here is Bob's opening:

It is good to have you guys come in from all over the territory for these sales meetings. I *like* to see you! There is not a man in here who doesn't know that I genuinely like him personally. I call you "my boys." And some of you call me "Pops," or the "Old Man." Sometimes when I trim the profit out of your expense statements, you call me other things. But you know I am always on the level with you. It makes me proud when you smile and say, "Same Old Bob!" I know that sometimes to shorten this, you say, "S.O.B." But we *understand* one another, and you are still *my boys*—even though I occasionally have to let some of you know you are of the illegitimate variety.

Now, the one thing that a man wants is to be *proud* of his children. The state penitentiary warden told one of my neighbors recently that his son was getting out of stir six months early on account of his good behavior, and my neighbor said, "I *knew* that boy would make good!"

A father in the Carolina mountains proudly told the census taker that his oldest boy was down at the state university. The census taker said, "What is he studying?"

And the mountaineer said,

"He ain't studyin' nuthin'. They're studyin' *him*. He's got two heads."

It was in those same mountains that I ran across a touching inscription on a gravestone. It said,

Here lies my daughter, Charlotte—
Born a virgin and died a Harlot.
For thirteen years she kept her virginity—
That's the all-time record for this vicinity.

The fathers in these three illustrations had one thing in common—
they wanted so much to be proud of their children that *they stretched
a point to do it*. Now, I want to be proud of my boys, too, but when
I look at your last quarter's sales record I have to do a hell of a lot of
stretching!

Frankly, the reason I am so glad to see you this morning is that I
thought some of you had died. We had company life insurance checks
ready to mail some of your wives. I see Howard Stickly here with his
arm in a sling. That explains why he hasn't been able to write any
orders, but we are going to find out in the next three days why the
rest of you haven't been writing any.

If there is any man in here who thinks he knows all about selling,
let him stand and say so. The rest of you are going to learn how. The
vacation is over, boys. School is starting *now*!

As a general rule, a speaker is safer *quoting* a stronger word
than he is in making it a part of his own text. While he was not
required to use the word in either case, the latter is more obviously his own choice. For example, in the story at the opening
of Chapter 10, page 151, the strong words are contained in the
statement by Parson Wilkes. The average audience would obviously be more tolerant of this language from the rough hewn
mountaineer than it would from you. To a degree, you enjoy
the objectivity of a reporter. Of course, you must take the
responsibility for what you report.

In addressing the so-called "Millionaires Club" in Florida, the
late Charles Kettering used a few words of profanity. Following
the meeting he was approached by an old friend, S. S. Kresge, the
distinguished founder of the Kresge Stores. Kresge, who had
earned his reputation as a straight-laced teetotaler said, "Ket,
your speech would have been better if you had omitted the cuss
words."

"Boss" Kettering responded by saying, "Sebastian, that wasn't
the real me saying those words. That was those damn Martinis
I had before the meeting!"

There are some stories that must contain the strong word to

retain their power and point. In such cases, the speaker must decide whether to use the whole story, or none of it. Other stories can undergo some alteration without losing a damaging percentage of their punch. There can be no set rules to govern such things. If you cannot *sense* the answers to such problems, you probably should not be telling stories.

One well-known speaker appraises the problem this way:

There are many good stories that are good for most any occasion. Other "good" stories are good for some occasions. And some stories are too "good" for any occasion.

### Test Yourself on What Is Appropriate

Let us take a test story of a type that does not contain strong language, but leaves an impression that is either funny, unfunny, or borderline:

For weeks a little girl had wanted to bathe with her mother. Finally the mother succumbed to the begging. The two had no sooner gotten in the tub together than the little girl burst out crying.

The mother exclaimed, *"Now,* what is the matter? You have pestered me all this time to take a bath with you, and here you are, embarrassed."

"It isn't that," said the little girl. "It's just that I am so *plain* and you are so *fancy!"*

Suppose you test your "story judgment" with the above story. Do *you* think it is funny? If so, would you use it for a P.T.A. meeting? County Medical Association? The Lion's Club? A college commencement? The Farm Bureau? The Sales Executives?

What about this one:

A backwoods preacher was discussing sin with a pipe-smoking hill woman who was a member of his church.

She said, "Parson, you are a fine preacher for us hill folks. We never really knowed what sin was until you come here."

Accepting this as the compliment he was sure she had intended, the preacher continued the discussion of wickedness by remarking, "Sister Smith, I think adultery is just as bad a sin as murder, don't you?"

The old lady puffed on her pipe while she contemplated that one, and finally she said, "I don't reckon I rightly know, Parson. I ain't never kilt nobody."

Do you think this story is funny?

In *your particular station in life,* can *you* tell this story and retain all the dignity you need to put over the most important parts of your speech? Could you tell it to some groups and realize a profitable gain, with no off-setting losses? Would the Elks Convention like it? The Business and Professional Womens Club? The American Legion? The American Association of University Women? The Audubon Society?

Let us try one more "preacher story." A minister had completed his morning service and was standing at the door, greeting his parishioners as they filed out. Presently a man stepped up, vigorously shook the minister's hand, looked admiringly into his eye, and said, "Parson that was a *damn* good sermon!"

The minister drew back in surprise, as did several of the parishioners who overheard. But the minister recovered quickly. Taking the man's hand warmly in both of his, the minister said,

"Friend—I call you 'friend,' although you are a stranger to me. I have never seen your face in my congregation until this morning. But I want you to know you are *welcome* here. And I want you to know, further, that I appreciate that fifty-dollar bill the usher tells me you dropped in the collection plate this morning. Some of the folks around here don't seem to understand it, but it takes a hell of a lot of money to run a church like this!"

Do you feel this story has *any* merit at all? Have you heard it before? Would you assume everyone has?

In *your total circumstances*—being *whom your are*—could you ever tell this story? If so, to what kind of a meeting would you feel safe in addressing it?

### Enrich Your Repertoire With Some "Quickie" Stories

In using humor there is an important place for the "quickies." They can be made to sweeten the mixture at most any time without seriously changing its consistency. If the quickie can be a new twist to an old tale, it is that much better. For example, there is the one about the man who said to his doctor,

"Doc, I never felt better in my life—and I think its high time I did."

Or take this one from Jack Parr:

"Washington's father did not punish him for cutting down the cherry tree because George still had the hatchet in his hand."

It is obvious what a clever clincher the Jack Parr quickie would be for a speech urging *preparedness* for some particular job, or eventuality. You could nail the preparedness point neatly by adding to the above joke the following serious fact:

"Last year there were 50,000 hold-ups in America. In not one case did a bandit hold up a uniformed policeman."

### Humor Can Save Sales

Humor has long been recognized as a great aid in selling. It is important to keep the customer in a buying mood. The old-time "salesmen" depended far too heavily upon humor. They knew all the latest stories but seldom improved their knowledge of their products. Some, like Myron Cohen, finally discovered their "customers" liked their stories better than their merchandise—so they quit selling merchandise and became professional story tellers.

Auctioneers often become artists in the quick change-of-pace, and in using quips that keep people buying. In the famous horse sale held annually at Lexington, Kentucky, the price of an old show horse had reached $465 when the bidding stopped cold. The auctioneer suddenly ceased his professional clatter, changed his voice to an intimate conversational tone, and over the loud speaker addressed the man who made the next-to-the-last bid. Said the auctioneer,

"Sam, I am trying to get $500 for this horse. If you will bid that, I'll sell him to you without any more argument. Sam, I want you to bid me $500. Then I want you to take this horse home and keep him for thirty days. If, at the end of thirty days, you don't like this horse—then you had better *get* to liking him—because *he is your horse!* You are not going to bring him back *here*—I'll tell you that *now!*"

This quick, humorous turn made the crowd laugh, the sale came to life, the bidding started, and the show horse sold to a new bidder at $750. There are many times when speakers can keep their hearers in a "buying mood," with the same psychological concept.

This chapter has attempted to demonstrate that humor is not an indispensable ingredient in a good speech, but it is a powerful aid when properly used.

I have said in an earlier chapter that *after* one prepares his own material, then he should go back and see if someone else has said the same thing before him, and said it better. I followed this procedure, and discovered Lorenzo Sears reached some of "my" conclusions before I was born. He declared humor is "an art that conceals an art," and added "needful lightness of expression may cover thoughts that are profound. Good humor may render palatable truths that are in themselves distasteful." And he concluded his discourse in humor as I shall conclude mine, by stating that "humorous stories and statements are *most useful* to illustrate, advance, and enliven a speech; especially when they seem to fall naturally into the line of remarks. Fortunate is the man who has his quiver full of these arrows and knows which one to draw, and when."

## Points to Ponder

Humor is a wonderful tool in the hands of the man who knows how to use it, but it can be fatal for the man who doesn't.

Humor should be used as a tool. It nails down ideas but is not a substitute for them.

Humor is tremendously useful to condition an audience, to clinch points, to accent illustrations, to provide changes of pace, and to occasionally use for conclusions.

Humor should come into your speech *naturally* because it is *yours* and fits into your situation.

No story is "good" that violates good taste or is inappropriate for the audience that hears it.

"Handle with Care" is the correct label for all stories involving race, religion, dialect, and politics.

Modern audiences want less build-up and more punch lines. Make it snappy. When correctly used humor will help sell both ideas and merchandise.

# 14

# The Indispensable Quality

I once addressed a convention of speech teachers, and in the question-and-answer period which followed I was asked,

"Can you state in one word what quality is most to be desired in public speaking?"

Had the question taken me completely by surprise, I think I could have answered in one word, "No." But fortunately I had pondered that point before. I was, therefore, able to give the group one of those "impromptu" answers upon which I had cogitated for years. I was able to defend my answer that day to the apparent satisfaction of the assembled experts, and I am more confident of it now. The answer I gave was *"Vitality."* It is the only word I know that embodies most of what is desired in the speaker, the content of the speech, and the delivery.

Both the dictionary and the book of synonyms will reinforce the contention that vitality is the best single ingredient to seek in speech. The word is found to mean "of critical importance," "truth," "imparting life and vigor," "animation," "living," "fundamental," "essential," "important," "significant," "necessary," "needful," "exhuberant," "something having vital force."

In the early chapters and throughout this book it has been stressed that the speaker cannot be separated from his speech. His words must ring true because he speaks from the *inner* convictions of a life that rings true. Both his life and his words must qualify as "something having vital force."

It is significant that the best of the periodicals in the speech field is entitled *Vital Speeches*.

The speaker should fairly exhume physical vitality, and his voice should be vibrant with it. The audience should be able to relax with the assurance that the speaker's reserve of physical power is many times more than he will need for the occasion. This personification of limitless power is consistently listed in the assets of great speakers.

In contrast, a friend of mine returned from a meeting to tell me he had just heard a "bang-up" speech. He said the speech was "banged-up" and the speaker was a "total wreck."

## Vitality Is Much More Than Enthusiasm

Whole chapters have been written on the necessity of the speaker possessing enthusiasm. But vitality is a bigger word than enthusiasm. It *contains* enthusiasm, along with *truth* and other "life giving qualities" that insure the proper *directing* of enthusiasm.

Norton points out that "Enthusiasm for art inspired Leonardo da Vinci, when he painted the Last Supper at Milan, but the French soldiers destroyed it with equal fervor." John the Baptist was enthusiastic, but so was Adolph Hitler. Nero's enthusiasm for playing the violin resulted in the burning of Rome. The Christians who died in the Roman Arena were enthusiastic about their objective, but so were the lions that devoured them. The Devil himself must be enthusiastic to carry on such an aggressive program, and Mark Twain became so enthusiastic over the Devil's managerial and leadership qualities that he paid Satan this tribute:

"Any man who can administer half of the world's spiritual life, and all of its political life, must be an administrator of the highest order."

Successful people are enthusiastic, but villains are, too. It is like saying the best things in life are free and ignoring the fact that there is no charge for the worst things, either.

A friend told me he was discouraged, and an enthusiastic acquaintance said, "Cheer up! Things could be worse."

"So," said my friend, "I cheered up—and sure enough—things got worse."

Enthusiasm is not enough. *Vitality* is the bigger word. One writer points out how easy it should be for a devoted minister of the gospel to acquire vitality—"a life-giving quality." The clergy-man *knows* God has changed his life. Therefore, he *knows* God can change any *life*. This *truth* fires him with missionary zeal—"something having vital force." He must tell the story to others. What wonderful news he has—the age of miracles is not past! With this vital knowledge and its limitless potential for doing good, the minister dedicates his life to his work, and the mission-ary goes forth. Then there arise such names as Dwight Moody, Billy Sunday, Billy Graham, Norman Vincent Peale, Bishop Sheen, and Rabbi Abba Hillel Silver. And in what form did they emerge before the world? *As great speakers.*

Is the quality of vitality—"possessing truth of critical impor-tance"—limited to the clergy? By no means! The insurance man can become vitalized when he sees a true vision of his potential for serving other people. He has the only method by which he can create an immediate estate to protect the future of those whom he loves more than life itself. And, if insurance can do that for *his* family, it can do it for *any* family. Another type of mis-sionary is born. Any educator worth his salt should be on fire with the fact that more and better education is mankind's only hope to win the race against world-wide catastrophe. How could a man in the transportation industry fail to comprehend that our civilization literally rolls on wheels, and thus be vitalized by the "critical importance" of his mission. The businessman, the sales-man, and the advertising man who sincerely study economics must see the *vital* importance of their work. They are the ones who keep the pipelines of the economy flowing. They are the "gas and oil" of the free enterprise vehicle that delivers all the wonderful things we call the "American standard of living." The soldier stands guard over this precious heritage. The journalist keeps the torch of freedom burning bright in the minds of our people, while the physician has the thrill of literally "imparting life and vigor"—*all of these* emerge in the all-embracing mag-nificent quality of *vitality!*

> Every mason in the quarry,
> > Every builder on the shore,
> Every chopper in the forest,
> > Every raftsman at the oar,

> Hewing wood and drawing water,
>> Splitting stones and cleaving sod,
> All the dusty ranks of labor,
>> In the regiment of God,
> March together toward His triumph,
>> Do the task His hands prepare:
> Honest toil is holy service:
>> Faithful work is praise and prayer.
>>>> —Author unknown.

## Speech Titles Should Reflect Vitality

Vitality should be reflected in the *title* of a speech. Speech titles often serve as the "advance man" for the speaker. The club or organization hears and reads that "next week Mr. Millard Wilson, local airline executive, will bring us a speech entitled 'Forty Years of Flying.'" If you did not know Mr. Wilson, how would you feel about this title? Would you be eager to attend next week's meeting? Perhaps the forthcoming meeting would have more appeal for you if Mr. Wilson were scheduled to "bring a sparkling speech" entitled *"Fasten Your Seat Belts!"* Or perhaps you would perk up if you saw this title for Mr. Wilson's air age speech: "You Can Eat Lunch Tomorrow *Anywhere!*" Animated titles alert the audience to the fact that you are coming. This is true whether the subject is announced a week in advance, or at the time you are introduced.

Some titles are so vital, so meaningful, and so perfectly fitted to the speech that they become monuments in their own right. Witness "Acres of Diamonds" and "The Cross of Gold."

One of the classic sermon titles of all time is Dwight Moody's, "Pontius Pilate's Question."

I never heard Mr. Moody speak. He died years before I was born. I read the sermon, "Pontius Pilate's Question," just one time and that was nearly thirty years ago. Yet its vitality was so great that it has *lived* with me all these years. Let us briefly examine this as a perfect example of fitting a title to a speech.

Pontius Pilate, the Roman governor before whom Christ was brought for "trial," had to make a decision. It was a decision like unto which all his other decisions were to be forever dwarfed into insignificance. The question he faced head-on was: *"What shall I do with the man called Jesus?"*

In Moody's great sermon he drives home the fact that the answer Pilate made to that question *determined his place in all eternity.* He had to decide between what was *right* and what was *popular.* Pilate first tried desperately to side-step the responsibility. Then he tried to settle for a partial answer. After that failed he suffered a complete collapse of character and made the wrong answer. Finally Pilate called for a vessel of water and attempted to literally wash his hands of the whole thing.

Now Moody is set up for the *vital scoring punch* of his sermon. *Every man* must answer Pilate's question: "What shall *I* do with the man Jesus?"—There is no escaping it. And how you answer it determines *your place in eternity!*

It is obvious that in this title and this speech we have a most vital theme for an evangelistic sermon. The objective of the speech is to make converts for Christianity, and the whole discourse hooks together in a manner that is vitalizing to the extreme.

Examples of other titles with spark and appeal are:

> How to Fail Successfully
> Sense, Common and Preferred
> Cats and Kings
>> ("A cat can look at a king," but only
>> through a cat's eyes.)
> The Hands of Esau
>> (A political speech accusing the state
>> party chairman of actually making the
>> appointments that were announced by
>> the governor.)
> The One Talent Man
> Cast Down Your Buckets Where You Are
> Wake The Town and Tell The People
> No Room at the Inn
> Keeping the White House White
> Alice in Blunderland

For some examples of threadbare titles that do not possess vitality consider these:

America at the Crossroads
Democracy and Education
Ten Rules of Success

## *Talk About Things* That Make a Difference

It cannot be over-stressed that to possess vitality your speech must be something you have lived.

The writer presided at a dinner meeting of educators honoring a missionary who had returned after many years of service in Africa. At the head table the missionary was a fascinating conversationalist. For example, he told of the war the farmers in certain sections of Africa carry on against the baboons who raid their fields. The farmers will drive off the raiders but the baboons sit out of gun range and wait for the farmers to leave the field. If five people came into the field and four leave, the baboons know one is hiding in wait for them, and they do not come back until he is gone. But the farmers have learned that the baboons cannot count beyond five. If six farmers go in the field and one hides, the baboons will fall for the trap. At the head table the missionary gave us wonderfully interesting accounts of the racial problems and other features of African life. Then he was introduced to speak. And what was his subject? "American Education." He was addressing a banquet meeting of teachers and he felt he had chosen a subject that would interest them. Actually, he had selected the one subject upon which he was undoubtedly the poorest prepared person in the room. The result was disastrous. The saddest thing about the situation was that he could have given his audience a real bell-ringer speech on almost any of the subjects he had discussed informally at the head table.

Many speeches are dull because they answer questions no one is asking. A speech should be good, but not "out of this world." Vitality comes with intense convictions about things that vitally affect both the speaker and the audience. In the little Kansas town where I grew up, there lived an old lady whose reactions to the town problems were always most intense. At one period of time the town was divided into a fight on local school issues. Someone said to the old lady, "Mrs. Green, which side of the school fight are you on?"

She said, "I haven't made up my mind yet, but when I do—I shall be very bitter."

I am sure even Mrs. Green made a more lasting impression on her fellow citizens than did the chameleon individuals who simply turned whatever color was necessary to harmonize with their surroundings.

### *When a Speech Is Sterilized of Its Vitality—Only Words Remain*

Job Hedges [2] humorously undertook to prepare a speech that would be "suitable for any occasion." His formula was simple—*sterilize* a speech. Make it *sound* like it had vitality, but still have it say *nothing*. Here is the result:

Mr. Chairman, Ladies and Gentlemen: It is indeed a great and undeserved privilege to address such an audience as I see before me. At no previous time in the history of human civilization have greater problems confronted and challenged the ingenuity of man's intellect than now. Let us look around us. What do we see on the horizon? What forces are at work? Whither are we drifting? Under what clouds of mist does the future stand obscured? My friends, casting aside the raiment of all human speech, the crucial test for the solution of all these intricate problems to which I have just alluded is the sheer and forceful application of those immutable laws which down the corridor of Time have always guided the hand of man, groping, as it were, for some faint beacon light for his hopes and aspirations. Without these great vital principles we are but puppets responding to whim and fancy, failing entirely to grasp the hidden meaning of it all. We must readdress ourselves to these questions which press for answer and solution. The issue cannot be avoided. There they stand. It is upon you—and you—and yet even upon me that the yoke of responsibility falls.

What, then, is our duty? Shall we continue to drift? No! With all the emphasis of my being I hurl back the message No! Drifting must stop. We must press onward and upward toward the ultimate good to which all must aspire. But I cannot conclude my remarks, dear friends, without touching briefly upon a subject which I know is steeped in your very consciousness. I refer to that spirit which gleams from the eyes of a new-born babe; that animates the toiling masses; that sways all the hosts of humanity past and present. Without this energizing principle all commerce, trade and industry are hushed and will perish from this earth as surely as the crimson sunset follows the

[2] Robert Davis in Lindgren, *Modern Speeches* (New York: F. S. Crofts and Company), 1930, pp. 66–67.

golden sunshine. Mark you, I do not seek to unduly alarm or distress the mothers, fathers, sons and daughters gathered before me in this vast assemblage, but I would indeed be recreant to a high resolve which I made as a youth if I did not at this time and in this place and with the full realizing sense of responsibility which I assume publicly declare and affirm my dedication and my concentration to the eternal principles and receipts of simple, ordinary, common-place *justice*.

For what, in the last analysis, is justice? Whence does it come? Where does it go? Is it tangible? It is not. Is it ponderable? It is not. Justice is none of these, and yet, on the other hand, in a sense it is all of these things combined. While I cannot tell you what justice is, this much I can tell you: that without the encircling arms of justice, without her shield, without her guardianship, the ship of state will sail through unchartered seas, narrowly avoiding rocks and shoals, headed inevitably to the harbor of calamity.

Justice! Justice! Justice! To thee we pay homage. To thee we dedicate our laurels of hope. Before thee we kneel in adoration, mindful of thy great power, mute before thy inscrutable destiny.

A room can be filled with such oratory as the above and yet be completely empty.

A newspaper reporter visited a nudist camp. In order to gain admittance and get his story, he had to go "au naturel" like the others. When he returned the reporter made a speech to the press club. His subject was announced in advance, and, of course, he attracted the biggest crowd in years. When he had finished his speech, he consented to a question-and-answer period. One eager reporter asked, "Of all the things in the nudist camp, what impressed you the most?"

With no hesitation the speaker answered, "Those cane bottom chairs!"

This is precisely the only kind of lasting impressions an audience could carry away from such a speech as the clever Job Hedges deliberately contrived "for all occasions." It is a speech designed *to make no difference*, and therefore is not *vital* to anyone.

*Some Examples of Vitality in Contemporary Speeches*

### CHARLES H. BROWER

Charles H. Brower,[3] president of a prominent New York adver-

---

[3] Charles H. Brower, President, Batten, Barton, Durstine and Osborn, Inc., New York, New York.

tising firm, delivered a vitalized address before the National Sales
Executives Convention in Washington, D. C., May 20, 1958,
from which the following is taken:

For this, in America, is the high tide of mediocrity, the great era
of the goof-off, the age of the half-done job. The land from coast to
coast has been enjoying a stampede away from responsibility. It is
populated with laundrymen who won't iron shirts, with waiters who
won't serve, with carpenters who will come around someday maybe,
with executives whose mind is on the golf course, with teachers who
demand a single salary schedule so that achievement cannot be rewarded, nor poor work punished, with students who take cinch courses
because the hard ones make them think, with spiritual delinquents of
all kinds who have been triumphantly determined to enjoy what was
known until the present crisis as "the new leisure." And the salesman
who won't sell is only a part of this over-all mess.

I think—and I hope to God it is true, that our people are becoming
sick of this goofing off. The reason I do not know, but I will guess that
we are gradually beginning to realize that history is repeating itself.
The Russians are doing a wonderful job as the barbarians in our
modern historical drama. But we are far outdoing them in our super-
lative imitation of Rome. We may lack a few of the refinements of
Rome's final decadence, but we do have the two hour lunch, the three
day weekend and the all-day coffee break. And, if you want to, you
can buy for $275, a jewelled pill box, with a built in musical alarm
that reminds you (but not too harshly) that it's time to take your
tranquilizer.

Unquestionably, we are in a battle for survival. We must get our
people into the battle. But first we have to get some battle into our
people.

What you and I have to do, patiently, and day by day, is to teach
those over whom we are given supervision, that work can be fun—that
the only real reward that life offers is the thrill of achievement, and
that the place where achievement amounts to most is on the job. A
hole in one isn't half as thrilling as landing a big order—a piece of
furniture built in your basement workshop will never be as thrilling as
a sales plan that works—a sailfish mounted on your wall will never
be quite as exciting as a well-earned promotion.

We are a nation of hobbyists, but believe me, there is a large element of escapism in hobbies. And too many of us get our vocations
all tangled up with our avocations. We have got to get to work, or a
stronger nation may put us to work. And to get to work, we have
got to re-discover what millions used to know: there is a great thrill
in work well done.

### ADLAI STEVENSON

For another example of the key quality that should be sought in speaking note the following paragraphs from a speech made by Adlai Stevenson when he accepted the Democratic Party's nomination for President, Chicago, July 26, 1952:

> . . . Let's talk sense to the American people. Let's tell them the truth, that there are no gains without pains, that we are now on the eve of great decisions, not easy decisions. . . .
>
> . . . The people are wise—wiser than the Republicans think. And the Democratic Party is the people's party, not the labor party, not the farmer's party, not the employer's party—it is the party of no one because it is the party of everyone.

### BRYSON REINHARDT

The following is a good example of how things that have been said many times before can be "injected with new life." Note how strikingly the speaker reveals the fallacy of "federal aid" with the illustration of the blood transfusion. This extract is from a speech that was delivered to the Lions Club in Ritzville, Washington, by Bryson Reinhardt.[4]

> Now, let's take another label: "federal aid to education." Whenever I hear that phrase used, I immediately correct the user as courteously as possible. I say, "Pardon me, sir, there is no such thing as federal aid to education. You must be thinking of federal control of education." When he protests in an injured tone, "Oh, no, I want federal aid without federal control," I patiently explain, "Sir, it is as absurd to speak of federal aid as it would be for your physician to offer to give you a blood transfusion by taking a pint of blood out of your left arm; spilling about 91% of it on the floor; and then putting the pitiful remainder into your right arm."
>
> All money for the support of our schools comes from the people—there just isn't any other way. *Friends* of the public schools want city, county, and state tax collectors to take money from the people and give it to our schools. *Enemies* of the public schools want federal tax collectors to take the money from the people, dilute it by about ten to one, and then ship back the pitiful remainder in a package fraudulently labeled "aid," for we are supposed to be grateful and to grovel at the feet of the bureaucrats.

[4] Bryson Reinhardt, *American Mercury*, August, 1959.

*Examples of Vibrant Writing in "Oral Style"*

Note the bold, virile way in which H. G. Wells [5] warned of World War II, in the words that follow. The warning of Mars was not heeded, and Mars came down upon us as he threatened:

Mars, the God of War, will sit like a giant above all human affairs for the next two decades, and the speech of Mars is blunt and plain. He will say to us, "Set your houses in order. If you squabble among yourselves, waste time, litigate, muddle, snatch profits, and shirk obligations, I will certainly come down upon you again.

"I have taken all your men between eighteen and fifty, and killed and maimed such as I pleased, millions of them. I have wasted your substance—contemptuously. Now, mark you, you have multitudes of male children between the ages of nine and nineteen running about among you—delightful and beloved boys. And behind them come millions of babies. Of these I have smashed and starved scarcely a paltry hundred thousand or so. But go on muddling, each for himself and none for the world, go on in the old way, stick to your rights, stick to your claims, each one of you, make no concessions nor sacrifices—and presently I shall come back again and take all the fresh harvest of life I have spared, all those millions that are now sweet little children and dear little boys, and I'll crush them into a red pulp, and I'll mix that pulp with the mud of trenches and feast upon it before your eyes more damnably than I have done before."

It should not be gathered from the samples we have quoted in this chapter that a speech cannot have vitality unless the speaker is "viewing with alarm." Note the vibrance of the following words of Don Herold: [6]

If I had my life to live over I'd try to make more mistakes next time. I would relax. I would limber up. I would be sillier than I have been this trip. I know of very few things that I would take seriously. I would be crazier. I would be less hygienic. I would take more chances. I would take more trips. I would climb more mountains, and swim more rivers. I would burn up more gasoline. I would eat more ice cream and less bran. I would have more actual troubles and fewer imaginary ones. You see, I am one of those fellows who live prudently and prophylactically and sensibly and sanely, hour after hour, day after day. Oh, I have had my moments,

[5] H. G. Wells, *What is Coming Up?* (New York: The Macmillan Company), 1916, pp. 93–94.

[6] Don Herold, "I'd Pick More Daisies" *College Humor.*

and if I had it to do over again, I'd have more of them—a lot more of them. In fact, I'd try to have nothing else. Just moments one after another, instead of living so many years, so many years ahead every day.

I have been one of those persons who never goes anywhere without a thermometer, a hot-water bottle, a gargle, a raincoat, and a parachute. If I had it to do over, I would go places and do things and travel lighter than I have.

If I had my life to live over, I would start bare-footed earlier in the spring and stay that way later in the fall. I would play hookey more. I wouldn't make such good grades except by accident. I would have more dogs. I would have more sweethearts. I would keep later hours. I would have more headaches. I would fish more. I would go to more circuses. I would go to more dances. I would ride on more merry-go-rounds. I'd pick more daisies.

The following extract is a good example of how a speaker made one point clear and then clinched it.

The preparation of a good speech requires years of living, experiencing, feeling, and thinking. Yet occasionally someone will complain that a speaker was paid several hundred dollars "for thirty minutes work." Speakers, like surgeons and other professional people, cannot be paid by the hour. They can "deliver" at their destination only what they carried with them the whole journey. They are not paid merely for the "unloading," but for using their total equipment for the total trip. A patient complained to a dentist for charging "five dollars for five seconds work" in pulling a tooth. The dentist said, "The next time I shall give you more for your money—I shall pull your tooth *slowly.*"

Note the lively way in which Charles T. Lipscomb [7] gets to the following point:

I want my son to be a salesman, because he will never be fenced in, never rolled in a rut, never headed for a dead end. And besides, he'll make money. The salesman is the foundation of free enterprise and the American standard of living. The guy who sells the goods is the one who will make a free, happy, successful world. I want my son to be a part of that world.

## Some *Examples of Making a Point With a Punch*

From speeches given by a diversity of speakers to a variety of

[7] Charles T. Lipscomb, "I Want My Boy to Be a Salesman," *Look,* February 24, 1953.

audiences I jotted down the following as examples of remarks whose sparkle demanded attention:

"Our studies have shown education increases the income of everyone excepting educators."

"According to Genesis, woman was the last thing made, and the product shows the result of both experience and fatigue."

"Your chairman's account of my long career would indicate that I have one foot in the grave. That may be true, but I am wearing a spat on the other."

"You may have observed that some speakers are good, and some are lousy. I am both—I'm good and lousy."

"Good public relations means you must treat your public differently than you treat your relations."

"In bringing new industries and new highways to our city it has been necessary to raze some private homes and destroy some old landmarks. These things are regrettable but unavoidable. When two elephants are fighting, a few ants are bound to get stepped on."

"When Congress is in session, I have the same feeling as when I see a baby get hold of a hammer."

"If history shows us anything it is this: you can build a throne with bayonets but you can't sit on it."

"When will the government learn you don't get production by pulling a rabbit out of a hat? If you want to produce something, you put two rabbits in the hat *and let them alone!*"

"At our college we teach the students the important thing is not to win the game—but to play fairly. Then we give the students a holiday when the team is victorious."

"When a man hesitates to buy life insurance, I ask him this: 'If you were depending upon *me* to support your family—*would you insure me?*'"

"When we started in business here we understood our competition was on its last legs. But, now we feel like the old mountaineer did about his wife. He said, 'Emily is failing dreadfully slow.'"

"I do not intend to engage in public debate with my critics. Theodore Roosevelt said that when you engage in such debate it is the same as though you were wrestling with a hog. You both get covered with mud, but the hog likes it."

"As you know we had just one week in which to prepare for this campaign. We moved faster than that nudist who spilled a cup of hot coffee in his lap."

"I am going to talk to you about *food*. If you want to know how important my subject is—then hear this: You men are solid, successful, civilized citizens. Yet just twelve meals stand between you and savagery. *One* day without food and you would lie. *Two* days without food and you would *steal*. *Three* days without food and you would *riot*. *Four* days without food and you would *kill!*"

"Babe Ruth hit 714 home runs in his big-league career. Everyone knows that record. But he made another big-league record. He struck out 1330 times. People remember him as the home-run king because he *kept swinging*."

"Knowing I am from Texas, people sometimes say, 'Is everything big in Texas? Aren't there any little things down there? What is the *smallest* thing in Texas?' When they ask me that way, I break an old Texas custom and tell them the truth. I tell them the smallest thing in Texas is the communist party."

"My partner and I went into business because we were just made for one another. He was rich and I was poor."

"My husband is like an oil lamp. In the first place he is not very bright. Secondly, he smokes all the time. Thirdly, he's been turned down by nearly everybody. Finally, he invariably goes out just when I need him the most."

"Back there in the Thirties we didn't have any H-Bombs and missiles. All we had to worry about was starving to death."

"In the old days when a man succeeded in business they knighted him—now they indict him."

"Our business was doing a nose dive. Up in the front office the ulcers were sprouting like dandelions."

"These old eyes of mine have seen almost half of our country's history. I suppose I shouldn't be shocked that they're gettin' a little tired. The things I'm going to tell you today are not things I read—or somebody said—they are things these eyes have seen."

"I am a teacher. Lately I am being told by my supervisor that

I should get 'down to the level of the students,' and that we should all 'explore' together.  Now hear this: I spent many years of my life and many thousands of dollars to get myself *above* the level of my students so I could *teach* them.  I am above the level of the students, and—by the eternal gods—I expect to *stay* there!"

"In the cattle business right now we're getting some comfort from an old cowpoke saying: 'You can't fall out of bed when you're sleepin' on the floor.' "

*And in Conclusion . . .*

As I come to the end of this book, I feel as Lincoln did in ending his first inaugural address—"I am loathe to close."  Speaking is such a vital and magnificent art that any treatment of it is inadequate and unworthy.

One of the most stupid procedures under the sun is to classify people as "talkers" and "doers."  The talking must always *precede* the doing.  No idea ever takes the form of achievement until after it has been formed into words.  Whether a man builds a temple, or dashes himself and his fellowmen to death over a precipice, depends solely upon what words he believes.  Through words we decide whether to pray for our fellowmen or to prey on them, whether to "follow our leaders or murder them."  The Scriptures say ". . . be ye doers of the word . . ."  *All* doers are doers of the word, *because the word must come first*.

Dr. E. C. Nance [8] puts it well:

Words, as symbols of ideas and ideals, have the power to make people fall in love or out of love; to be faithful or unfaithful to their vows and pledges.

Words can bring a song to the lips or a sting to the soul.  They can produce tears or laughter, success or disaster.  They can bring luster and brightness to the face of a child or send him to bed sobbing and sorrowful. . . .

Words can change the face of a city, build churches, schools, playgrounds, boys' clubs, scout troops, civic forums, civic clubs, Little Theaters, civic music organizations, garden clubs and better local governments.

[8] E. C. Nance, "The Power and Glory of the World," *Vital Speeches*, April 1, 1957.

Words can turn a sinner into a saint or a saint into a sinner. They can engender self-respect, hope, and constructive ambition in a friend, acquaintance, or employee; or words can discourage and frustrate him.

The force of words is great, good, glorious, or terrifying. . . .

Civilization is where it is today by the force of words. Man's present moral behavior is the fruit of the word. Everything on this earth created by the mind and hand of man was first an idea brought out in the minds of the world on the wings of a word . . .

We still remain dependent upon speech. We need words that will make us laugh, wonder, work, think, aspire, and hope. We need words that will leap and sing in our souls. We need words that will cause us to face up to life with a fighting faith and contend for those ideals that have made this the greatest nation on earth.

He who seeks to improve his proficiency in speech is arming himself with unlimited power for good or ill. This is why this book has not dealt alone with the *technique* of effective speech, but has also dwelt heavily upon the personal character and philosophy of the *individual* to whom so mighty a weapon is entrusted. There is a better goal than to become merely a speaker—it is to become a *spokesman*. Be a speaker who speaks *for* something— for things that are right, true, fair, honorable, and enduring. To be a good spokesman you must be proficient in the art of speaking, but you must also qualify on the last syllable of the word— you must be a *man*. This does not limit speakers to one gender, but it means the speaker should be a *good representative of mankind at its best*. This is why a religious and spiritual note was inevitably injected into this volume. If you would possess unlimited power, if you would put light in people's faces, you must hook on to the high line that leads to the Source of Power. You must chart your course by the fixed stars of the Eternal. *"In the beginning was the Word, and Word was with God."*

# Index